Praise for The Cadwaladr Quests

☆☆☆☆☆

It's been a constant battle finding an engaging read that will not only keep them interested in turning pages but will also compliment their preparation for grammar/ independent school entrance exams. This book ticked all the boxes. It's a fantastic story with a very clever and unique way of explaining the antonyms and synonyms within the text. This helped so much with my dyslexic son who reads very well but often misinterprets the meaning of the vocabulary. I would 100% recommend this book regardless of age and educational journey.

– ***Mum of three boys***

☆☆☆☆☆

S L Ager combines the use of effective and useful vocabulary with an in-built dictionary all in one book. Definitely a winner!!!

We introduced this book to our Year 5 students at our tuition centre last year when we read it as a group… The children loved it and wanted the story to continue… This book is now on our recommended list of books to prepare children for the 11+ exams.

– ***Mrs Win***

☆☆☆☆☆

My son loved reading this book, he couldn't put it down!! Excellent vocabulary list and perfect for those studying for 11plus exams. I highly recommend it. He's been asking for the second book *(Race for Gold)* EVERYDAY since he finished this one which we just purchased too! You won't regret purchasing this book.

– ***Nomi_smiles***

THE CADWALADR CHRONICLES

11+ VOCABULARY

BOOK 2: CIPHER

S. L. AGER

Developmental editor: Anna Bowles
Copyeditor and proofreader: Louis Greenberg
Cover design and interior formatting: Mark Thomas / Coverness.com

ISBN 978-1-913753-08-5 (paperback)
ISBN 978-1-913753-09-2 (ebook)

www.slager.co.uk

FOR ALL CHILDREN,
REGARDLESS OF DIFFICULT EXAMS

SPECIAL THANKS

I want to say a big thank you to some exceptional readers who helped me to develop *The Cadwaladr Chronicles.*

Thank you,

Janya Agarwal,

Arjun Pasumarti

and

Aaron Smith.

Table of Contents

PREFACE

I wrote *Cipher*, the second of *The Cadwaladr Chronicles*, prequels to *The Cadwaladr Quests*, after receiving so many requests from parents asking for books more suited to years two, three and four.

Some readers of the original *The Cadwaladr Quests* are in year three, but I don't recommend that for most children as the narrative is more suited to readers from late year four and above, including, of course, year six.

Although the prequels are aimed at younger readers, the narrative and vocabulary are as challenging as in *The Cadwaladr Quests* but they are age-appropriate.

Many of the words included and defined in this book come from the practice materials I covered and amassed with my two children when working towards the 11+ exams and SATs in primary school. We worked with both GL and CEM materials.

Of course, no published aids can guarantee that their material will appear on any exam paper, and neither can I. However, considering *The Cadwaladr Chronicles: Cipher* contains over 1,700 word definitions and hundreds of corresponding synonyms and antonyms (in a fun story for girls and boys), what does any parent or young reader have to lose?

I hope you enjoy Callwen's gripping adventure in the second book of *The Cadwaladr Chronicles*, but moreover, I hope it helps you and your children with any challenging vocabulary exams they are facing.

HOW TO USE THIS BOOK

This story has been specially written to help young readers prepare for their 11+, SATs and independent schools' entrance exams. It includes difficult vocabulary embedded in a fun narrative that provides context for the new words and makes them easier to learn and understand.

On every page, key words are in bold, and each has a correlated footnote with a concise definition. The words are defined using the context in which they appear in the text, and definitions are as child-friendly as possible. Chosen key words are defined only once, usually when they first appear in the story, unless they appear again in a different context.

Synonyms and antonyms, where applicable, are also provided.

This book does not aim to replace a dictionary or purport to be one, but dictionaries have been used to check the accuracy of each definition.

PS: There are a few Welsh words in the story. To learn how to pronounce them, please visit"
slager.co.uk/welsh-words

TOP READING TIPS

- Children, you may find it beneficial to read this book for the first time with an adult, but you and your parents can decide.
- The definitions are included for convenience and to guide the learning, not as a definitive 'must learn' list.
- Chosen key words are defined only once, usually when they first appear in the story, unless they appear again in a different context.
- To make learning difficult words easier, try to associate the words with the relevant scene in the book and to picture their meanings.
- Chapter lengths vary, so do not necessarily aim to finish a chapter in each sitting.
- Some pages have more definitions than others to fit in with the storytelling.
- Read the book as often as is needed, and continue to use its vast resource of definitions, synonyms and antonyms to reinforce learning.
- The best way to learn new words is to read as widely and with as much variety as possible. Every book is a world of adventure waiting for you to turn to the first page. I hope my book helps in this journey of discovery and learning.

KEY TO ABBREVIATIONS OF WORD TYPE

(v) verb

(n) noun

(adj) adjective

(adv) adverb

(prep) preposition

(con) conjunction

(int) interjection

(s) synonym

(ant) antonym

PARENTS, GET FIVE FREE COMPREHENSION EXERCISES

Parents, to receive your free comprehensions (with answers) based on *The Cadwaladr Chronicles: Book 2 – Cipher,* please leave a review for *Cipher* on Amazon and email a screenshot to:

freebies@slager.co.uk.

I will add you to my mailing list[1] and send you the comprehensions by email.

1 You can unsubscribe from the mailing list at any time. Further details will be emailed to you as soon as you are added.

INTRODUCTION TO THE KEY CHARACTERS, ITEMS AND LOCATIONS

Callwen (Cad) Cadwaladr. Adopted daughter of Prince Llywelyn and his wife, Siân.

The Knights Hawk. A magical order of hand-picked knights.

The Gwalch Gem bracelet. A magical combination of Welsh gold and emerald cut into the shape of a hawk.

Instinct. Powers bestowed by the bracelet which must be earned in order to become a Knight Hawk.

Cadwaladr Castle. Prince Llywelyn's residence.

Catrin Castle. Prince Dewi's residence. Cad's current home.

Prince Llywelyn. Knight Hawk. Ruler of Wales. Adoptive father to Cad and her baby brother, Prince John.

Princess Siân Cadwaladr. Wife of Prince Llywelyn. Mother to baby Prince John. Cad's adoptive mother.

Prince Dewi. Prince Llywelyn's younger brother.

Prince John. Baby son of Llywelyn and Siân. Cad's brother.

Gelert. Prince Llywelyn's faithful hound.

Dylan Rogers. Cad's friend and fellow page.

Rhys Price. Cad's friend and fellow page.

Ellis Williams. A groom and a page.

May. A hawk.

Bryn Davis. An older squire.

Jack Jones. Bryn's trainee.

Sir Robert Evans. Llywelyn's associate. A Knight Hawk.

Sir Owain Glyn. Llywelyn's second in command. A Knight Hawk.

Peggy (Hari). Prince Dewi's former henchman.

Goodwife Hughes. A servant in Anwen Cadwaladr's employ.

Hugh Hughes. Goodwife Hughes's son.

Fishy. A dog.

Midnight. Dewi's destrier.

Slippy. A snake.

Flash. A pony.

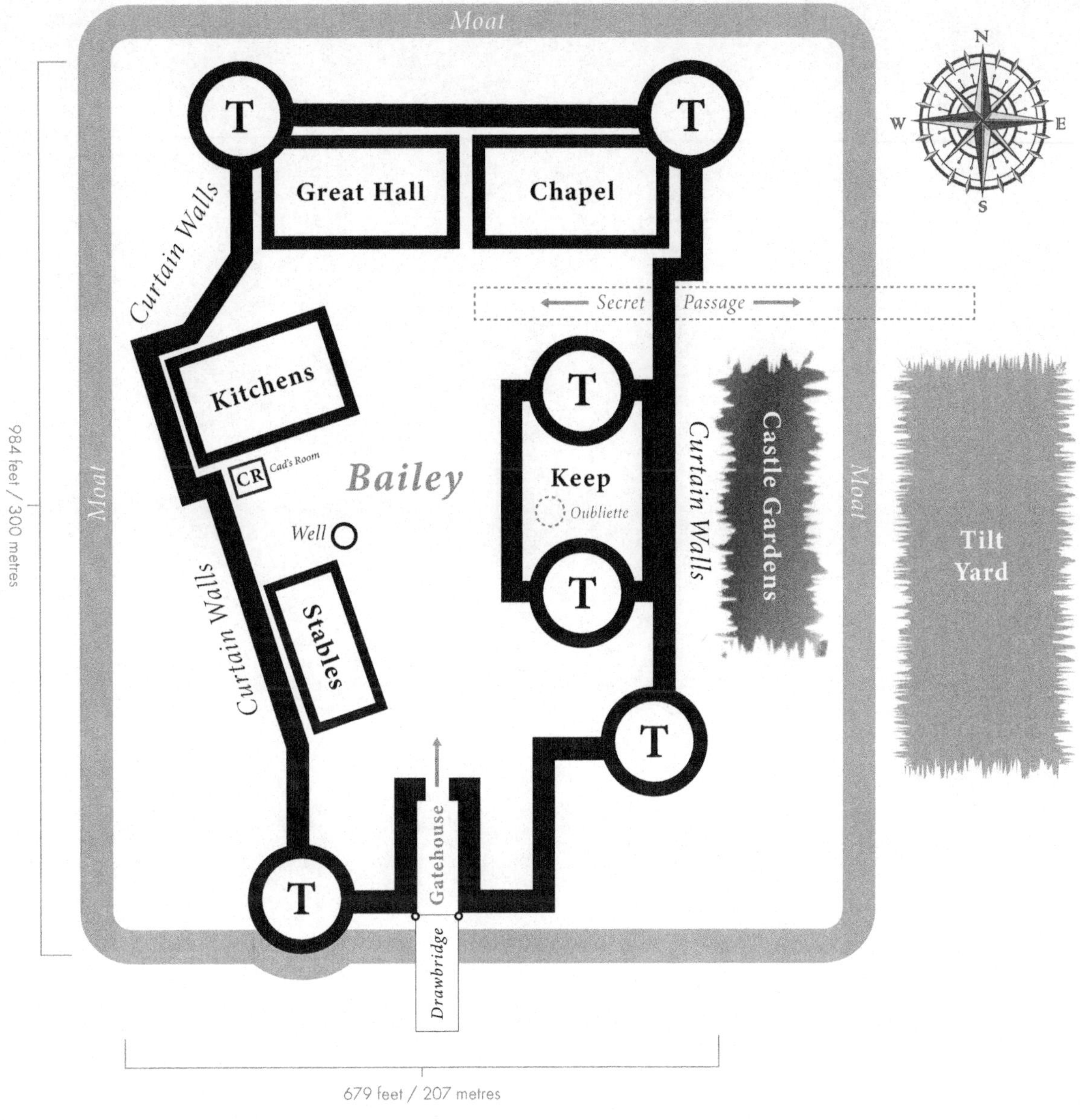

Map of Catrin Castle

TWELFTH-CENTURY WALES

CHAPTER ONE

Cipher

From beneath a loose hood, two black holes **peered**[1] at her. Below **gaped**[2] the space where a nose should be. **Bared**[3] teeth flashed, no lips left to cover them. The mouth grinned. No eyes **conveyed**[4] emotion, and no **flesh**[5] crinkled or **creased**[6]. Then, as always, the face took shape, **transforming**[7] before her eyes. Whose features would form upon tonight's bare bones? Whose laugh would ring from its cruel mouth? Its face held the **expression**[8] a nightmare wore.

Cad struggled for air. She kicked hard against the **biting**[9] water, the surface rippling above her as she **floundered**[10] in the well where **forsaken**[11] as a baby. Could she breathe before the bones formed flesh; escape the **oubliette**[12] before the skull spoke its **scornful**[13] words? Could Cad

---

1 **peer** *(v)* look with concentration. *(s)* stare, gape, gaze. *(ant)* glance.

2 **gape** *(v)* be or become wide open. *(s)* part, yawn. *(ant)* close, shut.

3 **bare** *(v)* reveal and expose something to view. *(s)* uncover, unveil, display. *(ant)* cover, hide.

4 **convey** *(v)* make known or understandable. *(s)* deliver, exude, communicate. *(ant)* obscure, conceal.

5 **flesh** *(n)* the muscle and fat of a human or an animal. *(s)* tissue.

6 **crease** *(v)* make a line in. *(s)* wrinkle, pucker. *(ant)* smooth, straighten.

7 **transform** *(v)* markedly change something. *(s)* alter, modify, remodel. *(ant)* preserve, sustain.

8 **expression** *(n)* a look that conveys (shows) a certain emotion. *(s)* face, appearance.

9 **biting** *(adj)* extremely cold. *(s)* freezing, bitter, glacial. *(ant)* balmy, warm.

10 **flounder** *(v)* struggle physically or mentally. *(s)* falter, blunder. *(ant)* succeed.

11 **forsake** *(v)* abandon (past participle: forsaken). *(s)* desert, leave, disown. *(ant)* welcome.

12 **oubliette** *(n)* a dungeon, especially in a medieval castle, with access only through a trapdoor in the ceiling.

13 **scornful** *(adj)* showing or feeling contempt (disrespect). *(s)* disdainful, derisive. *(ant)* admiring.

survive the **myriad**[1] mothers, none known to her, **morphing**[2] from skull to skin before her eyes? Or tonight, might she see Siân again? The cold grip of fear **subsided**[3], but in its place burned a hot fire of **despair**[4].

With a gasp, Cad shot upright, wide-eyed. Sweat soaked her body. In a heartbeat, reality **dawned**[5] on her. She had woken in time. Cad had beaten the **ghoul**[6] who invaded her nights, waking before it had fully **manifested**[7]. Tonight, she'd **thwarted**[8] the **fiend**[9] who appeared in her dreams. The cloaked **monk**[10] who had sealed her and John in the **dungeon**[11] to rot away forgotten.

Weak with relief, her chest **heaving**[12], Cad flopped back against her pillows, **grateful**[13] she had not seen Siân's face this time. Then like an **evaporating**[14] mist, the **tension**[15] left the air.

Since Cad's **ordeal**[16] in the oubliette, as though the images were nailed to her memory, she had suffered nightmares. And although they were now less regular, and she more able to wake before they **terrified**[17] her, too often she met that hooded figure **looming**[18] over her bed. Now, as she caught her breath, and dawn crept into her bedchamber, Cad **banished**[19] the **hideous**[20] images

---

1 **myriad** *(adj)* many. *(s)* numerous, multiple. *(ant)* few.

2 **morph** *(v)* undergo a gradual process of transformation. *(s)* convert, modify, transform. *(ant)* preserve.

3 **subside** *(v)* become less severe or intense. *(s)* diminish, ease, abate. *(ant)* increase.

4 **despair** *(n)* the loss of all hope. *(s)* hopelessness, desperation. *(ant)* hope, joy.

5 **dawn** *(v)* become evident, be perceived or understood by the mind. *(s)* strike, occur. *(ant)* obscure.

6 **ghoul** *(n)* a phantom or spirit, especially an evil one. *(s)* bogeyman, fiend, monster. *(ant)* angel.

7 **manifest** *(v)* appear. *(s)* show, display, present. *(ant)* hide.

8 **thwart** *(v)* successfully oppose. *(s)* foil, stop, defeat, overpower. *(ant)* aid, facilitate.

9 **fiend** *(n)* a cruel or wicked person. *(s)* baddie, monster. *(ant)* hero, angel.

10 **monk** *(n)* a member of a religious community. *(s)* brother, friar.

11 **dungeon** *(n)* a cell or room where prisoners are held. *(s)* prison, jail, oubliette, donjon.

12 **heave** *(v)* rise and fall. *(s)* roll, billow.

13 **grateful** *(adj)* feeling or showing appreciation for something. *(s)* thankful, glad, appreciative. *(ant)* ungrateful.

14 **evaporate** *(v)* dry out. *(s)* disperse, disappear. *(ant)* materialise.

15 **tension** *(n)* stress or unrest. *(s)* agitation, unease, apprehension. *(ant)* calmness.

16 **ordeal** *(n)* a prolonged and horrid experience. *(s)* trauma, nightmare. *(ant)* joy.

17 **terrify** *(v)* cause to feel great fear. *(s)* horrify, petrify. *(ant)* calm, soothe.

18 **loom** *(v)* appear over someone or something as a large, often threatening presence. *(s)* tower, rise. *(ant)* recede.

19 **banish** *(v)* get rid of. *(s)* dismiss, eliminate, eradicate, exclude. *(ant)* accept, allow.

20 **hideous** *(adj)* extremely unpleasant. *(s)* ugly, revolting, appalling, monstrous. *(ant)* attractive.

from her head, turning her thoughts over to the ever-present **cipher**[1] instead.

These days, when awake, she **pondered**[2] little else. **Symbols**[3] and letters formed in her mind, none wanting to be found and all **eluding**[4] her still.

Cad **scoured**[5] the puzzle for the hundredth time, still **stumped**[6]. **Exhaustion**[7] **impaired**[8] her **judgement**[9]. She longed to rip the **parchment**[10] apart, tear it to shreds cheering and whooping as she did so. As **rash**[11] as she was, Cad knew that would lead to regret once the red mist of anger, **fuelled**[12] by **lack**[13] of sleep, **anxiety**[14] and **frustration**[15], **inevitably**[16] lifted.

To **submit**[17] to this riddle's secrets was not an option. Instead, she **unfurled**[18] the **flimsy**[19] parchment she and Dylan had so often **pored**[20] over these last weeks since she'd **pilfered**[21] it from Sir Robert's **quarters**[22]. Cad's **brow**[23] creased as she studied the characters, twisting and

---

1 **cipher** *(n)* a disguised or secret way of writing something. *(s)* cryptograph, code, cryptogram.

2 **ponder** *(v)* think carefully about. *(s)* consider, contemplate, deliberate. *(ant)* disregard.

3 **symbol** *(n)* a mark or character that represents something. *(s)* sign, ideogram.

4 **elude** *(v)* avoid or escape. *(s)* evade, dodge. *(ant)* embrace.

5 **scour** *(v)* look or search thoroughly. *(s)* scrutinise, study, inspect. *(ant)* overlook.

6 **stump** *(v)* cause to be at a loss. *(s)* baffle, bewilder, confuse, confound, mystify. *(ant)* clarify, explain.

7 **exhaustion** *(n)* extreme mental or physical tiredness. *(s)* fatigue, weariness. *(ant)* vigour.

8 **impair** *(v)* damage or weaken. *(s)* reduce, lessen, decrease. *(ant)* improve, increase.

9 **judgement** *(n)* the ability to make decisions or come to conclusions. *(s)* sense, intelligence. *(ant)* recklessness.

10 **parchment** *(n)* prepared animal skin with a papery appearance used in ancient writing. *(s)* vellum, scroll.

11 **rash** *(adj)* acting without consideration of the outcome. *(s)* hasty, reckless, impulsive. *(ant)* careful, prudent.

12 **fuel** *(v)* power or inflame. *(s)* feed, provoke, stimulate, encourage. *(ant)* deplete.

13 **lack** *(n)* the state of being without or deficient. *(s)* need, want, dearth. *(s)* abundance.

14 **anxiety** *(n)* a worried and nervous feeling. *(s)* apprehension, unease, disquiet. *(ant)* calmness, reassurance.

15 **frustration** *(n)* the feeling of annoyance at something that one cannot change. *(s)* exasperation. *(ant)* satisfaction.

16 **inevitably** *(adv)* in an inevitable (unavoidable) way. *(s)* certainly, definitely. *(ant)* doubtfully.

17 **submit** *(v)* give in to. *(s)* succumb, acquiesce, yield, surrender, defer, buckle, capitulate. *(ant)* defy, resist.

18 **unfurl** *(v)* unroll or roll out. *(s)* open out, unfold, expand. *(ant)* furl, fold up.

19 **flimsy** *(adj)* light and easily damaged. *(s)* fragile, delicate. *(ant)* robust.

20 **pore** *(v)* be absorbed in reading or studying something. *(s)* examine, inspect, scrutinise.

21 **pilfer** *(v)* steal. *(s)* take, rob, thieve, snatch, purloin. *(ant)* give.

22 **quarters** *(n)* accommodation. *(s)* chambers, rooms, apartment.

23 **brow** *(n)* forehead.

turning their **intricate**[1] angles back and **forth**[2] in her head, noting their patterns, similarities and **anomalies**[3].

Neither Cad nor Dylan had dared make a copy for fear of losing the cipher's **accuracy**[4] in **translation**[5]. Both she and Dylan were **adept**[6] in coding and **deciphering**[7], as they'd created their **covert**[8] **communication**[9] language to help keep Cad's secret. **Nevertheless**[10], what she **suspected**[11] to be Sir Robert's **handiwork**[12], had **hitherto**[13] proved unbreakable, and it **infuriated**[14] and **consumed**[15] her too often.

Even in the **current**[16] **unseasonable**[17] warmth, Cad **shuddered**[18], for the parchment **evoked**[19] **ghastly**[20] memories of her ordeal in the oubliette with John. Thank heaven Rhys had found them in time. Thinking of that **gruesome**[21] place turned her **queasy**[22].

Weeks had passed, yet the man they'd left **unconscious**[23] in the oubliette, the man who'd

---

1 **intricate** *(adj)* detailed and complicated. *(s)* complex, elaborate. *(ant)* plain, simple.

2 **forth** *(adv)* forward in direction (or time). *(ant)* back.

3 **anomaly** *(n)* something that is different to normal. *(s)* oddity, irregularity. *(ant)* normality.

4 **accuracy** *(n)* correctness or precision. *(s)* certainty, exactitude. *(ant)* inaccuracy.

5 **translation** *(n)* the act of making something understandable, especially another language.

6 **adept** *(adj)* skilful or proficient. *(s)* competent, adroit, deft. *(ant)* inept.

7 **decipher** *(v)* succeed in understanding or identifying something. *(s)* decode, decrypt. *(ant)* cipher.

8 **covert** *(adj)* not openly displayed or acknowledged. *(s)* secret, concealed. *(ant)* obvious, overt.

9 **communication** *(n)* the exchange of information. *(s)* reporting, transmission.

10 **nevertheless** *(adv)* all the same. *(s)* however, even so, nonetheless.

11 **suspect** *(v)* believe in the existence or truth of something without proof. *(s)* assume, think, suppose. *(ant)* know.

12 **handiwork** *(n)* something made or done by someone. *(s)* design, creation, work, craft, action.

13 **hitherto** *(adv)* until this point. *(s)* previously, formerly, beforehand, yet, before, thus far. *(ant)* henceforth.

14 **infuriate** *(v)* anger greatly. *(s)* enrage, inflame, exasperate. *(ant)* soothe, calm.

15 **consume** *(v)* strongly affect or overwhelm with a feeling. *(s)* dominate, overpower, control. *(ant)* abandon.

16 **current** *(adj)* in the present. *(s)* ongoing. *(ant)* past.

17 **unseasonable** *(adj)* (of the weather) unusual for the time of year.

18 **shudder** *(v)* tremble unwittingly *(s)* shiver, shake, quiver, convulse.

19 **evoke** *(v)* bring something to the conscious mind. *(s)* induce, arouse, awaken, recall. *(ant)* suppress.

20 **ghastly** *(adj)* causing great fear or horror. *(s)* grim, dire, harrowing, hideous. *(ant)* pleasant.

21 **gruesome** *(adj)* causing horror. *(s)* grisly, hideous, ghastly, macabre. *(ant)* pleasant.

22 **queasy** *(adj)* feeling slightly sick (nauseous) or uneasy. *(s)* odd, unsettled. *(ant)* well.

23 **unconscious** *(adj)* not awake or aware of one's environment. *(s)* asleep, comatose. *(ant)* conscious.

beaten Bryn Davis so badly, had not reappeared. Perhaps he had **perished**[1], but she doubted that. Someone, an **accomplice**[2], the monk with the long, **slim**[3] fingers, had more likely moved him.

'Dylan,' Cad whispered to her sleeping friend. 'Dylan, wake up. You must see this.' But he didn't **stir**[4].

'Dylan,' she hissed, not wanting to wake Rhys, who'd shown no interest in the cipher and seemed ocean deep in sleep.

Nor did she want to disturb the snoring Fishy curled at the foot of Rhys's bed. She smiled **affectionately**[4] at her friends, both two-legged and four.

'Dylan,' she said, **prodding**[6] him.

He shot up. 'Ouch! Don't do that!' Dylan grumbled, clearly readying himself to pepper Cad with objections.

But, smoothing over the moment, Cad pressed her finger to her lips as she nodded towards Rhys, then shook her head. A **jab**[7] with her hairpin was the one thing that could **rouse**[8] Dylan, who slept like the dead. 'I need you to look at something with me, now.' Cad's heart raced: as if the shadows had come to life, she'd spotted something promising **scrawled**[9] on the parchment.

'Yes, yes. But, do not wake me with that hairpin again, ever.'

Not **burdened**[10] by **conscience**[11], Cad nodded in agreement, a look of **compliance**[12] on her face, but they both knew she would jab him again, and probably tomorrow if need be.

'Get the sticks,' Cad said, nodding to where she knew Dylan had hidden the pouch she'd fashioned from old leather **scraps**[13].

---

1 **perish** *(v)* die, especially suddenly. *(s)* expire, depart, pass away. *(ant)* live, survive.

2 **accomplice** *(n)* a person who helps another commit a crime. *(s)* co-conspirator, collaborator, abettor.

3 **slim** *(adj)* not fat. *(s)* slender, lean, thin. *(ant)* fat, stubby.

4 **stir** *(v)* move slightly. *(s)* disturb, budge. *(ant)* still.

4 **affectionately** *(adv)* in an affectionate (fond) manner. *(s)* benevolently, agreeably. *(ant)* unkindly.

6 **prod** *(v)* poke with something. *(s)* jab, push, nudge.

7 **jab** *(n)* a quick, sharp blow. *(s)* prod, dig, stab, push, nudge.

8 **rouse** *(v)* bring out of inactivity. *(s)* stimulate, prompt, provoke, arouse. *(ant)* calm, appease.

9 **scrawl** *(v)* write in a hurried way. *(s)* scribble.

10 **burden** *(v)* cause worry, hardship or distress. *(s)* afflict, overload. *(ant)* relieve.

11 **conscience** *(n)* one's internal moral sense of right and wrong. *(s)* integrity, morality. *(ant)* immorality.

12 **compliance** *(n)* the action of complying (agreeing) to or with something. *(s)* obedience, concurrence. *(ant)* refusal.

13 **scrap** *(n)* a small piece of something, especially one that is leftover. *(s)* morsel, bit.

Dylan rubbed his eyes, and with a yawn, reached beneath the bed's **slats**[1] where the tiny twigs they'd **painstakingly**[2] **whittled**[3] into **delicate**[4] markers, so they could repeatedly **replicate**[5] the cipher, lay **stowed**[6] away from **prying**[7] eyes. He passed the pouch to Cad, who removed the tiny **indicators**[8] that would **reconstruct**[9] and **deconstruct**[10] the mysteries of the cipher as and when they needed them. Cad knew the puzzle held the secret to the castle's **treachery**[11]. If it was the last thing she ever did, she would find who had **conspired**[12] with her mother, Siân, and her uncle, Dewi, to steal the Gwalch Gem bracelet and trick Llywelyn into killing his dog, Gelert.

Cad knelt, and Dylan **crouched**[13] beside her. With **diligence**[14], she laid out the thin sticks, **mimicking**[15] the parchment's symbols, twisting and turning the tiny twigs to **imitate**[16] the cipher's markings, until they might spot a sign that would unlock its secrets.

'Dylan. I think I saw something in my dreams. The code lined up for me. I'm almost there. What lies on this parchment is **crucial**[17], of that I am sure.'

Dylan rubbed sleep from his eyes, used to Cad's **obsession**[18] with breaking the code. She often

---

1 **slat** *(n)* a thin narrow piece of material such as wood, especially one that overlaps with another.

2 **painstakingly** *(adv)* done in a painstaking (careful) way. *(s)* thoroughly, diligently, meticulously. *(ant)* carelessly.

3 **whittle** *(v)* carve wood into an object. *(s)* pare, trim, shave, model.

4 **delicate** *(adj)* fine in structure. *(s)* dainty, frail, fragile. *(ant)* strong, durable.

5 **replicate** *(v)* make a copy of. *(s)* duplicate, reproduce, recreate.

6 **stow** *(v)* store, pack or keep neatly in a specific place. *(s)* stash, secrete, deposit. *(ant)* unload, remove.

7 **prying** *(adj)* looking or enquiring too closely. *(s)* inquisitive, curious, probing. *(ant)* disinterested.

8 **indicator** *(n)* something that shows or represents something. *(s)* gauge, symbol, signal.

9 **reconstruct** *(v)* make or form again. *(s)* restore, reassemble, rebuild. *(ant)* deconstruct.

10 **deconstruct** *(v)* take something apart. *(s)* dismantle, unravel, interpret. *(ant)* construct.

11 **treachery** *(n)* a breach of trust. *(s)* betrayal, deceit, disloyalty, dishonesty. *(ant)* loyalty, honesty.

12 **conspire** *(v)* make harmful secret plans with. *(s)* plot, scheme, collude.

13 **crouch** *(v)* to lower the body by bending one's knees. *(s)* squat, shrink, huddle. *(ant)* stand.

14 **diligence** *(n)* careful and persistent effort or work. *(s)* rigour, conscientiousness, zeal. *(ant)* laziness, carelessness.

15 **mimic** *(v)* resemble or imitate (copy or behave like). *(s)* mirror, impersonate, simulate. *(ant)* differ from.

16 **imitate** *(v)* copy or simulate. *(s)* mirror, resemble, replicate. *(ant)* differ from.

17 **crucial** *(adj)* of absolute (complete) importance. *(s)* critical, vital, key. *(ant)* trivial.

18 **obsession** *(n)* something one cannot stop thinking about. *(s)* passion, fixation. *(ant)* apathy.

woke him at night, or dragged him from **chores**[1] when she thought she was close to **resolving**[2] the cipher's mystery.

'And I think Sir Robert is more involved than he lets on,' said Cad for the thousandth time since **swiping**[3] the parchment from his rooms. 'You lie with dogs, you rise with fleas,' she muttered under her breath, unable to shake the distrust she **harboured**[4] towards her father's **associate**[5].

'Cad, do you not find this **somewhat**[6] tiresome now?' asked Dylan, **irritation**[7] creeping into his voice. 'We have puzzled over this for weeks,' he moaned, 'to no **avail**[8].'

Cad ignored him, **rummaging**[9] through all **viable**[10] explanations in the hope of finding a straw to cling to. If Sir Robert was worried about his lost cipher, he **concealed**[11] his **concern**[12] well. He'd **uttered**[13] not a word since its theft, and no one seemed to be searching for it. Cad wondered if he thought it lost. Cad often asked herself why she'd taken it, and she wasn't sure of the answer, but something had **rattled**[14] her when she'd seen it and with her father **absent**[15] she'd acted on her **hunch**[16].

To keep it safe, Cad ensured the parchment remained hidden within the secretly sewn folds of her **garments**[17] along with myriad other **miscellanies**[18]. Being raised as a **noble**[19] girl at Cadwaladr

---

1 **chore** *(n)* a task, often a household one. *(s)* job, work, errand, duty, drudgery.

2 **resolve** *(v)* find a solution. *(s)* solve, answer, fathom, unravel. *(ant)* mystify.

3 **swipe** *(v)* take without permission or payment. *(s)* steal, thieve, pilfer.

4 **harbour** *(v)* hold a thought or feeling in the mind. *(s)* nurture, foster.

5 **associate** *(n)* a business partner or companion. *(s)* ally, comrade, supporter.

6 **somewhat** *(adv)* a little but not a lot. *(s)* a bit, rather, quite, slightly. *(ant)* extremely.

7 **irritation** *(n)* the state of feeling impatient, annoyed or slightly angry. *(s)* exasperation, chagrin. *(ant)* delight.

8 **avail** *(n)* benefit or use. *(s)* advantage, reward, purpose, gain, profit. *(ant)* uselessness.

9 **rummage** *(v)* search in a haphazard (disorganised) way. *(s)* root, scrabble, dig.

10 **viable** *(adj)* capable of working or being. *(s)* feasible, possible. *(ant)* impossible.

11 **conceal** *(v)* hide or disguise. *(s)* screen, shroud, cloak, veil, camouflage. *(ant)* reveal, uncover.

12 **concern** *(n)* worry. *(s)* anxiety, disquiet, apprehension, unease. *(ant)* indifference, serenity, calm.

13 **utter** *(v)* speak. *(s)* say, express, breathe.

14 **rattle** *(v)* make someone nervous, uneasy, or annoyed. *(s)* unnerve, perturb, ruffle. *(ant)* calm.

15 **absent** *(adj)* not present. *(s)* out, gone. *(ant)* present.

16 **hunch** *(n)* an intuitive feeling or idea. *(s)* impression, suspicion, guess, notion. *(ant)* certainty.

17 **garment** *(n)* an item of clothing. *(s)* clothes, outfit, attire, dress.

18 **miscellany** *(n)* a group or mixture of different items. *(s)* assortment, variety. *(ant)* uniformity.

19 **noble** *(adj)* of high birth or rank. *(s)* aristocratic, patrician. *(ant)* humble, peasant.

Castle until the age of seven, had **sealed**[1] her **embroidery**[2] skills. But to this castle's **inhabitants**[3], who **assumed**[4] she was a **pageboy**[5] on knight's training, her expert **stitching**[6] skills remained **purposely**[7] hidden: boys didn't sew – much to her **chagrin**[8].

'This is the part that **baffles**[9] me,' Dylan **muttered**[10], **defeated**[11], the pinprick to his **rear**[12] now clearly **forgiven**[13] as he ordered the sticks into rows of symbols. 'See, just here.' He pointed to the patterns. 'The missing link is this one; I'm sure of it.'

Cad nodded. 'Mmm. I'm not so sure,' she replied, rearranging the pattern, hoping that might **prime the pump**[14], much to Dylan's irritation judging by the look on his face.

'You're such a bossyboots,' he **chided**[15], watching her **deftly**[16] move the tiny twigs into various positions, her face fixed in **concentration**[17].

Cad stared, her eyes narrowing in thought. She fiddled some more, but then shook her head, and in a **fit of pique**[18], **swiped**[19] at the pattern of sticks, destroying their arrangement.

'Why did you do that?' cried Dylan. 'You were close then. I **swear**[20] it.'

'I order these darned sticks to copy that code so often, I feel I am losing my mind,' she groaned,

---

1 **seal** *(v)* establish or conclude something in a definite way. *(s)* clinch, complete.

2 **embroidery** *(n)* the craft of sewing fabric in a decorative manner.

3 **inhabitant** *(n)* a person or animal that lives in a particular place. *(s)* dweller, resident, occupant.

4 **assume** *(v)* presume to be the case without any proof of it. *(s)* suppose, conclude, believe. *(ant)* prove.

5 **pageboy** *(n)* a boy in training for a knighthood, ranking one below a squire in a knight's personal service.

6 **stitch** *(v)* make or mend by sewing stitches. *(s)* sew.

7 **purposely** *(adv)* done with intention. *(s)* deliberately, wilfully. *(ant)* unintentionally, accidentally.

8 **chagrin** *(n)* annoyance or distress. *(s)* disappointment, exasperation, displeasure, irritation. *(ant)* delight, joy.

9 **baffle** *(v)* totally confuse. *(s)* perplex, bewilder, flummox, confound. *(ant)* enlighten, clear up.

10 **mutter** *(v)* say something that is difficult to hear. *(s)* murmur, mumble, whisper. *(ant)* shout.

11 **defeated** *(adj)* beaten. *(s)* conquered, vanquished, overcome. *(ant)* triumphant, victorious.

12 **rear** *(n)* backside. *(s)* bottom, bum, rump, butt, buttocks.

13 **forgive** *(v)* grant pardon to someone (past participle: forgiven). *(s)* excuse, absolve, exonerate. *(ant)* blame, resent.

14 **prime the pump** (phrase) stimulate something to start or continue.

15 **chide** *(v)* tell off, rebuke or scold. *(s)* reprimand, reproach, reprove. *(ant)* praise, applaud.

16 **deftly** *(adv)* in a deft (skilful) manner. *(s)* capably, adroitly, adeptly. *(ant)* clumsily.

17 **concentration** *(n)* the act of focusing all attention. *(s)* awareness, attentiveness. *(ant)* inattention.

18 **fit of pique** *(n)* a sudden feeling of annoyance.

19 **swipe** *(v)* hit or try to hit. *(s)* swing, slap, lash out.

20 **swear** *(v)* promise. *(s)* vow, affirm, attest.

frustrated[1] at her inability to solve this puzzle after such a lengthy study. 'It is so **perplexing**[2]. Maybe Evans knows it is unbreakable, and that is why he **frets**[3] not at losing it,' she added, **dispirited**[4].

Dylan was used to Cad's **outbursts**[5]. He'd known her since birth; Cad knew she tested his patience at times, but he was already organising the sticks again, applying his excellent eye for **detail**[6].

Resting her **weary**[7] eyes, Cad glanced over at Fishy, who was curled up at the foot of Rhys's bed and **comically**[8] appeared to be headless. Cad immediately relaxed at the sight of her **canine**[9] shadow, the pup she'd rescued from the **moat**[10], who was now, thanks to the meat pilfered from the kitchens on Cad's invisible night **jaunts**[11], a much larger dog than Cad had ever **anticipated**[12] she would be.

Cad stole a look at Rhys, who seemed to be sound asleep, but one never knew with Rhys and his **curious**[13] ways of silently watching and listening when **folks**[14] thought him stupid. Cad knew otherwise; the **taciturn**[15] boy, whom they'd recently **dubbed**[16] 'Lord Nosy', missed little.

'Look, Cad. Look again closely. Do you see what I'm seeing?' Dylan said, with the **enthusiasm**[17] of a young child.

---

1 **frustrated** *(adj)* feeling annoyed from being out of control. *(s)* exasperated, irritated. *(ant)* content.

2 **perplex** *(v)* completely confuse. *(s)* baffle, confound, flummox. *(ant)* enlighten.

3 **fret** *(v)* be constantly anxious. *(s)* worry, fuss, agonise, anguish.

4 **dispirited** *(adj)* feeling hopeless. *(s)* disheartened, dismayed. *(ant)* heartened.

5 **outburst** *(n)* a release of strong emotion. *(s)* eruption, flare-up. *(ant)* containment.

6 **detail** *(n)* an individual fact or item. *(s)* particular, circumstance.

7 **weary** *(adj)* extremely tired. *(s)* exhausted, fatigued, shattered. *(ant)* fresh, refreshed.

8 **comically** *(adv)* in a comical (funny or amusing) way. *(s)* hilariously, entertainingly. *(ant)* seriously, solemnly.

9 **canine** *(adj)* relating to or like a dog. *(s)* doggy, doggish.

10 **moat** *(n)* a defensive, water-filled trench surrounding a castle or town.

11 **jaunt** *(n)* a short journey or outing. *(s)* trip, tour.

12 **anticipate** *(v)* expect. *(s)* predict, foresee, forecast, foretell. *(ant)* neglect.

13 **curious** *(adj)* strange. *(s)* odd, unusual, funny, bizarre. *(ant)* ordinary, usual.

14 **folk** *(n)* people. *(s)* persons, individuals.

15 **taciturn** *(adj)* (of a person) quiet. *(s)* untalkative, silent. *(ant)* talkative.

16 **dub** *(v)* give a nickname to. *(s)* entitle, call, label, name, term, tag.

17 **enthusiasm** *(n)* eager enjoyment, approval or interest. *(s)* fervour, zeal. *(ant)* apathy.

Cad leaned over the sticks that imitated the cipher on the parchment, a flutter of unexpected excitement rising as she peered at them with such **intensity**[1], her eyes crossed. 'If we could just **identify**[2] these last two symbols, we may **crack**[3] it,' Dylan added.

She **stifled**[4] a groan – Cad knew this, and had for weeks, but was still unable to **fathom**[5] it. Hitherto, Evans's language had **evaded**[6] her. Then just as she was about to gather up the tiny twigs, something caught her eye. She blinked hard. In her mind, the symbols and letters took on beautiful curves like an unfurling **fern**[7], new shapes appearing as the sun streamed into the room, **illuminating**[8] the sticks on the floor before her. Then, like soldiers lining up to march into battle, like an arrow between the eyes, it hit Cad.

'Dylan,' she whispered, her heart **soaring**[9]. 'Dylan, I think I have it—'

But she stopped **abruptly**[10] as the door to their quarters burst open. Without thinking, she **automatically**[11] swiped the twigs beneath the bed and out of view. Cad's face **flushed**[12] with **fury**[13], her chest tightening with **rage**[14]. Bryn Davis, the **senior**[15] **squire**[16] whose **hide**[17] she'd saved from a cruel beating filled the doorway, wearing a **smug**[18] smile that was a work of art. Cad swallowed some ugly words, then swallowed some more.

---

1 **intensity** *(n)* the characteristic of being intense (powerful). *(s)* vehemence, vigour. *(ant)* apathy.

2 **identify** *(v)* work out who or what someone or something is. *(s)* establish, recognise, know.

3 **crack** *(v)* solve. *(s)* fathom, decipher, break, decode. *(ant)* encrypt.

4 **stifle** *(v)* restrain a reaction or stop oneself acting on an emotion. *(s)* suppress, repress, curb. *(ant)* encourage.

5 **fathom** *(v)* comprehend after much thought. *(s)* understand, grasp, perceive. *(ant)* misunderstand.

6 **evade** *(v)* avoid or escape. *(s)* elude, dodge. *(ant)* confront.

7 **fern** *(n)* a green flowerless plant which has leafy, feathery fronds.

8 **illuminate** *(v)* light up. *(s)* brighten, lighten. *(ant)* darken, dim.

9 **soar** *(v)* climb or fly rapidly above usual levels. *(s)* ascend, rise. *(ant)* plummet.

10 **abruptly** *(adv)* in an abrupt (unexpected and sudden) way. *(s)* hastily, quickly, immediately. *(ant)* gradually.

11 **automatically** *(adv)* done without thinking about beforehand. *(s)* spontaneously, impulsively. *(ant)* thoughtfully.

12 **flush** *(v)* become red. *(s)* blush. *(ant)* pale.

13 **fury** *(n)* wild anger. *(s)* rage, wrath, outrage, temper, frenzy. *(ant)* calmness.

14 **rage** *(n)* extreme anger. *(s)* wrath, fury, indignation, outrage. *(ant)* calmness.

15 **senior** *(adj)* high in rank or status. *(s)* superior, high-ranking. *(ant)* junior.

16 **squire** *(n)* a young noble man serving a knight in exchange for training to be a knight himself.

17 **hide** *(n)* the skin of an animal. *(s)* pelt.

18 **smug** *(adj)* having an overly high opinion of oneself. *(s)* self-satisfied, superior, complacent. *(ant)* humble, modest.

'You,' he said, pointing at Dylan. 'You're wanted to clean **armour**[1], now.' Then with a look of **utter**[2] **contempt**[3], his eyes turned to Cad. 'And *you,*' he snarled, are in the kitchens, *now*!'

Then Davis was gone. And as if he'd stolen the solution from Cad and taken it with him, the pattern she had clearly seen vanished from before her eyes.

---

1 **armour** *(n)* the metal plates worn to protect the body in battle. *(s)* covering, shield.

2 **utter** *(adj)* absolute. *(s)* total, complete, downright. *(ant)* partial.

3 **contempt** *(n)* the feeling that someone or something is worthless. *(s)* disdain, dislike, scorn. *(ant)* admiration.

CHAPTER TWO

Sick

Midday[1] dinner and the great hall **bustled**[2] with **ravenous**[3] **courtiers**[4], many who'd eaten nothing since last night's light supper.

'I bid you good **morrow**[5], **Goodwife**[6] Hughes,' said Cad, smiling at the kindly lady who had cared for her so well during her **stint**[7] in the tower. 'Hugh,' she added with a nod at Mrs Hughes's **scrawny**[8] son, Sir Robert's **apprentice**[9].

Cad **marvelled**[10] at such an unlikely mother-and-son pair: she **rotund**[11] and **jolly**[12], he **long-shanked**[13] and **dour**[14]. Hugh Hughes, what a mouthful that name was, and thank goodness he

---

1 **midday** *(n)* the middle of the day. *(s)* noon. *(ant)* midnight.

2 **bustle** *(v)* be full of activity. *(s)* hum, whirl, buzz. *(ant)* settle, quieten.

3 **ravenous** *(adj)* very hungry. *(s)* famished, starving, wanting. *(ant)* full, sated, satiated.

4 **courtier** *(n)* a person who attends a royal court. *(s)* aristocrat, noble, peer, attendant.

5 **morrow** *(n)* (archaic) the near future. *(s)* destiny, fate, prospect.

6 **goodwife** *(n)* the female head of a household, a term often used in the Middle Ages.

7 **stint** *(n)* a period of time. *(s)* stretch, spell, term.

8 **scrawny** *(adj)* bony and thin. *(s)* skinny, scraggy, spindly. *(ant)* fat, plump.

9 **apprentice** *(n)* a person learning from a skilled person. *(s)* learner, trainee, novice, pupil. *(ant)* veteran, master.

10 **marvel** *(v)* be filled with amazement and wonder. *(s)* gape, stare. *(ant)* disregard.

11 **rotund** *(adj)* plump. *(s)* chubby, portly, round, stout. *(ant)* thin, slender, skinny.

12 **jolly** *(adj)* happy. *(s)* cheerful, mirthful, merry. *(ant)* miserable, grumpy.

13 **long-shanked** *(adj)* (archaic) having long legs. *(s)* long-legged.

14 **dour** *(adj)* unfriendly, gloomy or miserable. *(s)* sour, stern, severe, grim. *(ant)* kindly, friendly, cheerful.

had survived the ordeal of riding Dewi's **stallion**[1], Midnight, when ordered to **retrieve**[2] Llywelyn by Sir Robert. Poor Mrs Hughes had been **despairing**[3] until Hugh had returned, **bedraggled**[4] yet thankfully in one piece.

Cad was not that hungry, and only picked at some bread; a morning's preparation – which included nibbling food in the castle's **vast**[5] kitchens – had **quashed**[6] her appetite.

Throughout her chores, she had closed her eyes, trying to picture the pattern that still eluded her: the **sequence**[7] that had formed in her head to then vanish when Bryn had **barged**[8] into their bedchamber, **doling**[9] out **duties**[10]. If only it had been kindly Goodwife Hughes who had popped her head in this morning.

Cad filled her cup and sipped some water. **Refreshed**[11] by its crisp coolness, she **appreciated**[12] how fortunate they were to have the natural well, which sat in Catrin Castle's **bailey**[13]. Catrin was a **unique**[14] castle, in that, although a vast **creation**[15] **boasting**[16] a **tilt yard**[17] and moat, Catrin rested **atop**[18] a naturally formed hill of rock. Due to an **abundance**[19] of rain in the mountains, in winter months, the moat would fill to its very top, and even in summer, it never failed Catrin.

---

1 **stallion** *(n)* a male horse that has not been gelded (neutered).

2 **retrieve** *(v)* bring or get something back. *(s)* fetch. *(ant)* lose, forfeit.

3 **despairing** *(adj)* feeling or showing the loss of all hope. *(s)* frantic, desperate. *(ant)* joyous.

4 **bedraggled** *(adj)* dishevelled (messy). *(s)* disarranged, unkempt, rumpled. *(ant)* neat, clean.

5 **vast** *(adj)* large or immense. *(s)* enormous, colossal, huge, gigantic. *(ant)* small, insignificant.

6 **quash** *(v)* suppress or put an end to. *(s)* quell, curb, subdue. *(ant)* allow.

7 **sequence** *(n)* a particular order. *(s)* arrangement, pattern, chronology. *(ant)* disorder.

8 **barge** *(v)* move with force. *(s)* push, shove, jostle.

9 **dole** *(v)* share something. *(s)* allocate, allot, assign.

10 **duty** *(n)* an action or task one must do as part of one's job. *(s)* chore, responsibility, obligation.

11 **refresh** *(v)* give new energy or strength. *(s)* enliven, revive, fortify. *(ant)* tire.

12 **appreciate** *(v)* understand or see the full worth of. *(s)* recognise, value, perceive. *(ant)* disregard.

13 **bailey** *(n)* a castle's inner courtyard, enclosed by an outer wall.

14 **unique** *(adj)* unlike anything else. *(s)* exclusive, distinctive, individual. *(ant)* common.

15 **creation** *(n)* something that has been made. *(s)* construction, design, building.

16 **boast** *(v)* possess a feature to be proud of. *(s)* have, own, enjoy.

17 **tilt yard** *(n)* a place or courtyard where jousts took place, sometimes enclosed.

18 **atop** *(prep)* on the top of. *(s)* upon.

19 **abundance** *(n)* a large quantity of something. *(s)* profusion, plethora, mass. *(ant)* lack, little, deficiency.

With no interest in food, and **distracted**[1] by the cipher, Cad fingered the parchment hidden up her sleeve. With Dylan's keen eye, they'd almost cracked it; just this **stubborn**[2] final **hurdle**[3] remained, yet thanks to Bryn's timing, it was one they must still **conquer**[4]. The **enigma's**[5] solution was the key to finding Catrin's **traitors**[6]; of that she was sure: a so-called **ally**[7] in this castle was bobbing with a bad apple.

'Hello, *girls*, what **fascinates**[8] you young *ladies* so?'

Why do they call us girls? thought Cad, instant rage rising as she almost spat her food at the **sneering**[9] boy. But, just about controlling herself, she shoved the parchment further up her sleeve, and with her mouth full of bread, snapped, 'Jack Jones, you're a noddle-headed worm.'

Jack's cod-thick lips flapped in a snigger. His shirt drifted from his trousers as he put his plate on the table and sat by Bryn, his **ample**[10] rear **greeting**[11] the bench with a thud. He and Bryn sat there as bold as two toads on a water lily. Cad could have slapped Jack's frog-like face, but went back to picking at her food and poking at the myriad **scored**[12] **grooves**[13] on the scarred table with her **gnawed**[14] fingernail.

Yet, unable to **resist**[15] checking on Bryn, she **glanced**[16] sideways and caught him staring at her with an odd look on his face. The moment he noticed her glance, his face changed. He **smirked**[17]

---

1 **distract** *(v)* deflect attention from something or someone. *(s)* divert, disturb, sidetrack. *(ant)* focus.

2 **stubborn** *(adj)* difficult to overcome. *(s)* persistent, lingering. *(ant)* fleeting.

3 **hurdle** *(n)* a problem which needs to be overcome. *(s)* obstacle, snag, difficulty. *(ant)* pleasure.

4 **conquer** *(v)* successfully overcome. *(s)* master, beat, control. *(ant)* lose to.

5 **enigma** *(n)* someone or something that is difficult to understand. *(s)* mystery, conundrum, riddle.

6 **traitor** *(n)* someone who betrays (double-crosser). *(s)* conspirator, turncoat, collaborator. *(ant)* loyalist.

7 **ally** *(n)* a person that helps another in a task. *(s)* aide, associate, supporter, friend. *(ant)* opponent.

8 **fascinate** *(v)* draw someone's close interest. *(s)* absorb, captivate, enthral. *(ant)* bore.

9 **sneer** *(v)* speak or smile in a nasty manner. *(s)* smirk, snigger, snicker. *(ant)* encourage.

10 **ample** *(adj)* large. *(s)* broad, extensive. *(ant)* small, meagre.

11 **greet** *(v)* become apparent to. *(s)* meet, approach. *(ant)* avoid.

12 **score** *(v)* cut. *(s)* nick, deface, gouge, mark. *(ant)* smooth.

13 **groove** *(n)* a long, narrow cut in a hard substance. *(s)* channel, hollow.

14 **gnaw** *(v)* chew persistently. *(s)* bite, nibble.

15 **resist** *(v)* hold back from doing something. *(s)* refuse, ignore. *(ant)* accept.

16 **glance** *(v)* take a hurried look. *(s)* glimpse, peep, peek. *(ant)* stare, peer.

17 **smirk** *(v)* smile, but in a smug, conceited or silly way. *(s)* grin, sneer, leer.

his finest and **slurped**[1] his beer, dashing away dribbles with his sleeve. After she'd rescued him from an **atrocious**[2] beating, he'd been **civil**[3] for a while, but as time slipped by, he'd **reverted**[4] to his **foul**[5] **taunting**[6] ways.

His **hapless**[7] **sidekick**[8], Jack Jones, did most of Bryn's dirty **bidding**[9] and **derived**[10] great pleasure from calling Cad, Dylan and Rhys 'girls' and 'ladies'. Cad mostly ignored their **catcalls**[11], but sometimes they caught her off guard, and like now, her hot head **threatened**[12] to rule her tongue.

'Ignore him. Swallow those words,' warned Dylan, as he sat beside her, a **hunk**[13] of bread in his hand.

'I know. I know,' Cad hissed, still wanting to swipe the smug smile off Bryn's face.

'Hold onto that bread, or you'll end up in the tower again,' muttered Dylan.

'You're right,' Cad answered, squashing her **seething**[14] temper, along with the bread in her fist.

However, inwardly **uneasy**[15], like a **treacherous**[16] river under a thin layer of ice, Cad suspected a sharper edge and hidden depths to Bryn and Jack's teasing. She wondered whether Bryn suspected she was *really* a girl, and was just waiting for an **opportune**[17] time to reveal her secret. But she suspected he dared not cross Robert Evans, the Knight Hawk left in charge whilst her

---

1 **slurp** *(v)* drink or eat noisily. *(s)* suck, guzzle. *(ant)* sip.

2 **atrocious** *(adj)* extremely unpleasant. *(s)* dreadful, appalling, vile. *(ant)* wonderful.

3 **civil** *(adj)* polite. *(s)* courteous, chivalrous, respectful. *(ant)* rude, discourteous.

4 **revert** *(v)* return to (a previous state, practice, topic). *(s)* regress, lapse. *(ant)* develop, grow.

5 **foul** *(adj)* bad. *(s)* wicked, immoral, wrongful. *(ant)* pleasant, righteous.

6 **taunt** *(v)* provoke or challenge someone. *(s)* criticise, mock, tease, goad, jibe, sneer, insult. *(ant)* compliment.

7 **hapless** *(adj)* unfortunate. *(s)* unlucky, luckless, wretched. *(ant)* fortunate, fortuitous.

8 **sidekick** *(n)* a helper of lesser rank. *(s)* accomplice, crony, aide. *(ant)* equal, colleague.

9 **bidding** *(n)* the asking or ordering of someone to do something. *(s)* request, command.

10 **derive** *(v)* come, or obtain from something specific. *(s)* acquire, attain.

11 **catcall** *(n)* a public insult. *(s)* boo, taunt, hiss, heckle, jeer, mockery. *(ant)* compliment.

12 **threaten** *(v)* produce an unpleasant result. *(s)* promise, herald, signify.

13 **hunk** *(n)* a large piece of something, often food. *(s)* chunk, wedge, portion. *(ant)* morsel, scrap.

14 **seething** *(adj)* full of intense anger. *(s)* furious, enraged, fuming. *(ant)* calm.

15 **uneasy** *(adj)* feeling troubled. *(s)* worried, anxious, nervous. *(ant)* calm, easy.

16 **treacherous** *(adj)* presenting hidden or unforeseen dangers. *(s)* hazardous, perilous. *(ant)* safe.

17 **opportune** *(adj)* (of a time) appropriate or convenient for an action or event. *(s)* advantageous. *(ant)* disadvantageous.

father continued on his **quest**[1] to recover the stolen Gwalch Gem bracelet.

Thoughts of Llywelyn, who'd saved her from a well's waters and raised her as his own, lifted Cad's heart. For although his mission remained unsuccessful, he would soon return here to Catrin for **respite**[2] and supplies.

And whilst she **masqueraded**[3] as a page, and could not **address**[4] him as her father, just the thought of his presence, in this now-**solemn**[5] castle, filled her with **hope**[6] and **joy**[7].

From beneath the bench where she sat, a wet nose nudged Cad's **calf**[8]. Cad's **surreptitious**[9] hand sneaked beneath the table, as Fishy, very gently, took the scraps from Cad's fingers. Cad had taught her pup well: do not snatch from your master; sit; stay; **recall**[10]; play dead and attack, all of which the clever little Fishy performed with **aplomb**[11].

When Cad had saved Prince John from Dewi's oubliette, Sir Robert, who'd worn a face like a **pinched**[12] **raven**[13], had been left with little choice but to allow Cad to keep Fishy – Cad was a hero and had been able to make some requests – for a while at least, **milking**[14] the **opportunity**[15] while it lasted.

Fishy was her shadow; she kept Cad warm at night, sometimes hopping over to Dylan or Rhys for extra cuddles. But no matter what, each morning when Cad opened her eyes, the first thing to greet her was Fishy, forever **beholden**[16] to her **saviour**[17].

---

1 **quest** *(n)* a long or difficult search for something. *(s)* mission, adventure, crusade, expedition, journey.

2 **respite** *(n)* a period of rest or relief from something difficult. *(s)* break, interval. *(ant)* continuation.

3 **masquerade** *(v)* make a false and deceptive show of pretence. *(s)* impersonate, pose, imitate.

4 **address** *(v)* name someone or talk to. *(s)* label, identify.

5 **solemn** *(adj)* not cheerful. *(s)* sombre, grave, serious. *(ant)* cheerful.

6 **hope** *(n)* expectation of good. *(s)* optimism, promise. *(ant)* pessimism.

7 **joy** *(n)* great happiness. *(s)* delight, jubilation. *(ant)* misery, unhappiness.

8 **calf** *(n)* the fleshy part at the back of a person's leg below the knee (plural: *calves*).

9 **surreptitious** *(adj)* something kept secret. *(s)* clandestine, stealthy, sneaky, furtive. *(ant)* open, blatant.

10 **recall** *(v)* (of a dog) come back when called. *(s)* return.

11 **aplomb** *(n)* self-confidence. *(s)* assurance, surety, composure. *(ant)* fear.

12 **pinched** *(adj)* tense because of an unpleasant situation or feeling. *(s)* fraught, stressed. *(ant)* relaxed.

13 **raven** *(n)* a large black bird.

14 **milk** *(v)* make the most of. *(s)* exploit, use, utilise.

15 **opportunity** *(n)* the chance to be able to do or achieve something. *(s)* prospect, occasion.

16 **beholden** *(adj)* owing thanks or duty to. *(s)* indebted, grateful, thankful, appreciative.

17 **saviour** *(n)* someone who saves someone else from peril or hardship. *(s)* rescuer, champion. *(ant)* condemner.

Ever grateful for Fishy's friendship, Cad **champed**[1] her tasteless bread and found herself staring at Bryn again, who noticed. For a **fleeting**[2] moment, a knowing glance passed between the two, before he then **glared**[3] back with a look as warm as a winter blizzard. Since she'd saved him from the beating, this often happened.

Cad **averted**[4] her eyes, and saw Jack Jones had pushed away his **trencher**[5]. Odd, as that boy ate for ten, and it seemed to show. **Albeit**[6] a muscled boy, his rotund face revealed his appetite, and she'd swear he'd grown **inches**[7] in weeks, and not just upwards.

It was a constant irritation to Cad that she struggled when **wrestling**[8] Jack in the tilt yard, who fought like a bulldog with a bone, and things would only get tougher. She must work harder **lest**[9] she be **deemed**[10] weak, but hand-to-hand **combat**[11] with the boys would never be a **cinch**[12]. However, nothing would stop her from proving to her father that she was worthy of a **knighthood**[13]. Worthy of joining his magical order, the Knights Hawk, to whom he'd **bestowed**[14] the powers of Instinct with the Gwalch Gem bracelet. She was heartsore at that thought because until he recovered the stolen bracelet, Llywelyn could knight no one. If he failed, the **order**[15] would eventually die out, and she would never join the Knights Hawk. That thought was **unbearable**[16].

Still not finding her appetite, Cad pushed away her plate. **Intrigued**[17] by a strange **retching**[18]

---

1 **champ** *(v)* chew noisily. *(s)* chomp, gnaw, munch.

2 **fleeting** *(adj)* lasting for a very short time. *(s)* brief, momentary, sudden. *(ant)* lasting, permanent.

3 **glare** *(v)* give an angry or fierce stare. *(s)* scowl, glower, frown. *(ant)* grin, smile.

4 **avert** *(v)* turn away. *(s)* turn aside, divert.

5 **trencher** *(n)* a plate for food. *(s)* dish, bowl, salver.

6 **albeit** *(con)* although. *(s)* though, even though, while.

7 **inch** *(n)* a unit of measurement which is equal to one twelfth of a foot.

8 **wrestle** *(v)* force or fight by grappling (tussling). *(s)* struggle, brawl, battle, scuffle.

9 **lest** *(con)* with the intention of preventing or to avoid the risk of. *(s)* in case, for fear that.

10 **deem** *(v)* consider, judge or regard in a specified way. *(s)* assume, believe, reckon, suppose. *(ant)* misjudge.

11 **combat** *(n)* fighting. *(s)* battle, action, conflict. *(ant)* peace.

12 **cinch** *(n)* an easy task. *(s)* breeze, gift, snap, cakewalk. *(ant)* difficulty, nightmare, hardship.

13 **knighthood** *(n)* the status, title or rank a knight.

14 **bestow** *(v)* offer or give an honour, gift or right. *(s)* confer, grant, present. *(ant)* withdraw.

15 **order** *(n)* a society of knights bound by a common rule of life. *(s)* organisation, company, group.

16 **unbearable** *(adj)* difficult or impossible to endure (suffer). *(s)* intolerable, unacceptable. *(ant)* bearable, tolerable.

17 **intrigue** *(v)* arouse curiosity or interest. *(s)* fascinate, captivate, attract, enthral. *(ant)* bore, disenchant.

18 **retch** *(v)* make the motion and sound of vomiting. *(s)* reach, heave, gag, convulse.

sound, she sat **erect**[1] and turned towards Jack Jones. A half-hiccup, half-**belch**[2] **emerged**[3] from his throat. Cad watched as his face turned grey and a **waxy**[4] **sheen**[5] oiled his skin. She knew the signs, and immediately leaped up from the bench, springing away just in time to dodge the **projectile**[6] vomit that sprayed forth, splattering Bryn Davis instead.

'Saviour's nails!' Bryn yelled, **vaulting**[7] to his feet.

The **chaos**[8] **elevated**[9] as people scattered to avoid the **spew**[10]. A smirk tugged at Cad's lips, a laugh boiling up from her belly. Bryn, dripping in his friend's stomach contents, stood and left the hall, giving a now **staggering**[11] Jack Jones an **almighty**[12] kick to the rear as he did, sending the boy **barrelling**[13] in the opposite direction.

'Come, Fishy,' Cad said, any remaining appetite now lost in the **stench**[14] of spew.

'Wait for me,' Dylan cried, grabbing an **unscathed**[15] apple, and following Cad with little Rhys **in tow**[16] before someone **bade**[17] them clean up the mess.

---

1 **erect** *(adj)* straight or rigidly upright. *(s)* bolt upright. *(ant)* horizontal, prone, prostrate.

2 **belch** *(n)* an emission of noisy wind from the stomach. *(s)* burp, eruct.

3 **emerge** *(v)* move out of or through something. *(s)* arise, arrive, surface. *(ant)* disappear, submerge.

4 **waxy** *(adj)* like wax in appearance. *(s)* ashen, pallid, blanched. *(ant)* flushed.

5 **sheen** *(n)* a soft shine. *(s)* lustre. *(ant)* dullness.

6 **projectile** *(adj)* something flying through the air, especially a weapon. *(s)* airborne.

7 **vault** *(v)* leap or spring by supporting or propelling oneself with one's hands. *(s)* jump, bound.

8 **chaos** *(n)* total disorder and confusion. *(s)* mayhem, pandemonium. *(ant)* order, tranquillity.

9 **elevate** *(v)* increase the level of something. *(s)* raise. *(ant)* decrease, diminish.

10 **spew** *(n)* vomit. *(s)* sick.

11 **stagger** *(v)* move unsteadily. *(s)* sway, lurch, reel, stumble.

12 **almighty** *(adj)* great or enormous. *(s)* massive, supreme, mighty. *(ant)* weak, insignificant, feeble.

13 **barrel** *(v)* move quickly and in a way that is out of control. *(s)* career, hurtle, fly.

14 **stench** *(n)* a strong and horrid smell. *(s)* stink, reek, malodour. *(ant)* perfume, fragrance.

15 **unscathed** *(adj)* without suffering, harm or injury. *(s)* safe, unhurt. *(ant)* injured, harmed.

16 **in tow** (phrase) following or accompanying a person or thing. *(s)* in convoy.

17 **bid** *(v)* (archaic) command (past tense: *bade*). *(s)* tell, order, direct, instruct.

CHAPTER THREE

Rhys

'Master Cad, w–w–what caused Jack Jones's sickness?' **stuttered**[1] Rhys, who was perched on the edge of his bed, his **complexion**[2] paling to grey, his fingers **wringing**[3] the **hem**[4] of his **tunic**[5].

'I don't know, Rhys. Jack's a greedy **hog**[6]. He probably stuffed too much down too quickly. You know what he's like, and don't call me *master*. I am your friend,' Cad **reassured**[7] him, throwing a side-eyed glance at Dylan, for she knew Rhys had a strange fear of vomit: it terrified him.

Rhys had odd ways about him, but she and Dylan knew of his good heart, **hence**[8] she'd shared her secret with him. **Orphaned**[9] like her, and even though he infuriatingly called her 'master', Cad knew Rhys saw Dylan and her as **siblings**[10], for that is what they were to him: his **surrogate**[11] family.

---

1 **stutter** *(v)* struggle to say one's words. *(s)* stammer, falter, hesitate. *(ant)* enunciate.

2 **complexion** *(n)* the natural state of a person's skin, especially that of the face.

3 **wring** *(v)* squeeze and twist. *(s)* knead, screw.

4 **hem** *(n)* the edges of clothing which has been turned under and sewn into place. *(s)* edge, border.

5 **tunic** *(n)* a loose garment, often sleeveless and worn with a belt. *(s)* surcoat, robe.

6 **hog** *(n)* pig. *(s)* swine, grunter, porker.

7 **reassure** *(v)* do or say something to remove someone's fears or doubts. *(s)* comfort, hearten. *(ant)* unnerve.

8 **hence** *(adv)* for this reason. *(s)* therefore, consequently, thus, so.

9 **orphan** *(v)* make a child an orphan (without birth parents).

10 **sibling** *(n)* a brother or sister.

11 **surrogate** *(adj)* substitute. *(s)* replacement, stand-in.

Given the **spate**[1] of unexplained sickness in the last few days, Cad worried about the shy lad. Several people had suffered repeated vomiting, and although Catrin Castle, like Llywelyn's Cadwaladr Castle, was one of the cleanest in the **realm**[2], it seemed to be spreading and much too fast for her liking. It was odd, for the weather had been dry and sunny for weeks, which often **prevented**[3] sickness from taking hold. Llywelyn's moats boasted clean water, as did the castle's **internal**[4] well. And thanks to Sir Robert's **ingenious**[5] drainage plans, waste from the **latrines**[6] flowed away from the castle into deep underground **chambers**[7] beyond its walls, where it **rotted**[8] without **polluting**[9] the area.

Thinking of Evans, Cad took the parchment from her tunic and unfolded it.

'As we're forbidden to train today, we may as well work on the cipher,' she said to Dylan.

In return, Dylan, who had clearly been hoping to nap away his afternoon, rolled his eyes and frowned all the way up to his forehead.

'Fishy, sit with Rhys,' ordered Cad, ignoring Dylan's **sour**[10] look and pointing at Rhys's bed.

Deciphering codes did not interest Rhys, but Fishy did. Rhys would pet her for hours, and Fishy happily **obliged**[11], waiting patiently for the **morsels**[12] Rhys retrieved from the folds of his **filthy**[13] tunic. He was not a boy much keen on soap and water, and Cad worried he'd not make a knight, but she'd never share those thoughts and **crush**[14] the boy who was here due to

---

1 **spate** *(n)* a series of similar things happening one after the other. *(s)* outbreak, wave.

2 **realm** *(n)* an area of responsibility or rule. *(s)* kingdom, domain, monarchy.

3 **prevent** *(v)* stop something from happening. *(s)* check, halt, arrest. *(ant)* allow, cause, permit.

4 **internal** *(adj)* relating to the inside. *(s)* interior, inner. *(ant)* external, outer.

5 **ingenious** *(adj)* clever, inventive and original. *(s)* innovative, creative. *(ant)* unimaginative, uncreative.

6 **latrine** *(n)* a toilet, especially one that is shared by many. *(s)* privy, garderobe.

7 **chamber** *(n)* an underground space. *(s)* compartment, hollow, cell.

8 **rot** *(v)* cause to decay (break down). *(s)* degrade, decompose.

9 **pollute** *(v)* contaminate with hazardous substances. *(s)* poison, taint, foul. *(ant)* purify, clean.

10 **sour** *(adj)* expressing disappointment or anger. *(s)* resentful, irritable. *(ant)* pleasant, amiable.

11 **oblige** *(v)* do as someone asks to make them happy. *(s)* indulge, serve, gratify.

12 **morsel** *(n)* a small piece or amount. *(s)* mouthful, bite, nibble, bit. *(ant)* entirety, total.

13 **filthy** *(adj)* extremely dirty. *(s)* grimy, mucky. *(ant)* clean.

14 **crush** *(v)* make someone feel incredibly embarrassed or disappointed. *(s)* humiliate, devastate. *(ant)* cheer.

Llywelyn's kindness, another of his rescued **waifs**[1] and **strays**[2].

Until the birth of his only son, Prince John, Llywelyn and his wife, Siân, had been childless for years. In treating Cad as their own, they'd allowed Rhys to follow her when she'd **insisted**[3], **begged**[4] and **pleaded**[5] with her **adoptive**[6] father to **sanction**[7] her knight's training at his brother's castle.

Thinking of her family, Cad tried to ignore what she knew was coming, but Siân popped into her head: her beautiful, kind mother, who had so cruelly **absconded**[8] with Llywelyn's brother, leaving her only son, Prince John, behind. Cad could no longer bear to think of Siân, and finally pushed the image from her mind and turned to the cipher.

'Dylan,' she said, **rotating**[9] the parchment and **observing**[10] its intricate symbols from all angles. 'I had it this morning. I saw it as clear as day before that **wantwit**[11] Davis burst in on us.'

'How frustrating,' Dylan replied, his smile fading into a serious look. He sat beside her, removing the delicately whittled twigs from the leather pouch and began laying them on the floor between their beds.

'I know this cipher is trying to tell us something. Something about the Gwalch Gem …' Cad muttered, the wheels in her head spinning.

Cad hadn't shared what her father had revealed before he'd left for his quest. Not even Dylan knew that Llywelyn and Evans suspected the bracelet could **manipulate**[12] time – that both of them had been working on something before Dewi stole the bracelet.

'Come, Cad. Let us study the patterns now before Bryn has time to wash off the spew and

---

1 **waif** *(n)* a homeless, neglected or abandoned person, often a child. *(s)* orphan, stray.

2 **stray** *(n)* a person or animal that has no home or carer and struggles to survive.

3 **insist** *(v)* demand forcefully without allowing refusal. *(s)* command, require, persist. *(ant)* give up.

4 **beg** *(v)* ask honestly. *(s)* beseech, implore, plead, request. *(ant)* offer.

5 **plead** *(v)* make an emotional appeal. *(s)* beg, beseech, implore, request. *(ant)* offer.

6 **adoptive** *(adj)* (of a person) related by adoption (legally raising someone else's child).

7 **sanction** *(v)* approve or permit. *(s)* allow, authorise, endorse. *(ant)* veto, disallow.

8 **abscond** *(v)* leave in rushed secret. *(s)* flee, run away, make off. *(ant)* remain, stay.

9 **rotate** *(v)* move in a circle. *(s)* turn, revolve, spin.

10 **observe** *(v)* watch carefully. *(s)* view, study, regard. *(ant)* miss, ignore.

11 **wantwit** *(n)* a person in need of wit. *(s)* fool, halfwit, dolt, clod, ninny. *(ant)* genius.

12 **manipulate** *(v)* alter, control or influence. *(s)* direct, affect, change.

return for **vengeance**[1] with **vile**[2] chores for us.' Dylan sat arranging the twigs as they'd been that morning, his fingers as careful as a bishop's.

Over in a corner of the room, gentle snores rose from Rhys's bed. Fishy was snoozing; whether Rhys was, or was only pretending to, Cad was unsure, but she knew the boy **barely**[3] missed a trick.

Her eyes owlish, Cad placed the parchment on the floor and **gazed**[4] at the **array**[5] of twigs, **mustering**[6] the patience and skills needed to solve a puzzle **thus**[7]. She gently prodded and pushed the slim sticks, **manoeuvring**[8] them into new **designs**[9] and figures, noting which she felt worked, **discarding**[10] those that seemed to fail, and then recording the results on another piece of parchment. One more detail, and they might solve this **conundrum**[11]. For sure, she'd seen something earlier, **materialising**[12] like a long-lost ship from a **fog**[13], and now it was gone.

After a lengthy stretch of **staunch**[14] concentration, frustrated and weary, her head **throbbed**[15] and her eyes ached from staring at the ordered twigs. Dylan pulled a bored face, and she knew he'd lost interest and was daydreaming of the tilt yard's combat and **jousting**[16].

'Lord save us all!' she **cursed**[17], swiping at the twigs and **strewing**[18] them between the beds.

---

1 **vengeance** *(n)* punishment for a wrongdoing. *(s)* revenge, retribution. *(ant)* forgiveness.

2 **vile** *(adj)* very unpleasant. *(s)* nasty, foul, horrid. *(ant)* pleasant.

3 **barely** *(adv)* hardly, almost not. *(s)* rarely, scarcely. *(ant)* easily, often.

4 **gaze** *(v)* look steadily. *(s)* stare, gape, peer. *(ant)* glimpse.

5 **array** *(n)* a significant display or range of something. *(s)* selection, arrangement, group. *(ant)* individual, one.

6 **muster** *(v)* summon up (a response, attitude or feeling). *(s)* gather, raise, call on. *(ant)* disperse.

7 **thus** *(adv)* in this way. *(s)* like so, like this.

8 **manoeuvre** *(v)* guide or move carefully. *(s)* direct, steer.

9 **design** *(n)* a pattern or plan. *(s)* arrangement, composition, layout.

10 **discard** *(v)* throw something aside, as it is no longer useful or desirable. *(s)* abandon, reject, scrap. *(ant)* retain.

11 **conundrum** *(n)* a difficult or confusing question or problem. *(s)* puzzle, mystery.

12 **materialise** *(v)* appear or become present. *(s)* occur, turn up. *(ant)* disappear.

13 **fog** *(n)* a thick cloud of water droplets forming in the air which restricts or obscures visibility.

14 **staunch** *(adj)* committed. *(s)* dedicated, stalwart. *(ant)* unreliable.

15 **throb** *(v)* experience a feeling of pain which comes in regular beats. *(s)* pulsate, pound.

16 **joust** *(n)* a medieval contest in which two opponents fought on horseback using lances. *(s)* tourney, tilt.

17 **curse** *(v)* speak bad words or blaspheme (speak disrespectfully about God). *(s)* swear.

18 **strew** *(v)* scatter or spread things untidily. *(s)* throw, cast, toss. *(ant)* gather, assemble.

'Cad, rest your eyes a while,' said Dylan, **seeking**[1] an excuse to stop, and she didn't really blame him for that as he climbed onto his bed.

Murmuring a **vexed**[2] sigh, Cad flicked the stray twigs into a pile, and was about to gather them up into the pouch when she froze. One pattern gave her pause. She sucked in a breath, afraid to **exhale**[3], lest what she now saw vanished along with it. Too scared to blink, she whispered, 'Dylan, come. *Now!*'

With an **exaggerated**[4] groan, Dylan rolled across his bed and plopped onto the floor beside her.

Wide-eyed, she nodded her chin at him. 'Do you see it?'

Blank, Dylan looked at her. 'Not me, you nonny. Look at the pattern. What do you see?'

He stared at the twigs, blinked, scratched his head, then said, 'Twigs.'

'Here, here,' she **urged**[5], with good-natured patience, pointing and **adjusting**[6] slightly. 'There.'

Just then, Rhys's head popped over the side of Dylan's bed.

'I think I see it,' he said quietly. 'It is just there.' He pointed at the last pattern of twigs lying in a row.

Cad stopped. Her chin dropped, almost touching her chest in shock.

Silently, Rhys slid off the bed onto the floor, and with his slim little fingers, arranged the twigs in an intricate pattern, pointed to the parchment and said, 'See, it is here. Slot this shape into the central part, turn it twice, and count along using the shape's corners to **alert**[7] you to its meaning. Then you have your missing pieces. Now you might be able to read the message. I think each pattern stands for letters.'

Like a fish hooked on a line, Cad's mouth flapped, but silence **ensued**[8] as she quickly grabbed Sir Robert's parchment.

---

1 **seek** *(v)* try to find. *(s)* look for, hunt for, search for, pursue. *(ant)* lose.

2 **vexed** *(adj)* annoyed. *(s)* displeased, irked, riled, irritated. *(ant)* pacified, calm.

3 **exhale** *(v)* breathe out. *(s)* emit, expel, expire, respire. *(ant)* inhale, breathe in.

4 **exaggerated** *(adj)* increased beyond normal proportions. *(s)* overstated, embellished. *(ant)* understated.

5 **urge** *(v)* try to persuade someone. *(s)* encourage, press. *(ant)* dissuade, deter, discourage.

6 **adjust** *(v)* change to achieve a desired outcome. *(s)* alter, modify, regulate.

7 **alert** *(v)* warn of a problem or danger or notify someone of something. *(s)* advise, disclose. *(ant)* ignore.

8 **ensue** *(v)* happen afterwards or as a consequence. *(s)* arise, develop, follow. *(ant)* precede.

Rhys, who suddenly seemed to fill the whole room, was already back on his bed stroking Fishy, whose tail happily slapped its blankets.

Cad's eyes **scanned**[1] the symbols, her mind **reckoning**[2] and remembering, slotting letters into place and removing others, switching patterns, checking the fit.

'Well, I never, Rhys Price,' she eventually muttered, any **prior**[3] **opinion**[4] she'd held of him immediately rolling back.

'What? What is it?' asked Dylan, **sorely**[5] **lagging**[6].

As the **scales fell**[7] from Cad's eyes, she shook her head in astonishment. Rhys couldn't even read properly, but **evidently**[8] that mattered not. On the **brink**[9] of seeing the answer for herself, he'd gently tipped her over the edge, and there it was, that ship emerging from the fog. The cracked code lay before her on the floor.

Without delay, Cad scribbled the solution onto her parchment and scoured Evans's document for the answer she'd sought for weeks. Her mind clicked and whirred, its wheels spinning like a wagon rolling down a hill.

'What is it?' asked Dylan, staring, clearly confused at the startling mix of anxiety and excitement that had swept across Cad's face.

But Cad didn't answer as the letters swirled before her eyes, lining up into words, sentences and paragraphs to be read and understood. And just in case she'd misunderstood their meaning, she read that very last line over and over again.

---

1 **scan** *(v)* look carefully. *(s)* study, scour, search, inspect.

2 **reckon** *(v)* work something out. *(s)* calculate, appraise.

3 **prior** *(adj)* coming or existing before. *(s)* earlier, previous. *(ant)* later, subsequent.

4 **opinion** *(n)* a view not always based on fact. *(s)* belief, judgement, perspective. *(ant)* fact.

5 **sorely** *(adv)* to a large degree. *(s)* badly, severely, woefully.

6 **lag** *(v)* fall behind others. *(s)* delay, dally, dither. *(ant)* keep up.

7 **scales fall** (from one's eyes) (phrase) one is no longer deceived.

8 **evidently** *(adv)* clearly. *(s)* obviously, plainly, manifestly. *(ant)* doubtfully.

9 **brink** *(n)* the point at which something is about to happen. *(s)* threshold, verge.

CHAPTER FOUR

Weapons and Thieves

'Cad, what is it?' Dylan asked for a fourth time, his brows becoming one.

Cad **scrutinised**[1] the **penultimate**[2] and last lines of Sir Robert's pilfered parchment; the **obstinate**[3] code that had fought them **furiously**[4], that had taken weeks to **surrender**[5], finally lay here defeated, **smitten**[6] by the **might**[7] of Rhys's hidden **talents**[8]. Rhys, the boy who **apparently**[9] snoozed on his bed in the corner of their chamber, had cracked the code they'd **teetered**[10] on the brink of for weeks.

'*Cad!*' Dylan barked. '*What is it?*'

Cad stared at Dylan, her eyes like **saucers**[11], her mind double-checking – no, triple-checking – her results before she jumped in with both big feet. She glanced over at Rhys and Fishy. Rhys

---

1 **scrutinise** *(v)* inspect or examine closely. *(s)* study, explore.

2 **penultimate** *(adj)* last but one in a series of things. *(s)* second last.

3 **obstinate** *(adj)* unwilling to give in. *(s)* stubborn, tenacious, unyielding. *(ant)* compliant.

4 **furiously** *(adv)* in a furious (energetic) manner. *(s)* energetically, feverishly, frantically. *(ant)* slowly.

5 **surrender** *(v)* stop resisting an enemy or opponent. *(s)* submit, concede, capitulate, yield. *(ant)* fight, win.

6 **smite** *(v)* conquer or defeat (past participle: smitten). *(s)* beat, quash, crush. *(ant)* lose to.

7 **might** *(n)* impressive power. *(s)* strength, force, vigour. *(ant)* weakness, feebleness.

8 **talent** *(n)* a natural skill or ability. *(s)* gift, flair, aptitude, forte, expertise. *(ant)* inability.

9 **apparently** *(adv)* as far as one knows or can see. *(s)* supposedly, seemingly. *(ant)* implausibly.

10 **teeter** *(v)* move back and forth. *(s)* sway, lurch, reel.

11 **saucer** *(n)* a shallow dish on which a cup is placed, but in the Middle Ages was used for serving sauces.

snored, but Cad now knew he was listening – to everything. Did he ever sleep, she wondered. All those times she and Dylan had discussed castle business, their heads huddled together, voices a **mere**[1] whisper. As they'd **mulled**[2] over the cipher, albeit always in their own invented **pig Latin**[3] **gibberish**[4], perhaps Rhys had been **privy**[5] to it all. If Rhys could crack Sir Robert's code, he probably understood their **crude**[6] gibberish conversations.

'Ouch!' **yelped**[7] Cad, rubbing her shoulder and whirling.

'Now you know what it feels like,' said Dylan, **wielding**[8] Cad's emerald hairpin, his white teeth filling his grin.

Cad snatched it from him, **unimpressed**[9], stowing it away in a secret **seam**[10] of her tunic. She must be more **prudent**[11] with her **precious**[12] jewels: the magical pieces given to her by her father and mother.

'I need a second pair of eyes on this,' Cad muttered, quashing all surfacing thoughts of Siân. 'Look here.' She pointed to the cipher. 'Now I've written the solution, do you see what I see?'

'What do you see?' asked Dylan.

Cad tutted. 'That's the whole point,' she snapped. 'I don't want my opinions to **influence**[13] yours. Apply the key and decipher the code into words, then **recite**[14] that last line to me.' She immediately regretted her tone, but not enough to apologise; a swirl of **arrogance**[15] got in her way.

---

1 **mere** *(adj)* having no greater extent than, barely. *(s)* meagre, scant.

2 **mull** *(v)* think about. *(s)* ponder, consider, contemplate, reflect. *(ant)* disregard.

3 **pig Latin** *(n)* a language game in which English words are reordered and understood by those privy to its attributes.

4 **gibberish** *(n)* nonsense speech. *(s)* blather, drivel, balderdash. *(ant)* sense.

5 **privy** *(adj)* having knowledge of something secret. *(s)* wise to, in on.

6 **crude** *(adj)* rudimentary (basic) or makeshift. *(s)* simple, rough, unsophisticated. *(ant)* sophisticated.

7 **yelp** *(v)* make a short, sharp cry, especially of pain or alarm. *(s)* squeal, squeak, yell.

8 **wield** *(v)* hold and use. *(s)* brandish, wave, flaunt, display.

9 **unimpressed** *(adj)* feeling no respect or admiration for. *(s)* indifferent, unamused. *(ant)* impressed.

10 **seam** *(n)* a line formed where two pieces of fabric are sewn together. *(s)* join, closure.

11 **prudent** *(adj)* acting with care. *(s)* cautious, wise. *(ant)* unwise, imprudent.

12 **precious** *(adj)* of great value or importance. *(s)* valuable, rare, special. *(ant)* worthless, unimportant.

13 **influence** *(v)* have an effect on someone's behaviour or something. *(s)* control, sway, impact.

14 **recite** *(v)* say aloud. *(s)* narrate, repeat, detail, describe.

15 **arrogance** *(n)* a sense of self-importance. *(s)* ego, pride, hubris. *(ant)* humility.

Cad cared not if Rhys now overheard. He'd probably solved the code ages ago and had known all along what it meant. **Ego**[1] now aside, Cad **lamented**[2] that fact because if what she now read on the parchment was true, maybe she could have prevented any unfortunate outcomes.

Dylan's blue eyes **squinted**[3], his bushy brows **merging**[4] as he gnawed his bottom lip in **contemplation**[5].

His **musing**[6] infuriated Cad, and her impatience almost **overwhelmed**[7] her, but she, too, bit her lip and waited. Unlike Cad, Dylan almost always took his time **committing**[8] to decisions. She watched, **itching**[9] to **spur**[10] him on, but bit down and re-read those last two lines. Her stomach swirled – she knew what they said; she just needed **confirmation**[11].

As if bored by a **preacher's**[12] **tedious**[13] **sermon**[14], Dylan finally said, 'I think it's a plan for something.'

'What do you mean?' she asked, her **tone**[15] **brusque**[16].

'It's a plan,' said Dylan, looking **bemused**[17]. 'And it mentions Prince Dewi's name, so that *must* mean bad news.'

---

1 **ego** *(n)* a person's sense of self-importance or esteem. *(s)* self, character, self-pride.

2 **lament** *(v)* feel or express disappointment or regret. *(s)* deplore, rue. *(ant)* celebrate.

3 **squint** *(v)* look with one's eyes screwed up or partly closed. *(s)* narrow.

4 **merge** *(v)* meet or mix together. *(s)* join, unite, combine. *(ant)* separate.

5 **contemplation** *(n)* deep thought. *(s)* reflection, consideration.

6 **muse** *(v)* consider. *(s)* wonder, contemplate, ponder.

7 **overwhelm** *(v)* overcome, overload.

8 **commit** *(v)* decide to do something. *(s)* engage, give, allocate.

9 **itch** *(v)* experience an overwhelming desire to do something. *(s)* yearn, hanker, crave.

10 **spur** *(v)* encourage. *(s)* urge, hurry, motivate, drive. *(ant)* discourage.

11 **confirmation** *(n)* the action of making sure something is true. *(s)* poof, verification.

12 **preacher** *(n)* a person who speaks about certain subjects, especially of religion. *(s)* priest, cleric.

13 **tedious** *(adj)* tiresome or monotonous. *(s)* long, slow, dull, boring, dreary. *(ant)* interesting.

14 **sermon** *(n)* a religious talk. *(s)* preaching, speech, monologue.

15 **tone** *(n)* the sound of one's voice. *(s)* pitch, timbre, intonation.

16 **brusque** *(adj)* blunt and abrupt in manner. *(s)* curt, direct, tactless, offhand. *(ant)* polite.

17 **bemused** *(adj)* confused or muddled. *(s)* bewildered, perplexed, stumped. *(ant)* clear, definite.

Cad's eyes **bulged**[1] with **unforeseen**[2] shock, and she was sure she had heard Rhys **flinch**[3] in his bed as Dylan spoke.

'Are you sure?' asked Cad, taken aback. 'Check again,' she urged, searching his calm eyes for answers. That's not what she'd seen when she'd read the symbols.

'As sure as I'll ever be,' he said.

Dylan ran his fingers along each line. Cad could see his mind working as terrible doubts **spiralled**[4] into hers. She was a **competent**[5] **scholar**[6], but her reckoning speed was slower than Dylan's.

'It's this pattern here that I ponder upon,' he said, pointing to a **cluster**[7] of symbols.

'What about it?' replied Cad, in a would-be calm voice, but with **panic**[8] **surging**[9] through her body, her eyes hungry for answers.

'It's **ambiguous**[10], but it talks of **weaponry**[11], I believe.' Dylan studied the symbols. 'It's almost **poetic**[12]. I can't be entirely sure, but it seems to be some sort of weapon. A vast beast of a machine, and one unknown to me. I am not certain why, but it talks of dragons breathing fire.'

'Dylan, talk me through what you see. I want to understand why I **misread**[13] it,' Cad snapped, **furious**[14] at her **inadequacy**[15].

'Maybe you didn't misread it,' replied Dylan. 'Perhaps it is I who misunderstand, for why would they talk of a fire-breathing beast?'

---

1 **bulge** *(v)* to swell or extend. *(s)* protrude, balloon, expand. *(ant)* contract.

2 **unforeseen** *(adj)* not seen beforehand. *(s)* unexpected, unpredicted. *(ant)* expected.

3 **flinch** *(v)* shy away from instinctively. *(s)* move, twitch, wince. *(ant)* stand firm.

4 **spiral** *(v)* show a continuous but significant increase. *(s)* escalate, mount. *(ant)* fall, decrease.

5 **competent** *(adj)* capable, able and efficient (good at something). *(s)* proficient, adept. *(ant)* incompetent.

6 **scholar** *(n)* a highly educated person. *(s)* intellectual, academic, authority.

7 **cluster** *(n)* a group of things positioned close together. *(s)* collection, bunch.

8 **panic** *(n)* uncontrollable anxiety or fear. *(s)* fright, dread, alarm, horror. *(ant)* calm, self-control.

9 **surge** *(v)* increase suddenly and with more power. *(s)* rise, gush, course. *(ant)* decline, ebb.

10 **ambiguous** *(adj)* open to misinterpretation. *(s)* unclear, vague. *(ant)* clear, unambiguous.

11 **weaponry** *(n)* weapons. *(s)* arms, munitions.

12 **poetic** *(adj)* written as verse rather than prose (ordinary language). *(s)* lyrical. *(ant)* prosaic.

13 **misread** *(v)* read something incorrectly. *(s)* misunderstand, misinterpret. *(ant)* understand.

14 **furious** *(adj)* extremely angry. *(s)* enraged, fuming, seething. *(ant)* calm, mild.

15 **inadequacy** *(n)* lacking the quality or quantity required. *(s)* want, lack, inability. *(ant)* adequate.

But once Dylan talked her through his **reasoning**[1], she felt **convinced**[2] his **interpretation**[3] was **accurate**[4]. The cipher was a design – the likes of which Cad had never seen before – **commissioned**[5] by her uncle, Dewi. Why had it been in Sir Robert's **suite**[6] of rooms? She had no answer to that, but she suspected Evans swam with razor-toothed **pikes**[7] in a dark and shady pool.

'Dylan, make a copy best you can, and **stash**[8] it somewhere safe.'

'It will be tricky to **transcribe**[9] accurately, but I'll try.' Dylan, who had a great eye for detail, got to work immediately.

'Please, just do your best,' said Cad, grateful to Dylan. For it would be a task she would **loathe**[10].

Black despair uncoiled itself in Cad's mind like a worm in a grave; she flopped back against her bed. She had broken the cipher but **misconstrued**[11] its meaning, most likely **precisely**[12] as its **inventor**[13] had **intended**[14]. Cad had seen only the obvious: the words on the parchment, but not the true meaning hiding in the empty spaces between them. Sir Robert was ingenious; she knew that. If he'd written the code, knowing the cipher may be broken, he'd seemingly written the real meaning as **riddles**[15], poetic problems, and he'd **duped**[16] her, as he'd planned. No wonder he showed no anxiety over the cipher's loss. But like Cad herself, Evans had not **bargained**[17] on the

---

1 **reasoning** *(n)* the action of thinking logically.

2 **convinced** *(adj)* sure about something. *(s)* certain, assured, satisfied. *(ant)* unconvinced.

3 **interpretation** *(n)* way of understanding. *(s)* conclusion, inference, supposition.

4 **accurate** *(adj)* correct. *(s)* exact, right, precise. *(ant)* inaccurate, wrong.

5 **commission** *(v)* order the production of something. *(s)* instruct, authorise.

6 **suite** *(n)* a set of rooms. *(s)* living quarters.

7 **pike** *(n)* a long predatory fish with large teeth and a pointed snout.

8 **stash** *(v)* keep in a hidden place. *(s)* hide, conceal, stow, secrete. *(ant)* reveal, unpack.

9 **transcribe** *(v)* put into written form. *(s)* duplicate, reproduce, rewrite.

10 **loathe** *(v)* feel intense dislike or disgust for. *(s)* hate, despise, abhor, detest. *(ant)* adore, love.

11 **misconstrue** *(v)* understand incorrectly. *(s)* misunderstand, misinterpret. *(ant)* understand.

12 **precisely** *(adv)* in a precise (exact) way. *(s)* absolutely, just. *(ant)* vaguely.

13 **inventor** *(n)* a person who designs or makes something never before seen or used. *(s)* creator.

14 **intend** *(v)* make for a specific purpose. *(s)* plan, aim, expect, want, desire.

15 **riddle** *(n)* a statement whose meaning must be solved. *(s)* puzzle, enigma, mystery.

16 **dupe** *(v)* deceive and trick. *(s)* fool, hoodwink, mislead, cheat, beguile.

17 **bargain** *(v)* expect. *(s)* anticipate, imagine, envisage, foresee, predict.

combination[1] of the odd boy, Rhys Price, and his hidden talents, plus Dylan's swift **analytical**[2] mind. Evans didn't know this because he didn't care to know his **charges**[3]. That was his **downfall**[4] – **presumption**[5]. If Evans held plans for a weapon mentioning Dewi's traitorous name, and even more terrifying, one that breathed fire, did her father know about it? Until she had that answer, she would trust no one, especially Sir Robert.

Cad's mind whirled into action, but she must resist the urge to rush and make rash decisions. She must **rein in**[6] her **rowdy**[7] thoughts and **contemplate**[8] carefully.

'Dylan,' she said, **despite**[9] knowing Rhys would be listening. 'I must use my ring to revisit Sir Robert's rooms in search of further clues. I found the parchment there. Hopefully, I will find more answers.'

Pensive[10], Dylan nodded.

'As we are **confined**[11] to our rooms, I will go today before dark. A search without **reliance**[12] on torches will be easier,' added Cad, feeling for the emerald ring she'd sewn into her tunic's hem. Wherever she went, her magic jewels went with her, stowed in the ingenious hems, seams and pockets she'd created for every garment she **possessed**[13].

At first, fiddling about, Cad **presumed**[14] she'd **stashed**[15] the ring in a different pocket, so her

---

1 **combination** *(n)* the joining of two separate things. *(s)* union, merger.

2 **analytical** *(adj)* using logic (sense) to work things out. *(s)* systematic, methodical. *(ant)* illogical.

3 **charge** *(n)* a person given over to the care of someone else. *(s)* ward, dependent, trainee. *(ant)* guardian.

4 **downfall** *(n)* the cause of one's loss or decline, a significant flaw. *(s)* undoing, failure. *(ant)* rise.

5 **presumption** *(n)* something which is accepted without proof. *(s)* belief, assumption. *(ant)* fact.

6 **rein in** *(v)* control something. *(s)* gather, adjust, collect, compose. *(ant)* free.

7 **rowdy** *(adj)* disordered and noisy. *(s)* unruly, turbulent. *(ant)* quiet, restrained.

8 **contemplate** *(v)* think about. *(s)* ponder, consider, deliberate. *(ant)* disregard.

9 **despite** *(prep)* in spite of, regardless of. *(s)* even though, even with, undeterred by. *(ant)* because of.

10 **pensive** *(adj)* thoughtful. *(s)* reflective, contemplative, preoccupied. *(ant)* thoughtless.

11 **confine** *(v)* keep within certain limits. *(s)* enclose, trap, imprison. *(ant)* release.

12 **reliance** *(n)* a need for something or someone. *(s)* dependence.

13 **possess** *(v)* have or own a characteristic or thing. *(s)* acquire, obtain. *(ant)* lack.

14 **presume** *(v)* assume something but without certainty. *(s)* suppose. *(ant)* confirm.

15 **stash** *(v)* keep in a hidden place. *(s)* hide, conceal, stow, secrete. *(ant)* reveal, unpack.

eager[1] fingers sought elsewhere, **fishing**[2] about the **fabric**[3], covering all the familiar folds. But a creeping panic began to **afflict**[4] Cad's fingers as she **exhausted**[5] her usual hiding places. Now **numbed**[6] by fear, her hands **dithered**[7] as she **fumbled**[8]. With despair taking hold, she shook as she tore at her tunic, ripping the delicate stitching and perfectly disguised hems. The panic wasn't creeping now; it was racing, sprinting, winning, overwhelming her with a blind **terror**[9] she'd not felt since being trapped in the oubliette.

'Cad! Cad! Stop! What is it?'

Dylan's voice reached her ears as though **muffled**[10] through a tunnel. Only when he grabbed her arm, trying to stop her from tearing off her tunic, did she breathe and meet his fearful gaze.

'Cad. What is it?' Dylan cried.

Cad saw her panic reflected in his eyes. She shook her head, trying to force back the words she didn't want to say. Her hands **frantically**[11] patted at her tunic, the seams of her **woollen**[12] **hose**[13] were now twisted and ripped where she'd clawed in search of the ring, even though she knew it would not be there, and still, her head shook in silence, her face as pale as a cod steak.

Only when Rhys crawled off his bed and joined them with Fishy did Cad accept what lay before her. In a pinch, her plans **imploded**[14].

Cad's misting eyes **flitted**[15] from boy to boy. Fishy sat silently with Rhys, **doe-eyed**[16], sensing

---

1 **eager** *(adj)* wanting to do or have something keenly. *(s)* impatient, enthusiastic, ready. *(ant)* unenthusiastic.

2 **fish** *(v)* search by feeling for something concealed. *(s)* fumble, grope. *(ant)* find.

3 **fabric** *(n)* cloth. *(s)* fibre, material, textile, drapery.

4 **afflict** *(v)* cause pain or trouble to and affect adversely. *(s)* bother, ail, plague. *(ant)* aid.

5 **exhaust** *(v)* use something up completely.

6 **numb** *(v)* stop someone feeling or thinking properly. *(s)* paralyse, stupefy. *(ant)* feel.

7 **dither** *(v)* act indecisively or waver between. *(s)* hesitate, teeter. *(ant)* decide.

8 **fumble** *(v)* move the hands about clumsily. *(s)* scrabble, search, root, dig, rummage.

9 **terror** *(n)* great fear. *(s)* horror, dread, trepidation.

10 **muffled** *(adj)* not loud due to being obstructed or muted in some way. *(s)* faint, suppressed. *(ant)* loud.

11 **frantically** *(adv)* in a frantic (panicked) way. *(s)* desperately, madly, uncontrollably. *(ant)* calmly.

12 **woollen** *(adj)* made from wool, partly or wholly.

13 **hose** *(n)* leg and feet coverings such as stockings, socks and tights. *(s)* hosiery.

14 **implode** *(v)* fail or end suddenly. *(s)* cave in, fold. *(ant)* explode.

15 **flit** *(v)* move swiftly. *(s)* dart, flick, dance. *(ant)* remain, still.

16 **doe-eyed** *(adj)* having eyes that are large and gentle, and especially those that are dark like a doe's (female deer).

something **foreboding**[1], her tail tucked away and her ears pinned flat to her head.

'Cad,' Dylan whispered, his skin **wan**[2], his eyes now wide with anxiety, 'what is it?'

'My ring—', she eventually whispered, stuttering over the sentence. 'Siân's emerald invisibility ring. It is gone.'

---

1 **foreboding** *(adj)* implying that something bad is about to happen. *(s)* dreadful, alarming. *(ant)* heartening.

2 **wan** *(adj)* pale-faced and giving the impression of illness or exhaustion. *(s)* pallid, ashen, drawn. *(ant)* glowing.

CHAPTER FIVE

Accusations and Guilt

Although the friends **ransacked**[1] the bedchamber, their search proved **futile**[2]: Cad's ring was gone. The ring which had **rendered**[3] her invisible when she'd found Prince John. The ring given to her by Siân when Cad had left home to train at Catrin Castle.

Cad **recalled**[4] Siân's parting words: 'Keep this gift safe, sweet girl, and use it wisely. For one day, you may need it.'

At the time, Cad had admired the pretty piece, but confused by her mother's words, had shown it **scant**[5] **regard**[6]: jewellery held no interest for her. It didn't even fit Cad, who feared she might lose it. But when Siân had pricked Cad's thumb, with what Cad now knew was the emerald-hawk hairpin, drawing a **bead**[7] of blood and dropping it onto the centre of the hawk in the ring, Cad had realised this was no ordinary jewel. She had regarded Siân, about to ask her why, but Siân had smiled that **stunningly**[8] sweet smile and shook her head saying, 'Callwen,

---

1 **ransack** *(v)* search thoroughly, often stealing and causing damage. *(s)* rifle, comb, turn over.

2 **futile** *(adj)* useless and pointless. *(s)* ineffective, fruitless. *(ant)* useful.

3 **render** *(v)* cause to become. *(s)* make, leave.

4 **recall** *(v)* bring something back into one's mind. *(s)* remember, recollect. *(ant)* forget.

5 **scant** *(adj)* barely sufficient or adequate. *(s)* little, negligible. *(ant)* extensive.

6 **regard** *(n)* concern or attention. *(s)* consideration, thought. *(ant)* disregard, neglect.

7 **bead** *(n)* a drop of something. *(s)* droplet, dot. *(ant)* pool.

8 **stunningly** *(adv)* in a way that is stunning (beautiful or shocking). *(s)* extraordinarily. *(ant)* negligibly.

why ask? Experiment. A Knight Hawk must be **resourceful**[1] if they are to become an Instinctive **servant**[2] of the realm.'

But why the blood, Cad had wanted to **blurt**[3]. Why prick my thumb and drop my blood into the centre of the hawk? But Cad had known better; if Siân offered no answer, Cad must accept that. Siân did nothing without **intent**[4], and at the time, Cad trusted Siân with her life.

Had trusted her with my life, Cad thought, as a pearl-shaped tear splashed onto Fishy's fluffy fur. Cad lay exhausted, **bewildered**[5] at the loss of her **beloved**[6] ring, with Fishy's head flopped on her chest. The dog hadn't moved since a **devastated**[7] Cad, as numb as a snowdrift, had collapsed onto her bed in defeat, and Dylan and Rhys on theirs, their belongings strewn around them.

Cad understood her friends' present painful silence.

Bones mend but regret doesn't, Cad thought, now **drowning**[8] in her own **guilt**[9]. She searched for the phrases to form a worthy apology. The words to **atone**[10] for the dreadful **accusations**[11] she'd flung at her friends as she'd torn apart their **honour**[12] along with their bedchamber. The words needed to say, *Sorry I blamed you. Sorry I suspected, even for an **instant**[13], that my best friends could **betray**[14] me in such a way as to steal my **cherished**[15] ring.* Yet, apart from Llywelyn, Sir Robert, Dylan and Rhys, who knew about her invisibility ring – who?

The **culprit**[16] was neither Dylan nor Rhys; she had **concluded**[17] that in the depths of despair

---

1 **resourceful** *(adj)* able to overcome difficulties. *(s)* capable, ingenious. *(ant)* unimaginative.

2 **servant** *(n)* someone employed by a ruling body. *(s)* public servant. *(ant)* governor.

3 **blurt** *(v)* say something suddenly and without consideration. *(s)* announce, exclaim, cry.

4 **intent** *(n)* a purpose. *(s)* intention, objective, plan. *(ant)* reluctance.

5 **bewildered** *(adj)* perplexed or confused. *(s)* baffled, mystified, confounded. *(ant)* enlightened.

6 **beloved** *(adj)* much loved. *(s)* adored, prized, favourite, treasured.

7 **devastated** *(adj)* feeling overwhelming shock or grief. *(s)* traumatised, overcome. *(ant)* comforted.

8 **drown** *(v)* feel something is too great to deal with. *(s)* overwhelm, overcome. *(ant)* tolerate.

9 **guilt** *(n)* a bad feeling about one's wrongdoing. *(s)* regret, remorse, shame. *(ant)* innocence.

10 **atone** *(v)* make up for a wrongdoing. *(s)* compensate.

11 **accusation** *(n)* a claim that someone has done something wrong or illegal. *(s)* allegation, blame, criticism.

12 **honour** *(n)* respect and self worth. *(s)* esteem, integrity, honesty. *(ant)* shame.

13 **instant** *(n)* a moment of time. *(s)* second, minute.

14 **betray** *(v)* deceive someone. *(s)* mislead, trick, double-cross, cheat. *(ant)* be faithful.

15 **cherish** *(v)* hold dear and protect. *(s)* prize, treasure, adore, appreciate, value. *(ant)* neglect.

16 **culprit** *(n)* a person or thing responsible for a wrongdoing. *(s)* offender, criminal, baddie. *(ant)* victim.

17 **conclude** *(v)* decide on or judge something by reasoning. *(s)* deduce, infer, determine. *(ant)* reject.

just now. Such **callous**[1] betrayal was beyond them; the five of them were family – she, Dylan, Rhys, Fishy and, of course, May, Cad's blind **goshawk**[2]. No, the culprit must be Robert Evans, for why would Llywelyn steal the ring that protected her? He had no **motive**[3], but nor did Sir Robert, at least not one obvious to Cad. But since Evans had **assumed**[4] the command of Catrin Castle, Prince John had been **abducted**[5], and she'd discovered a secret cipher that seemed to contain plans for a weapon which could cause **mass**[6] **devastation**[7].

But why would Evans, to whom Llywelyn had entrusted the **governance**[8] of his castle, betray him so cruelly? With no **discernible**[9] motive, she could neither fathom nor accept an explanation of Sir Robert's guilt. Then Cad's mind snapped to Bryn Davis and the **abhorrent**[10] beating from which she'd saved him during John's **kidnapping**[11].

Bryn had never revealed his **assailant's**[12] **identity**[13], and Cad had not pushed the point. Bryn's **initial**[14] civility towards Cad had vanished in the weeks following the attack. He was not one to be pressed, and since their **relationship**[15] was so **fragile**[16], she had resisted **harrying**[17] him, lest it worsen. This way, he owed her a **favour**[18], and she wanted it to remain so.

Bryn had been Prince Dewi's squire before Dewi had absconded with the bracelet. Could

---

1 **callous** *(adj)* cruel and heartless. *(s)* hard, unfeeling, uncaring. *(ant)* compassionate.

2 **goshawk** *(n)* a large white-grey hawk with cream-coloured underwings. *(s)* raptor.

3 **motive** *(n)* an incentive for acting or behaving in a certain way. *(s)* grounds, basis, reason. *(ant)* deterrent.

4 **assume** *(v)* take power or responsibility of. *(s)* accept, undertake. *(ant)* relinquish.

5 **abduct** *(v)* take away by force. *(s)* kidnap, seize. *(ant)* release.

6 **mass** *(adj)* involving a large number of things or people. *(s)* widespread, extensive. *(ant)* meagre.

7 **devastation** *(n)* great destruction. *(s)* ruin, suffering, desolation. *(ant)* creation.

8 **governance** *(n)* control. *(s)* rule, command, administration. *(ant)* lawlessness.

9 **discernible** *(adj)* able to be recognised, seen or found out. *(s)* noticeable, detectable. *(ant)* imperceptible.

10 **abhorrent** *(adj)* causing disgust and loathing. *(s)* loathsome, despicable. *(ant)* agreeable.

11 **kidnapping** *(n)* the act of taking someone and holding them captive against their will. *(s)* abduction. *(ant)* release.

12 **assailant** *(n)* a person who physically harms or attacks another. *(s)* assaulter, aggressor. *(ant)* ally.

13 **identity** *(n)* someone's naming or individuality. *(s)* identification.

14 **initial** *(adj)* to start with. *(s)* beginning, early, first. *(ant)* final.

15 **relationship** *(n)* the way in which people are connected or get along. *(s)* association, bond.

16 **fragile** *(adj)* easily damaged. *(s)* delicate, flimsy, weak. *(ant)* sturdy, robust.

17 **harry** *(v)* bother or pester. *(s)* hound, badger, annoy. *(ant)* leave in peace.

18 **favour** *(n)* an act of kindness. *(s)* goodwill, benevolence.

Bryn be working for Dewi now? she **mused**[1], straightening up. It was **feasible**[2]. Had Cad been shaking the wrong tree?

Her mind **ventured**[3] back to the oubliette and the hooded figure who had locked her in there; those long, slim fingers grasping that **grille**[4], forever **etched**[5] in her mind. She still had no idea who that hooded figure was, nor thankfully had she seen it since. **Indisputably**[6], she knew it was not the same man who had attacked Bryn; the same man she had left for dead in the oubliette. His build was too **stocky**[7] compared with those bony hands. At different times, there had been two people in the oubliette that day. Still, someone in this castle had wanted **rid**[8] of John, and without her invisibility ring, finding that person would be much harder to do.

Cad thought of her baby brother John, now guarded in **isolation**[9] at Llywelyn's Cadwaladr Castle by a hand-picked **troop**[10] of Knights Hawk. Even with John **sequestered**[11] there, Cad didn't **take** her own safety **for granted**[12]. But one question battling in her mind always fought to be heard; had she been an **innocent**[13] **bystander**[14] when trapped in the oubliette with John, or had her assailant wanted her trapped and forgotten too?

Regardless of the **uneventful**[15] weeks that had followed her ordeal, that question **simmered**[16] away, but she'd raised her **hackles**[17], and raised they would stay. Now as her thoughts drifted back

---

1 **muse** *(v)* ask oneself in a thoughtful manner. *(s)* wonder, ponder, contemplate. *(ant)* disregard.

2 **feasible** *(adj)* possible. *(s)* likely, probable, conceivable, imaginable. *(ant)* impossible.

3 **venture** *(v)* begin a journey or undertaking. *(s)* proceed, go, move, wander.

4 **grille** *(n)* a screen or grating of metal bars or wires placed in front of something to allow ventilation or observation.

5 **etch** *(v)* impress, carve or cut on a surface. *(s)* mark, print, stamp, score, imprint.

6 **indisputably** *(adv)* in a way that cannot be disputed (challenged). *(s)* undoubtedly. *(ant)* questionably.

7 **stocky** *(adj)* broad and heavily built. *(s)* thickset, stout, chunky, burly, hefty, squat. *(ant)* slight, slender.

8 **rid** *(v)* take action to be free of someone or something. *(s)* do away with. *(ant)* keep.

9 **isolation** *(n)* the situation of being alone. *(s)* seclusion, separation. *(ant)* contact.

10 **troop** *(n)* a group of soldiers or armed forces. *(s)* company, unit, team.

11 **sequester** *(v)* keep apart or hide away from. *(s)* isolate, seclude, segregate. *(ant)* integrate.

12 **take for granted** *(v)* assume to be happening or given. *(s)* believe. *(ant)* doubt.

13 **innocent** *(adj)* not guilty. *(s)* blameless, honourable. *(ant)* guilty.

14 **bystander** *(n)* a person who is present but not involved. *(s)* onlooker, witness. *(ant)* participant.

15 **uneventful** *(adj)* not denoted by interesting events. *(s)* routine, ordinary. *(ant)* eventful.

16 **simmer** *(v)* exist in a lesser way. *(s)* bubble, churn, stew. *(ant)* boil.

17 **hackles** *(n)* upright hairs on an animal's back, risen when it is alarmed. *(s)* spikes, spines, bristles.

to the present, she regarded her friends. Guilt, **remorse**[1] and anger at her own stupidity still rendered her unable to find the words she needed.

*I'm such a **reckless**[2] wantwit*, she **scolded**[3] herself, **cringing**[4] inside.

Then, as her fog of confusion and anger steadily cleared, an obvious pathway emerged before her.

'Dylan, Rhys,' she mumbled, fiddling with her tunic, her eyes lowered.

Neither boy replied but they **levelled**[5] their gaze her way, both looking **wary**[6] of a looming **tirade**[7].

When Cad saw their pained expressions, **shame**[8] shook her, for both boys stared at her, fear in their eyes.

*How could I have made you both feel so **wretched**[9]?* Her guilt hung like an unfinished argument. She drew her knees to her chest like a shield, then readied herself.

'I—' Cad cleared her throat with a loud cough. **Rarely**[10] lost for words, they eluded her now, but she tried her best. 'I'm so sorry for exploding as I did.' She swallowed hard, her voice **catching**[11]. 'I know neither of you would hurt me like that. I'm so s—'

'It's all right, Cad,' interrupted Dylan to save her **embarrassment**[12]. 'It's all right.'

Abashed[13] and crushed by remorse, she forced back her tears, her smile watery-weak. Rhys said nothing but flashed his gap-toothed grin at her. All three sat in silence, listening to the **rhythmic**[14] thud of Fishy's tail on the bed.

---

1 **remorse** *(n)* guilt or regret. *(s)* shame, repentance, ruefulness. *(ant)* remorselessness.

2 **reckless** *(adj)* heedless of danger or the consequences of an action. *(s)* irresponsible, wild, rash. *(ant)* cautious.

3 **scold** *(v)* tell someone off angrily. *(s)* reprimand, admonish, chastise. *(ant)* praise.

4 **cringe** *(v)* shiver inwardly with embarrassment or disgust. *(s)* wince, squirm, blush.

5 **level** *(v)* aim. *(s)* direct, train, turn.

6 **wary** *(adj)* cautious about a problem or danger. *(s)* cagey, guarded, careful. *(ant)* unwary.

7 **tirade** *(n)* a lengthy, angry speech, criticism or accusation. *(s)* outburst, rant. *(ant)* praise.

8 **shame** *(n)* a feeling of distress and humiliation caused by one's own wrongdoing. *(s)* embarrassment. *(ant)* pride.

9 **wretched** *(adj)* (of someone) being in a very unfortunate or unhappy state. *(s)* miserable. *(ant)* happy.

10 **rarely** *(adv)* not often. *(s)* seldom, infrequently. *(ant)* frequently, often.

11 **catch** *(v)* (of the voice) to change due to emotion. *(s)* tremor, hitch, quiver.

12 **embarrassment** *(n)* a feeling of shame or awkwardness. *(s)* unease, discomfort, humiliation. *(ant)* confidence.

13 **abashed** *(adj)* embarrassed, ashamed or disconcerted. *(s)* humiliated, deflated, mortified. *(ant)* undaunted.

14 **rhythmic** *(adj)* having rhythm (a repeated pattern of sound). *(s)* regular. *(ant)* irregular.

'Boys,' she eventually said, lifting her voice, 'thank you for being my friends.'

And then as if she'd **unravelled**[1] a complicated knot, she chirped, 'Come, help me clear up this **shambles**[2] before Goodwife Hughes calls by and sees the chaos. Then I will share my plan with you.'

1 **unravel** *(v)* undo something that is tangled. *(s)* unsnarl, disentangle. *(ant)* tangle.

2 **shambles** *(n)* a total mess. *(s)* disorder, chaos, disarray. *(ant)* order.

CHAPTER SIX

Slippy Clears the Decks

Despite people being confined to their sick rooms and supper being taken in **shifts**[1], the great hall bustled with **famished**[2] courtiers and **servants**[3]. They **gossiped**[4] and laughed **amid**[5] the **scent**[6] of **rich**[7] rabbit **pottage**[8] and the **din**[9] of castle **joviality**[10]. The ever-prudent Sir Robert had **kennelled**[11] all dogs, so Fishy was locked safely in Cad's bedchamber. Cad would feed her after supper.

With their target in sight, Cad sat beside Dylan and quickly stuffed her secret pockets with food, for she knew she'd have no time to eat if their plan **prevailed**[12]. Jack Jones, the boy who'd vomited at midday dinner, was confined to his room, but the rest of Bryn's **tribe**[13] surrounded him, hanging onto his every word.

---

1 **shift** *(n)* something done in relays. *(s)* stint, stretch, bout, period.

2 **famished** *(adj)* very hungry. *(s)* ravenous, starving, underfed. *(ant)* full, sated, satiated.

3 **servant** *(n)* someone who works for another person, often doing household tasks. *(s)* houseboy. *(ant)* master, mistress.

4 **gossip** *(v)* engage in conversation not based on proof. *(s)* tattle, chatter, prattle.

5 **amid** *(prep)* surrounded by, in the middle of. *(s)* among, amidst. *(ant)* outside.

6 **scent** *(n)* a distinctive smell (often a pleasant one). *(s)* trace, whiff, aroma. *(ant)* stench, stink.

7 **rich** *(adj)* (of food) containing, fat, spices and, or, sugar. *(s)* heavy, flavoured. *(ant)* light.

8 **pottage** *(n)* stew or soup. *(s)* casserole.

9 **din** *(n)* a loud, irritating and prolonged noise. *(s)* uproar, racket, commotion. *(ant)* silence.

10 **joviality** *(n)* cheer. *(s)* gaiety, animation. *(ant)* dullness, gloom.

11 **kennel** *(v)* put a dog into a kennel (place for a dog). *(s)* house.

12 **prevail** *(v)* succeed or win. *(s)* triumph. *(ant)* fail, lose.

13 **tribe** *(n)* social group. *(s)* folk, clan, people.

Cad, **smouldering**[1] like a hot coal, flashed an unseen snarl his way, poured water from a **ewer**[2] into her cup and sipped. It was warmer than usual, **lacking**[3] the refreshing bite of the water pulled up from the well. Perhaps with so many sick, there was a **dearth**[4] of folks to fetch water. Hitherto, Cad had managed to avoid all water duties, that being her only **concession**[5] ordered by Llywelyn to Dewi. Cad shuddered at the thought of leaning into the well's **shaft**[6] and **hauling**[7] the bucket's rope, just as Llywelyn and Owain had pulled her from the well as a baby.

Now **plagued**[8] by dark thoughts, Cad pictured Jack Jones's midday vomit and **abandoned**[9] her **tepid**[10] water in place of a small beer. Dylan's eyes widened.

'Not like you to **quaff**[11] beer,' he whispered.

Many pages and squires **supped**[12] small beers, but Cad liked a clear head, especially since the oubliette.

'I fancied a change,' she muttered, with an **unwarranted**[13] bite of irritation in her voice.

Cad hoped Rhys was holding his nerve. They'd **strategically**[14] sat him on the opposite side of the table, near Bryn and his followers. Cad regarded her trencher and gnawed on a chicken bone. **Sumptuous**[15] **spit-roast**[16] meats would soon be off the menu if Catrin were indeed at risk

---

1 **smoulder** *(v)* feel or show barely suppressed negativity. *(s)* seethe, simmer, fume. *(ant)* rage.

2 **ewer** *(n)* a big jug with a wide opening, formerly used for carrying water. *(s)* urn, vessel.

3 **lacking** *(adj)* wanting. *(s)* missing, deficient. *(ant)* having.

4 **dearth** *(n)* a lack of. *(s)* shortage, scarcity, deficiency. *(ant)* abundance.

5 **concession** *(n)* a thing that is allowed. *(s)* adjustment, compromise.

6 **shaft** *(n)* a long, narrow hole that gives access to something. *(s)* borehole, tunnel, passage.

7 **haul** *(v)* drag or pull with force or effort. *(s)* heave, yank, wrench. *(ant)* push, shove.

8 **plague** *(v)* cause continual distress to. *(s)* afflict, torment, harass. *(ant)* soothe, support.

9 **abandon** *(v)* leave alone or behind. *(s)* discard, ditch, dump. *(ant)* keep.

10 **tepid** *(adj)* slightly warm. *(s)* lukewarm, warmish. *(ant)* cold, icy, boiling.

11 **quaff** *(v)* drink with enthusiasm. *(s)* indulge, down, swig. *(ant)* sip.

12 **sup** *(v)* drink. *(s)* consume, imbibe.

13 **unwarranted** *(adj)* not justified, having no basis in fact. *(s)* unjustified, undue. *(ant)* warranted, justified.

14 **strategically** *(adv)* in a way relating to strategy (skill or long-term plan). *(s)* tactically. *(ant)* randomly.

15 **sumptuous** *(adj)* extremely pleasant. *(s)* lavish, splendid, extravagant. *(ant)* plain.

16 **spit-roast** *(adj)* describing meat turned on a long spit (rod) over a fire until cooked.

of **siege**[1] from a monstrous weapon. And right now, food wasn't her focus. She needed a **ruckus**[2], and was about to start one.

Keeping her head down, she **swivelled**[3] her eyes towards Bryn, who quaffed back a beer. She noted he wasn't drinking the water either, but then he rarely did at supper, once he'd completed his daily tasks.

Cad nodded at Rhys, her heart gathering pace. Then she winked twice to signal *Get ready*. One wink and he must act.

The senior courtiers, who ate before squires and servants, were tucking into bread and cheeses, all washed down by **undiluted**[4] wines. Cad knew the **overindulgent**[5] by the colour of their flushed faces – the courtiers who were **fond**[6] of the more **potent**[7] **brews**[8] and **fortified**[9] wines. The usual suspects who stumbled away from the supper table, their **gaits**[10] swaying in **accord**[11] with their wine **intake**[12].

Sir Robert Evans was not of this **cohort**[13]. He was too sharp a knife to be blunted that easily. Cad had never seen him red-faced, nor heard his words **slur**[14], or noticed his gait sway to the **rhythm**[15] of wine **consumption**[16]. No. Sir Robert's hawk eyes remained **crystal clear**[17], **beady**[18]

---

1 **siege** *(n)* the surrounding and blocking of a castle or other place by a force cutting off essential supplies.

2 **ruckus** *(n)* a commotion (noisy disturbance). *(s)* tumult, racket, uproar. *(ant)* peace.

3 **swivel** *(v)* turn around a point. *(s)* rotate, pivot, spin.

4 **undiluted** *(adj)* not weakened by adding water. *(s)* strong, full strength. *(ant)* diluted.

5 **overindulgent** *(adj)* allowing oneself too much of something. *(s)* immoderate. *(ant)* moderate.

6 **fond** *(adj)* having a liking for. *(s)* keen, partial. *(ant)* disinterested, indifferent.

7 **potent** *(adj)* having greater influence, strength or power. *(s)* strong, formidable. *(ant)* weak.

8 **brew** *(n)* a variety of beer. *(s)* ale.

9 **fortified** *(adj)* stronger. *(s)* strengthened, bolstered. *(ant)* weakened.

10 **gait** *(n)* the way a person walks or strides. *(s)* step, posture, carriage, movement.

11 **accord** *(n)* agreement. *(s)* harmony. *(ant)* disagreement.

12 **intake** *(n)* the amount of food or drink one consumes. *(s)* consumption.

13 **cohort** *(n)* a group of people with a shared characteristic. *(s)* unit, contingent.

14 **slur** *(v)* mumble words so that sounds run into one another. *(s)* garble. *(ant)* enunciate.

15 **rhythm** *(n)* a regular pattern of movement or sound. *(s)* beat, cadence, flow, pace.

16 **consumption** *(n)* the amount used, eaten or drunk. *(s)* intake.

17 **crystal clear** (phrase) completely free of impurities. *(s)* transparent, unclouded.

18 **beady** *(adj)* (of the eyes) small, round and gleaming, keen and observant. *(s)* watchful, bright. *(ant)* dull.

and **alert**[1], just like May's should have been – except poor May's no longer worked, as she'd been blinded by Dewi's cruel **falconers**[2]. Anger rose at the thought of what they'd done to her beloved goshawk, but Cad couldn't heal May's eyes now. Instead of **dwelling on**[3] negative thoughts, Cad sneaked more chicken into the secret pocket of her tunic. She would call May to her bedchamber after dark to sleep with her and the boys.

Cad glanced over at Goodwife Hughes, who was chatting to her bored-looking son, Hugh. If only Mrs Hughes knew of the real **menagerie**[4] **residing**[5] in Cad's bedchamber at night, she would have heart failure. Without fail, Cad and Rhys cleaned up any **evidence**[6] of their animals well before Goodwife Hughes ever got there.

After one more scan of the hall, Cad knew it was time. She looked straight at Rhys, who picked at a pear. Beneath the wooden table, his leather pouch was strapped to his belt and **writhing**[7] with life, his **exotic**[8], secret pet, Slippy, was inside. Thank goodness it was late summer; in cold weather, Rhys's pet would be **hibernating**[9] beneath the **rushes**[10] in their chamber.

Like Cad, Rhys loved animals and had rescued this odd pet from near death, sneaking it into their room one day. Cad's heart had almost stopped when she'd been presented with Rhys's **adder**[11], but when he'd explained why his find was near to death, due to a complete lack of teeth, Cad had **relented**[12]. **Thus**[13] Rhys's new-found friend, Slippy, shared their room with Fishy and May, much to Dylan's chagrin, whose sharp analytical mind could not **comprehend**[14] people's

---

1 **alert** *(adj)* quick to notice unusual situations and danger. *(s)* vigilant, cautious, attentive. *(ant)* inattentive.

2 **falconer** *(n)* someone who keeps, trains or hunts with falcons or other birds of prey.

3 **dwell on** (phrase) think about something for too long to one's disadvantage. *(s)* brood on.

4 **menagerie** *(n)* a collection of animals, usually kept in captivity to be exhibited.

5 **reside** *(v)* permanently have a home in a specific place. *(s)* occupy, inhabit, dwell. *(ant)* visit.

6 **evidence** *(n)* facts or information presented to support the truth. *(s)* proof, confirmation.

7 **writhe** *(v)* twist and turn, contort the body. *(s)* squirm, thrash. *(ant)* still, relax.

8 **exotic** *(adj)* something that is striking because it is not ordinary. *(s)* unconventional. *(ant)* conventional.

9 **hibernate** *(v)* (of an animal) sleep through the winter months. *(s)* overwinter.

10 **rush** *(n)* a type of plant, cut, dried and strewn on floors in medieval castles and dwellings to absorb unwanted substances.

11 **adder** *(n)* the only poisonous snake found in Britain.

12 **relent** *(v)* give in to something. *(s)* capitulate, yield, concede. *(ant)* stand firm.

13 **thus** *(adv)* as a result of this. *(s)* so, consequently, therefore, hence, ergo.

14 **comprehend** *(v)* understand. *(s)* get, fathom, grasp. *(ant)* misunderstand, misinterpret.

sentimentality[1] for animals. But then, he was not an orphan **plucked**[2] from the jaws of death like she and Rhys. How could he understand, for he was the **privileged**[3] son of a noble training to be a knight in the castle of a prince?

When Rhys finally made eye contact with her, Cad gave him one slow, **deliberate**[4] wink. Rhys placed down his pear and **casually**[5] observed his neighbours, who, **oblivious**[6] to the **squirming**[7] pouch at his belt, chatted and **dined**[8], enjoying the kitchen's offerings. Her eyes now like slits, and her jaw a **vice**[9], Cad watched as Rhys, wearing his most **inane**[10] grin, surreptitiously slid his hands beneath the table and deftly drew back the leather pouch's neck.

Cad saw Rhys scan the room. No doubt he was checking that stray dogs had not sneaked into the hall for **titbits**[11], and was **bracing**[12] himself to stash his pet rapidly. Then Rhys released Slippy onto the floor right beneath the legs of Goodwife Hughes, who sat opposite him with Hugh. Rhys, clearly anticipating the screams, was focused only on readying to rescue Slippy and exit the hall; he knew he must be swift lest Slippy be bashed over the head and fed to the dogs. Rhys loved Slippy, and it had tested Cad's powers of **persuasion**[13] **to the hilt**[14] as she had convinced him to **jeopardise**[15] his snake for her plan.

As Goodwife Hughes's screams sliced through the air, filling the hall like those of a threatened piglet, the diners scattered, shocked by the sudden **commotion**[16]. **Per**[17] their plan, Dylan slipped

---

1 **sentimentality** *(n)* feelings of pity or love, especially for past things. *(s)* mawkishness.

2 **pluck** *(v)* suddenly or quickly remove someone from a bad situation. *(s)* pull, take, extract. *(ant)* insert.

3 **privileged** *(adj)* having special advantages or rights. *(s)* fortunate, prosperous. *(ant)* disadvantaged.

4 **deliberate** *(adj)* careful and unhurried. *(s)* measured, steady. *(ant)* hasty, careless.

5 **casually** *(adv)* in a casual (relaxed and informal) manner. *(s)* nonchalantly. *(ant)* formally.

6 **oblivious** *(adj)* unaware or unconcerned about what is happening. *(s)* ignorant, unconscious. *(ant)* conscious.

7 **squirm** *(v)* twist and move the body. *(s)* writhe, wriggle. *(ant)* still.

8 **dine** *(v)* eat a meal, especially dinner. *(s)* consume, feast.

9 **vice** *(n)* a metal tool with jaws for holding an object firmly in place. *(s)* clamp, brace, clasp.

10 **inane** *(adj)* lacking meaning or sense. *(s)* senseless, witless. *(ant)* sensible, intelligent.

11 **titbit** *(n)* a little piece of tasty food. *(s)* goody, snack, treat, bite.

12 **brace** *(v)* prepare for something difficult or unpleasant. *(s)* steady, prime, ready. *(ant)* weaken.

13 **persuasion** *(n)* the act or process of making someone do or believe something. *(s)* convincing.

14 **to the hilt** (phrase) to the utmost degree or as much as possible.

15 **jeopardise** *(v)* cause or put into a dangerous situation. *(s)* risk, endanger, imperil. *(ant)* safeguard.

16 **commotion** *(n)* a noisy disturbance and confusion. *(s)* uproar, tumult. *(ant)* calm, peace.

17 **per** *(prep)* by way of. *(s)* by means of, through, according to.

stealthily[1] away while Cad enjoyed the unfurling **furore**[2]. Stifling a grin, she observed Goodwife Hughes, who in one **uncharacteristic**[3] leap, mounted the bench where she'd sat, **kirtle**[4] now raised above her knees. In a complete **tizzy**[5], the woman frantically shook its fabric, stamping her feet like a **court jester**[6] in mid-dance. The hall fell silent, as Mrs Hughes, now a rich shade of plum, her arms **pinwheeling**[7], screeched like an owl, her feet working as though treading grapes in a **vat**[8].

Titters[9] turned into **chortles**[10]. Hugh Hughes, turning the colour of boiled **beetroot**[11], glared at his mother, who flashed her **undergarments**[12] to an **enthralled**[13] **audience**[14] scattered about the hall. His jaw **slackened**[15] and he gaped in horror, his eyes wide with a mixture of embarrassment and fury.

'Mother,' he yelled, 'whatever are you doing?', his sour, vinegary face **distorting**[16] into that of a **gargoyle**[17].

But she flapped and hissed like an angry swan, blind and deaf to the onlookers, who were now **howling**[18] with laughter. It was obvious to Cad that Goodwife Hughes knew exactly what she'd seen slithering beneath her legs, even if the surrounding folks had not. Hand to her

---

1 **stealthily** *(adv)* done in a stealthy (undetected) way. *(s)* clandestinely, furtively. *(ant)* openly, publicly.

2 **furore** *(n)* a disturbance caused by excitement or anger. *(s)* commotion, rumpus. *(ant)* tranquillity.

3 **uncharacteristic** *(adj)* in a way that is not usual. *(s)* unexpected, novel. *(ant)* characteristic.

4 **kirtle** *(n)* an outer petticoat or gown. *(s)* surcoat, skirt.

5 **tizzy** *(n)* nervous excitement or agitation. *(s)* flap, state, panic. *(ant)* calm, control.

6 **court jester** *(n)* an employee of the royal household paid to entertain guests by acting the fool. *(s)* clown, merryman.

7 **pinwheel** *(v)* turn continuously. *(s)* twirl, pirouette.

8 **vat** *(n)* a big tank used for holding liquid. *(s)* drum, barrel, cask.

9 **titter** *(n)* a short laugh which someone is trying to suppress. *(s)* giggle, snigger. *(ant)* howl.

10 **chortle** *(n)* a noisy, happy laugh. *(s)* chuckle, guffaw. *(ant)* howl.

11 **beetroot** *(n)* a root vegetable which is deep red when cooked.

12 **undergarment** *(n)* clothing worn beneath other clothing. *(s)* underwear, underclothes. *(ant)* overgarment.

13 **enthral** *(v)* capture or fascinate. *(s)* rivet, captivate, engross, grip. *(ant)* bore.

14 **audience** *(n)* a group of people who listen or watch something. *(s)* spectators, onlookers.

15 **slacken** *(v)* become or make slack (without tension). *(s)* loosen, relax. *(ant)* tighten.

16 **distort** *(v)* pull or twist out of shape. *(s)* contort, deform. *(ant)* straighten.

17 **gargoyle** *(n)* a grotesque (ugly) carving or sculpture which typically protrudes from the gutter of a grand building.

18 **howl** *(v)* make a howling (crying) sound. *(s)* yowl, bay, yelp.

mouth, Cad struggled to contain her **burgeoning**[1] giggles.

Hugh Hughes, looking close to heart failure, grabbed his mother by the arm, **yanking**[2] her from the bench. Then shaking her, and trying to hide his **disdain**[3], said, 'Mother, you are making a **laughing stock**[4] of us.'

But Goodwife Hughes, distracted and **hysterical**[5], continued to check her skirts for **stowaway**[6] adders.

Sir Robert, sitting on the **dais**[7] at the top of the table, stood and began marching towards the ruckus, his **jagged**[8] eyebrows, disappearing lips, and threatening steps spreading quiet amongst the **revellers**[9].

Time to end this, thought Cad, when she saw Rhys dive beneath the table to retrieve and stow Slippy away. That was Cad's **cue**[10] to leave, and as swift as a **swallow**[11] through sky, she quietly slipped off before anyone realised she was gone.

All but one, that was. For as Cad left the great hall, she didn't see the **crook-backed**[12] man who **shuffled**[13] slowly after her, his **lame**[14] leg dragging along the ground behind him.

---

1 **burgeoning** *(adj)* growing or increasing rapidly. *(s)* accelerating, escalating. *(ant)* dwindling.

2 **yank** *(v)* pull with a sudden, hard movement. *(s)* wrench, heave, haul. *(ant)* push, shove.

3 **disdain** *(n)* the feeling that something is unworthy of respect. *(s)* contempt, derision, scorn. *(ant)* admiration.

4 **laughing stock** *(n)* a person of ridicule. *(s)* fool, spectacle.

5 **hysterical** *(adj)* affected by uncontrolled emotion. *(s)* frenzied, frantic, wild. *(ant)* calm.

6 **stowaway** *(adj)* hidden. *(s)* concealed, obscured. *(ant)* revealed.

7 **dais** *(n)* a low platform for a throne or lectern. *(s)* stage, rostrum, stand.

8 **jagged** *(adj)* rough or sharp. *(s)* spiky, ragged. *(ant)* smooth.

9 **reveller** *(n)* a person who is enjoying themselves in a noisy way. *(s)* partygoer. *(ant)* party-pooper.

10 **cue** *(n)* a signal to act. *(s)* prompt, indication.

11 **swallow** *(n)* a swift-flying songbird.

12 **crook-backed** *(adj)* having a back which is not straight due to disease or injury.

13 **shuffle** *(v)* walk with one's feet dragging on the ground. *(s)* shamble, lumber, dodder.

14 **lame** *(adj)* unable to walk properly due to injury or disease. *(s)* gammy, maimed. *(ant)* able-bodied.

CHAPTER SEVEN

Caught Red-Handed

Goodwife Hughes's hysterical screeching in the great hall **wrenched**[1] the castle's guards from their **stations**[2] just as Cad had planned. Many sprinted past her and Dylan as they rushed in the opposite direction towards Sir Robert's rooms in the **keep**[3]. Cad had not been near these rooms since she'd found the cipher there weeks ago.

'We won't have long before the guards realise it's just the goodwife **ranting**[4] and return to their **posts**[5],' panted Cad. 'I must be in and out before then. I wonder if Evans has further plans in his rooms; if so, I'll find them. The question is, why does he have plans that seemingly belong to that traitorous snake, Prince Dewi? Evans is my father's friend. Or could he, indeed, be helping the **foe**[6]?'

Dylan nodded, struggling to keep up with Cad, who almost broke into a trot.

'Cad, slow down. We'll raise **suspicions**[7],' he muttered.

But Cad ignored him, striding on. 'I hope Rhys managed to rescue Slippy before they saw him,' Cad said.

---

1 **wrench** *(v)* pull suddenly. *(s)* jolt, yank, wrest, heave.

2 **station** *(n)* the place where someone is put to guard someone or something. *(s)* post, location.

3 **keep** *(n)* the strongest (sometimes highest) tower of a castle. *(s)* donjon, stronghold, fort, dungeon.

4 **rant** *(v)* speak or shout in a lengthy and passionate way. *(s)* bluster, bellow, rage. *(ant)* sweet-talk.

5 **post** *(n)* a position from where a person can guard or lookout for someone or something. *(s)* station.

6 **foe** *(n)* an enemy, nemesis or opponent. *(s)* antagonist, rival, opposition. *(ant)* friend, ally, comrade.

7 **suspicion** *(n)* a state of doubt or distrust. *(s)* mistrust, uncertainty. *(ant)* certainty.

'Before someone bashed it on the head, you mean,' Dylan replied.

Cad meant precisely that, and she prayed that Slippy, the gummy adder, was alive to see another day. Cad knew Rhys would be **distraught**[1] if he lost Slippy, for she felt the same about May and Fishy.

'When he wants to, Rhys moves like a **startled**[2] **fawn**[3],' said Cad.

Without warning, Cad froze, grabbing Dylan's arm.

'What is it?' he whispered, his face greying.

Cad whirled, her legs a little watery, but the shadowy passageway seemed empty. 'I thought I caught a **glimpse**[4] of something,' she replied, quickly quashing her **paranoia**[5].

Since the **trauma**[6] in the oubliette, Cad had suffered from visions of that **cowled**[7] monk's figure **stalking**[8] her in the shadows as well as in her dreams. Now her nerves **lurched**[9] her back to that day; they crackled as her **limbs**[10] **tensed**[11] for fight or flight. Whoever had intended to seal her and John in that hellhole probably still resided in this castle. Even though it **tormented**[12] her, she had mulled over the ordeal many times since, and concluded that the long slim fingers may well have belonged to the hands of a woman.

'False alarm. Come.' She signalled to Dylan with a **tilt**[13] of her chin. 'The guards will soon return.'

Both friends continued down the passageway towards Sir Robert's rooms. Neither spotted the half-man, half-shadow following them, dragging his leg behind him.

---

1 **distraught** *(adj)* extremely worried and upset. *(s)* distressed, fraught, desperate. *(ant)* calm, serene.

2 **startle** *(v)* cause to feel sudden alarm or shock. *(s)* scare, frighten, surprise, perturb. *(ant)* calm, ease.

3 **fawn** *(n)* a deer in its first year of life.

4 **glimpse** *(n)* a quick or partial view. *(s)* glance, peep, peek. *(ant)* stare.

5 **paranoia** *(n)* feelings and thoughts that are unsubstantiated (not proven). *(s)* delusion. *(ant)* reality.

6 **trauma** *(n)* a distressing occurrence or experience. *(s)* agony, anguish, hurt, upset. *(ant)* healing.

7 **cowled** *(adj)* wearing a cowl (hood). *(s)* hooded.

8 **stalk** *(v)* pursue (follow, chase) or approach stealthily (unseen). *(s)* hunt, trail, shadow.

9 **lurch** *(v)* move abruptly without control. *(s)* toss, pitch.

10 **limb** *(n)* an arm, leg or wing. *(s)* appendage, offshoot.

11 **tense** *(v)* become rigid, usually from anxiety. *(s)* tighten, stiffen. *(ant)* relax.

12 **torment** *(v)* cause severe suffering. *(s)* distress, cause pain, torture. *(ant)* soothe.

13 **tilt** *(n)* a sloping movement. *(s)* slant, incline.

'I'll be as quick as I can,' Cad said to Dylan as they turned into the passageway **housing**[1] Sir Robert's rooms.

Candles flickered outside the grand quarters, **casting**[2] **eerie**[3] dancers onto the walls, their **accumulating**[4] wax forming **craggy**[5] **glaciers**[6] about the **sconces**[7]' bases.

'Wait here as planned,' Cad told Dylan, wondering if she might find her missing ring in Sir Robert's rooms along with more information on the cipher. When they had studied the cracked code together further, it had seemed incomplete, and they'd been unable to fathom the weapon it described.

'When the guard returns, **proceed**[8] as agreed. You know of his **gambling**[9] **passion**[10]; he won't refuse to play you. If Evans returns first, revert to plan two,' Cad said.

'Plan two?' asked Dylan, his face screwed up into a question.

'Plan two is if I hear the lock turn, then I hide, and you distract whoever is coming through the door.' Cad hoped Sir Robert's four-poster bed still boasted the floor-length skirts where she'd hidden last time.

Dylan nodded.

'What I mean is, don't let anyone come through that door without giving me the time to hide.'

Dylan nodded again.

Using her magical emerald hairpin, as her hands danced an unwelcome jig, Cad managed to unlock Evans's door and entered his room. With her heart in her throat, she scanned the **locale**[11], which was empty, the wooden shutters at the windows closed, rendering the place a

---

1 **house** *(v)* provide space for or accommodate (keep in a certain place). *(s)* hold, contain. *(ant)* expose.

2 **cast** *(v)* cause to appear on the surface of something. *(s)* emit, project.

3 **eerie** *(adj)* strange and scary. *(s)* spooky, creepy, weird, peculiar. *(ant)* normal.

4 **accumulate** *(v)* build up. *(s)* amass, increase, accrue. *(ant)* dissipate.

5 **craggy** *(adj)* rough and uneven. *(s)* bumpy. *(ant)* smooth.

6 **glacier** *(n)* a river of ice slowly moving down a mountain.

7 **sconce** *(n)* a fixture mounted onto a wall to hold a candle or oil lamp.

8 **proceed** *(v)* begin an action. *(s)* start, move, act. *(ant)* stop.

9 **gamble** *(v)* play games for money. *(s)* bet, chance, wager.

10 **passion** *(n)* a strong enthusiasm for something. *(s)* obsession, fervour. *(ant)* indifference.

11 **locale** *(n)* a place. *(s)* area, location, setting, position.

gloomy[1], **drab**[2] **environment**[3].

Once **satisfied**[4] she was alone, Cad locked the door behind her and **thrust**[5] open the shutters. The last of the day's light streaked through, punishing her eyes. Illuminated dust **motes**[6] danced in the dying sun, whose rays lit the parchments strewn about the table that **dominated**[7] the room.

Cad knew she should check the parchments first; still, the **lure**[8] of finding her stolen ring prevailed as she **rifled**[8] through Evans's wardrobe, chest and drawers, but to no avail. Her search was **fruitless**[9], and now regretful at having strayed from her plan, she wasted more precious time rearranging the belongings as she'd found them. Once finished, she listened carefully to the silence around her, **ruing**[10] the time she'd **squandered**[11].

My ring won't prevent this weapon's ***construction***[12], she **admonished**[13] herself, studying the scattered parchments for clues. With any luck, Evans would have **encrypted**[14] more **vital**[15] information, hopefully using the same coding Rhys had deciphered. She must prove the **decryption's**[16] **authenticity**[17] and accuracy before alerting Llywelyn to its contents and their suspicion of this weapon. But with Dewi's name on the cipher, there was little chance she was wrong.

---

1 **gloomy** *(adj)* dark and dismal. *(s)* bleak, dreary, miserable. *(ant)* bright, clear.

2 **drab** *(adj)* lacking brightness. *(s)* dull, dreary, gloomy. *(ant)* bright.

3 **environment** *(n)* one's surrounding conditions. *(s)* setting, ambiance.

4 **satisfy** *(v)* to make or to be happy with something. *(s)* content, please. *(ant)* dissatisfy.

5 **thrust** *(v)* move forcefully. *(s)* shove, push, drive.

6 **mote** *(n)* a tiny piece of something. *(s)* particle, speck, spot, fleck.

7 **dominate** *(v)* be the most conspicuous (stand out most) thing. *(s)* command.

8 **lure** *(n)* something used to tempt. *(s)* pull, temptation, enticement, attraction.

8 **rifle** *(v)* search through something in a hasty way. *(s)* hunt, rummage, scour.

9 **fruitless** *(adj)* not achieving the desired results. *(s)* useless, pointless, futile. *(ant)* fruitful.

10 **rue** *(v)* regret something you wish you could undo. *(s)* lament, deplore. *(ant)* celebrate.

11 **squander** *(v)* waste. *(s)* lose, misuse, misspend. *(ant)* gain.

12 **construction** *(n)* the act of building or making something. *(s)* assembly, development.

13 **admonish** *(v)* reprimand (tell off) firmly. *(s)* warn, chide, caution. *(ant)* praise.

14 **encrypt** *(v)* convert into code to make secret. *(s)* encipher, encode. *(ant)* decrypt.

15 **vital** *(adj)* completely necessary. *(s)* essential, key, crucial. *(ant)* unimportant, secondary.

16 **decryption** *(n)* the act of making a code or mystery intelligible. *(s)* decipherment. *(ant)* encryption.

17 **authenticity** *(n)* the quality of being authentic (genuine). *(s)* legitimacy. *(ant)* inaccuracy.

The scattered parchments were similar to those she'd seen when searching for Prince John: intricate maps **resembling**[1] tunnels, marked with **cryptic**[2] symbols. Cad **sifted**[3] through them, wishing she could study the pieces and appreciate them more, but now was not the time. She was still vexed at being so distracted by searching for her ring, when a sound from the corridor froze her blood. Cad knew that voice too well. Why was Bryn Davis outside Evans's rooms, and where was Dylan? Something was wrong, and even though she'd locked the door from the inside, no doubt a key would be turning in it very soon. The shock suddenly hit, as her legs wobbled and her stomach seemed to empty.

Panic rose as Cad **scoped**[4] the **regal**[5] bed with its skirts. She could dive beneath it like last time. Then if need be, she could exit **via**[6] the tunnel leading from these rooms. But the thought of crawling through those **suffocatingly**[7] **cramped**[8] tunnels without the help of the kitten, filled her with a terror too **grotesque**[9] to contemplate. She hadn't **encountered**[10] the cat since she'd been stuck in the oubliette, and without its **guidance**[11], those tiny tunnels were **unthinkable**[12] to Cad.

Liquid fear **coursed**[13] through her veins as her gaze slid towards the door. **Horrified**[14], she watched, her heart **somersaulting**[15] as its **ornate**[16] handle slowly lowered. Little time remained before a key would turn and someone pushed it open. Here she was in Sir Robert's rooms again,

---

1 **resemble** *(v)* look or seem like something else. *(s)* feature, simulate. *(ant)* differ from.

2 **cryptic** *(adj)* having a meaning which is difficult to understand. *(s)* confusing, enigmatic. *(ant)* straightforward.

3 **sift** *(v)* look or work through something carefully. *(s)* go through.

4 **scope** *(v)* investigate something. *(s)* scan, check, examine.

5 **regal** *(adj)* fit for a ruler. *(s)* royal, grand, majestic, impressive, splendid. *(ant)* humble.

6 **via** *(prep)* through. *(s)* by, by way of.

7 **suffocatingly** *(adv)* in such a way to make one feel trapped or oppressed.

8 **cramped** *(adj)* uncomfortably small or restricted. *(s)* confined, tight, limited. *(ant)* spacious.

9 **grotesque** *(adj)* extremely unpleasant. *(s)* monstrous, absurd. *(ant)* pleasant.

10 **encounter** *(v)* meet unexpectedly. *(s)* run into, come across. *(ant)* avoid.

11 **guidance** *(n)* advice given to help someone or something to find a way. *(s)* instruction, direction.

12 **unthinkable** *(adj)* too horrid to be thought possible. *(s)* unimaginable, inconceivable. *(ant)* desirable.

13 **course** *(v)* move through without obstruction. *(s)* flow, gush, race, surge, stream. *(ant)* trickle.

14 **horrify** *(v)* to fill someone with horror. *(s)* scare, alarm, panic. *(ant)* please.

15 **somersault** *(v)* perform a flip. *(s)* overturn.

16 **ornate** *(adj)* decorative. *(s)* fancy, elaborate. *(ant)* dull, plain.

empty-handed and trapped between the horns of capture and hiding once more.

'Callwen, can I help you?'

Cad's legs threatened to **buckle**[1].

Rooted to the spot, and with little time to think, she grasped her thoughts, her eyes fixed on the door handle, which now remained still.

'Callwen?'

Cad had recognised the voice at once, but she couldn't fathom how it was in this room and behind her: no one had come through its door.

Composing[2] herself, Cad arranged her face into the sweetest smile she could muster, hid the terror from her eyes, then **pirouetted**[3] on her heel to face the voice.

'Sir Robert,' she said with a **respectful**[4] **bow**[5] of her head, while trying to **interpret**[6] the look on his unreadable face.

'Callwen, as I asked, can I help you?' he repeated, his voice, almost pleasant, but with accusation just below the surface and, sounding like a thin stream of icy water, it matched the frozen look in his **unfathomable**[7] eyes.

Caught red-handed, feeling like a sheep facing a wolf, Cad battled to **arrest**[8] the flush creeping up her chest, but its **telltale**[9] heat rose, finally pricking her face and turning it pink. With no **plausible**[10] answer, and truth now the only option, Cad sucked in a deep breath as she lined up her words, and said, 'Sir Robert, I owe you an apology.'

---

1 **buckle** *(v)* bend and give way under strain or pressure. *(s)* crumple, fold. *(ant)* straighten.

2 **compose** *(v)* settle or calm oneself. *(s)* gather, collect, contain. *(ant)* agitate.

3 **pirouette** *(v)* perform a pirouette. *(s)* twirl, spin, rotate, turn, circle.

4 **respectful** *(adj)* showing manners and politeness for someone or something. *(s)* courteous, gracious. *(ant)* disrespectful.

5 **bow** *(n)* a respectful bend of the head or upper body. *(s)* bob, nod.

6 **interpret** *(v)* understand the meaning of. *(s)* comprehend, decipher. *(ant)* misinterpret.

7 **unfathomable** *(adj)* not capable of being understood. *(s)* mystifying, puzzling. *(ant)* fathomable, clear.

8 **arrest** *(v)* stop. *(s)* halt, end, prevent. *(ant)* start, begin.

9 **telltale** *(adj)* indicating or revealing something. *(s)* significant, giveaway.

10 **plausible** *(adj)* seeming probable (likely) or reasonable (sensible). *(s)* believable, feasible. *(ant)* implausible.

CHAPTER EIGHT

Sir Robert

Much to Cad's chagrin, as she spoke to Sir Robert, her voice **quavered**[1], stubbornly refusing to settle as she continued with her **confession**[2]. Her tone **expressed**[3] remorse, but it was also stretched with fear.

'Sir Robert, weeks back, whilst distraught and searching for my brother, I happened upon your unguarded quarters. However, I was unaware they were yours until I entered them.' Cad forced herself not to wring her hands, but clenched them together so hard, her knuckles whitened.

Evans, face like **granite**[4], peered at her, his already narrow eyes turning to slits. He said nothing, leaving her words hanging in the air like an unfinished argument, but she knew they **rankled**[5] as he silently chewed them over. Cad swallowed, ruing the sound it made at her neck as his gaze **roamed**[6] over her.

'Why did you conclude the rooms were mine?' Evans, his tone **probing**[7], likely didn't believe

---

1 **quaver** *(v)* shake or tremble. *(s)* quiver, tremor. *(ant)* steady.

2 **confession** *(n)* an admission of guilt. *(s)* disclosure, acknowledgment. *(ant)* denial.

3 **express** *(v)* convey (show) a thought or feeling in gestures, words or conduct. *(s)* indicate. *(ant)* hide.

4 **granite** *(n)* a hard rock often used as a building stone.

5 **rankle** *(v)* cause ongoing irritation. *(s)* bother, annoy, upset. *(ant)* placate.

6 **roam** *(v)* (of the eyes) look over something without stopping. *(s)* drift, prowl. *(ant)* flit.

7 **probe** *(v)* try to uncover information. *(s)* explore, examine.

a word she said, especially after the **desperate**[1] **yarn**[2] she'd spun with Rhys following the oubliette ordeal.

Forcing stillness, Cad blinked too slowly and swallowed hard again, **gulping**[3] even louder this time.

'The … the parchments that lay on your table. I guessed,' stuttered Cad, dipping her chin in its direction, 'along with your **personal**[4] belongings,' she added quickly, glancing across at the **portrait**[5] which hung above his bed and hoping he'd buy her **tale**[6].

Evans rocked back and forth from heel to toe, then cleared his throat with a **pompous**[7] cough.

His eyes, yellowish **beads**[8] pricked with black, shone with something **akin**[9] to **malice**[10]. He enjoyed **interrogation**[11]; this much Cad knew from the last time he'd questioned her and Rhys about the **incident**[12] in the oubliette.

'And this … this *apology* you wish to make.' He waved his hand as if **wafting**[13] away an unpleasant **odour**[14]. 'For what **deed**[15] must you **make amends**[16], *Callwen*?'

Cad wasn't sure, but had **threat**[17] **lurked**[18] when he'd **emphasised**[19] her true name, Callwen? The name, and the girl, she must hide from the world lest she fail in her quest to become a Knight Hawk.

---

1 **desperate** *(adj)* done with daring and recklessness. *(s)* audacious, rash. *(ant)* cautious.
2 **yarn** *(n)* a far-fetched story. *(s)* tale, lie, tall story. *(ant)* truth.
3 **gulp** *(v)* swallow or breathe noisily due to emotion. *(s)* gasp.
4 **personal** *(adj)* affecting or belonging to a certain person (yours). *(s)* own, private. *(ant)* public.
5 **portrait** *(n)* a painting of someone's face and upper body. *(s)* likeness, image.
6 **tale** *(n)* a true or fictitious story. *(s)* account, anecdote, gossip, hearsay.
7 **pompous** *(adj)* self-important or affectedly grand. *(s)* pretentious, vain. *(ant)* modest.
8 **bead** *(n)* a small piece of material like glass, that is threaded with others to make jewellery such as a necklace.
9 **akin** *(adj)* similar in character. *(s)* related, close, comparable. *(ant)* unlike, dissimilar.
10 **malice** *(n)* the desire to hurt or harm someone. *(s)* spite, malevolence, badness. *(ant)* kindness.
11 **interrogation** *(n)* the act of questioning someone. *(s)* probing, investigation. *(ant)* debrief.
12 **incident** *(n)* an instance of something happening. *(s)* event, occurrence, episode.
13 **waft** *(v)* move with a waving motion. *(s)* fan.
14 **odour** *(n)* a distinctive, often unpleasant, smell. *(s)* aroma, stink, stench.
15 **deed** *(n)* a performance or action. *(s)* feat, act.
16 **make amends** (phrase) make up for a wrongdoing.
17 **threat** *(n)* a statement of intention to take hostile action. *(s)* warning, menace. *(ant)* benefit, boon.
18 **lurk** *(v)* be or remain hidden, hang about. *(s)* prowl, hide, skulk. *(ant)* appear, materialise.
19 **emphasise** *(v)* stress a word when speaking. *(s)* highlight, accentuate. *(ant)* understate.

His face **unnerved**[1] Cad; it was like that of a starving **falcon**[2].

'That day, I took something from your rooms that did not belong to me.' **Drooping**[3] her head in **feigned**[4] shame, Cad struggled on. 'I took this parchment.'

From its hiding place in her tunic, she presented the cipher as a magician might a hidden coin. His slit eyes widened, his head tilting in **realisation**[5] as his claw-like hand hooked the parchment from hers. Cad's shoulders **slumped**[6] as she waited for the **onslaught**[7].

'Ahh!' he spat through thin lips. 'So that is what became of it.'

His **flinty**[8] eyes **bored**[9] into hers.

'Yes,' she whispered, her gaze falling towards her feet.

Sir Robert unfolded the parchment with his **wrinkled**[10] fingers as her eyes tracked back to him.

'Ahh, **vellum**[11], the queen of parchments,' he muttered, squinting at the now **grubby**[12] piece in his **wizened**[13] hand.

Cad forced a **penitent**[14] expression as she waited for Evans to **mete**[15] out another stint in the tower, for she was sure it was coming.

He's definitely enjoying this, Cad thought, studying him with disdain.

---

1 **unnerve** *(v)* cause to lose confidence or courage. *(s)* alarm, worry. *(ant)* calm, encourage.

2 **falcon** *(n)* a type of bird of prey. *(s)* raptor.

3 **droop** *(v)* hang down loosely. *(s)* sag, drop.

4 **feign** *(v)* simulate or pretend. *(s)* affect, fake, bluff, sham.

5 **realisation** *(n)* the act of becoming aware that something is a fact. *(s)* understanding, awareness. *(ant)* ignorance.

6 **slump** *(v)* fall, sit or lean heavily. *(s)* sag, slouch, collapse. *(ant)* lift, straighten.

7 **onslaught** *(n)* a vicious or destructive attack. *(s)* bombardment, barrage. *(ant)* defence.

8 **flinty** *(adj)* hard. *(s)* unyielding, steely, stony, inflexible. *(ant)* soft, gentle, flexible.

9 **bore** *(v)* (literally or figuratively) drill a hole in something.

10 **wrinkle** *(v)* make lines or folds in. *(s)* crease, crinkle. *(ant)* smooth, straighten.

11 **vellum** *(n)* quality parchment made from the skin of a calf.

12 **grubby** *(adj)* dirty. *(s)* grimy, soiled, unwashed. *(ant)* clean.

13 **wizened** *(adj)* showing signs of old age. *(s)* wrinkled, creased. *(ant)* smooth, young.

14 **penitent** *(adj)* showing regret. *(s)* sorry, apologetic, remorseful. *(ant)* unrepentant.

15 **mete** *(v)* give out punishment. *(s)* issue, assign, allocate.

Evans **savoured**[1] the moment, taking his time. He **inspected**[2] the vellum, **emitting**[3] strange noises like those of an owl as he turned it over in his hands and lifted it to the **shaft**[4] of light pouring in through the window. Cad, with **waning**[5] patience, quashed a rising **quip**[6] of cheekiness.

Just get on with it, she raged inside, hoping he would imprison her in the 'better cells' like last time. Thank goodness she had concealed various **mercy**[7] notes on her person. The moment Evans locked her up, she would call on May to deliver her messages to Dylan and Llywelyn.

'Mmm,' muttered Evans, his **calculating**[8] eyes meeting Cad's once more.

'And what think you of the symbols inked onto this vellum?'

Eh? Cad thought, blinking in surprise.

Rattled by his question, Cad **weighed up**[9] her answer, perplexed by his **genuine**[10] tone and open expression. She studied his face. Was Sir Robert asking *her* for information about the cipher – *his* cipher?

Evans waited, but his gaze never left Cad's. Again, she blinked far too slowly, trying to mask her thoughts.

Cad, the one caught red-handed, was forced to answer his questions.

Is he trying to trick me? she thought, wondering if his words carried a double meaning, and deciding she must **temper**[11] her answer.

'Maybe the symbols **portray**[12] a message. I don't know,' she said, her eyes alight with thought.

Then, playing cat and mouse, she remained **mute**[13], innocence shining from her face.

What is this man up to?

---

1 **savour** *(v)* enjoy and linger over. *(s)* relish, delight in. *(ant)* dislike.

2 **inspect** *(v)* look at something closely and with care. *(s)* examine, scrutinise, check.

3 **emit** *(v)* make a sound. *(s)* issue, produce, utter, voice. *(ant)* silence.

4 **shaft** *(n)* a ray of light. *(s)* streak, beam.

5 **wane** *(v)* decline in extent. *(s)* decrease, dwindle, diminish. *(ant)* grow, increase.

6 **quip** *(n)* a witty (humorous) remark. *(s)* witticism, retort, jest, jibe.

7 **mercy** *(n)* forgiveness and compassion. *(s)* clemency, sympathy. *(ant)* cruelty.

8 **calculating** *(adj)* describing ruthless and determined behaviour. *(s)* shrewd, cunning. *(ant)* innocent.

9 **weigh up** *(v)* assess something or someone carefully. *(s)* evaluate, gauge. *(ant)* calculate.

10 **genuine** *(adj)* real, truthful or sincere. *(s)* honest, candid. *(ant)* insincere, false, hypocritical.

11 **temper** *(v)* weaken the influence of something. *(s)* moderate, soften, assuage. *(ant)* strengthen.

12 **portray** *(v)* represent or describe something in a certain way. *(s)* depict, show, reveal. *(ant)* obscure.

13 **mute** *(adj)* remaining speechless. *(s)* silent, taciturn, quiet. *(ant)* vocal, speaking.

'Callwen,' Evans said, his voice soft, 'perhaps you misunderstand me.'

Cad had no idea where this headed, but her face gave nothing away.

'Do you think the cipher on this vellum to be my work?' Evans asked with a tilt of his head, concern burning bright in his eyes.

What in heaven?

She was so surprised by his question, she **skirted**[1] his look while she searched for a reply.

'Yes. That was my **assumption**[2], as I found it on your table,' she finally answered, her eyes flicking across to it as she spoke.

'Callwen bach,' he cooed, speaking the name used by her mother, making Cad **wince**[3]. 'This parchment is not of my hand.'

Is he telling the truth? Cad thought, **confounded**[4] by Evans.

'This code is not my creation,' he continued, his voice even and without malice. 'And nor am I able to translate its markings **adequately**[5] to understand them.'

His searching gaze rested on hers.

'Callwen, if you have fathomed this code, then share it with me,' he pleaded, his arms floating up to the level of his waist, his palms turned out in **supplication**[6] like a preacher in the **pulpit**[7].

Now the **prey**[8] of complete confusion, Cad's mind whirled as she explored his eyes for the truth. If what Evans said was true, she had no choice: she must help Llywelyn's **kingdom**[9]. She glanced about the room, its parchments and **priceless**[10] books, a **hoard**[11] of learning. Torn, she regarded the man whom she'd known throughout her childhood. The man in whom her father had placed all trust in his **absence**[12]. The man she must now decide whether to trust, the

---

1 **skirt** *(v)* try to ignore or avoid dealing with. *(s)* evade, dodge. *(ant)* face.

2 **assumption** *(n)* something that is accepted as true but without proof. *(s)* belief, guess. *(ant)* reality.

3 **wince** *(v)* grimace slightly in reaction to pain or distress. *(s)* flinch, cringe, recoil. *(ant)* smile.

4 **confounded** *(adj)* surprised or confused. *(s)* puzzled, baffled, perplexed. *(ant)* clear.

5 **adequately** *(adv)* in a way that is adequate (enough). *(s)* sufficiently. *(ant)* inadequately.

6 **supplication** *(n)* the action of appealing or pleading. *(s)* plea, prayer, appeal. *(ant)* offer.

7 **pulpit** *(n)* a raised platform in a church or chapel from where a preacher delivers a sermon. *(s)* stage, platform, dais.

8 **prey** *(n)* the victim of. *(s)* target, gull, dupe. *(ant)* predator, hunter.

9 **kingdom** *(n)* a place ruled by a monarch (king or queen). *(s)* realm, dominion. *(ant)* republic.

10 **priceless** *(adj)* so precious that a value cannot be put on it. *(s)* invaluable, rare, high-priced. *(ant)* worthless.

11 **hoard** *(n)* a store of valuable objects, often one that is hidden. *(s)* stock, cache, mass, collection.

12 **absence** *(n)* the state of not being at an occasion or a place. *(s)* absenteeism. *(ant)* presence, attendance.

Knight Hawk, Sir Robert Evans. But one more question burned.

'Sir Robert,' Cad said, with an almost **indiscernible**[1] bow of her head, 'if you did not **pen**[2] this cipher, then who did?'

'Ahh,' replied the knight, his arms now shoulder height, his palms turned upwards in contemplation. 'Callwen bach, if you can crack the conundrum, then perhaps you might answer your own question.'

Cad studied his face again, her stare steady and **contemplative**[3], her mind battling with **indecision**[4].

Why are you not angry with me? Cad asked herself, unable to comprehend his reaction.

Perhaps what he said was true: he could not interpret the code without her help.

Cad met his gaze to see a **complexity**[5] that was absent before. His open expression and sharp eyes, which were now soft, almost to the point of **beseeching**[6], convinced her. She had no choice but to help him. For her father's **sake**[7], just for now, she must trust Sir Robert Evans. However, she would not mention the name, Dewi, that appeared amongst the symbols. If Sir Robert truly could not read the cipher, then she would keep that information just for her friends and her father.

---

1 **indiscernible** *(adj)* difficult to see or distinguish. *(s)* unnoticeable, undetectable. *(ant)* discernible.

2 **pen** *(v)* write. *(s)* compose, draft.

3 **contemplative** *(adj)* involving prolonged thought. *(s)* pensive, thoughtful. *(ant)* unreflective.

4 **indecision** *(n)* the inability to make a decision. *(s)* hesitancy, doubt. *(ant)* decision.

5 **complexity** *(n)* the state of being complex (not simple). *(s)* intricacy. *(ant)* simplicity.

6 **beseech** *(v)* ask someone urgently or fervently. *(s)* implore, beg, plead. *(ant)* offer.

7 **sake** *(n)* the well-being and success of. *(s)* benefit, welfare, gain.

CHAPTER NINE

Peggy Saves the Day

'Callwen, come **hither**[1]. Sit.'

Sir Robert, reading that something in Cad had given way, pulled over a spare chair, and patting it, **beckoned**[2] her to his desk. Then, using **embers**[3] from the **grate**[4] of the dying fire, he lit two beeswax candles and placed their holders on his desk. They flickered in **hues**[5] of **Titian**[6], softening the room's **dimming**[7] light. After **stoking**[8] and then piling more wood onto the **dwindling**[9] fire and gently blowing in life with **bellows**[10], Evans joined Cad at his **bureau**[11].

---

1 **hither** *(adv)* to, towards or closer to this place. *(s)* here, nearer. *(ant)* thither.

2 **beckon** *(v)* make a gesture with the hand, arm or head to instruct someone. *(s)* signal, sign.

3 **ember** *(n)* a small piece of glowing material in a dying fire. *(s)* ash.

4 **grate** *(n)* a metal frame used for holding fuel, such as coal or wood, in a fireplace.

5 **hue** *(n)* colour, tone or shade. *(s)* aspect, tinge, tint.

6 **Titian** *(adj)* a warm reddish, brownish colour.

7 **dim** *(v)* make less bright. *(s)* darken, fade. *(ant)* brighten.

8 **stoke** *(v)* add fuel to a burning fire. *(s)* tend.

9 **dwindle** *(v)* lessen in size or strength. *(s)* decrease, decline, diminish. *(ant)* increase.

10 **bellows** *(n)* a device that puffs air into a fire when squeezed together.

11 **bureau** *(n)* a writing desk. *(s)* roll-top desk.

His desk was an **elaborate**[1] **affair**[2] of highly **polished**[3] and **exquisitely**[4] **carved**[5] oak, which he'd **transported**[6] from Cadwaladr Castle when he'd assumed command of Catrin. Cad regarded the ink pot and grinned inwardly, remembering how, weeks back, his face had dripped with its contents after she'd shot the pot with her **sling**[7].

That was a ***mighty***[8] *fine aim*, she thought, *especially as I was stuck underneath his bed.*

'Sire, if I may request something of you, please?' asked Cad, trying not to think of the ink and **dousing**[9] the fire in her eyes.

'Of course, Callwen.'

Cad **bristled**[10] at that and said, 'I think it more prudent **henceforth**[11], sire, that you address me only as Cad.' She hesitated a moment, **gauging**[12] his reaction at what might appear to be **impudence**[13]. 'I fear someone might overhear, sire. Perhaps the **wainscot**[14] has ears,' she added with a **wry**[15] grin.

With a **blank**[16] face, and his pupils like pinpricks, Sir Robert **inched**[17] his chair closer to his desk, cleared his throat and said, 'As you wish, Callwen. Henceforth, you will be Cad.'

'Thank you, sire. I want more than anything to be as you, a Knight Hawk, and help my father. I fear certain folks in this castle suspect that I am a girl and wish failure for me.'

With a kink of his eyebrow, his gaze met hers.

---

1 **elaborate** *(adj)* detailed in design. *(s)* fussy, extravagant, ornate. *(ant)* plain, simple.

2 **affair** *(n)* an object of a specific type. *(s)* thing.

3 **polish** *(v)* make something shiny by rubbing it. *(s)* buff, gloss, shine. *(ant)* dull.

4 **exquisitely** *(adv)* in an exquisite (perfect and beautiful) way. *(s)* flawlessly, supremely, elegantly. *(ant)* crudely.

5 **carve** *(v)* cut a hard material to make an object or design. *(s)* sculpt, form.

6 **transport** *(v)* take from one place to another. *(s)* bring, fetch

7 **sling** *(n)* a simple weapon in the shape of a loop, used to throw stones, etc. *(s)* catapult, slingshot.

8 **mighty** *(adv)* extremely. *(s)* exceedingly, markedly, frightfully.

9 **douse** *(v)* extinguish. *(s)* smother. *(ant)* ignite, light.

10 **bristle** *(v)* recoil or react defensively. *(s)* stiffen, shiver, flinch. *(ant)* calm.

11 **henceforth** *(adv)* from this or that time forward. *(s)* hence, hereafter, subsequently.

12 **gauge** *(v)* measure or estimate the amount of. *(s)* judge, assess, evaluate, determine, calculate.

13 **impudence** *(n)* the quality of being cheeky (rude). *(s)* insolence, disrespect. *(ant)* respect.

14 **wainscot** *(n)* an area of panelling on the lower walls of a room, especially that made of wood.

15 **wry** *(adj)* expressing dry humour. *(s)* ironic, sarcastic, humorous. *(ant)* straightforward.

16 **blank** *(adj)* showing a lack of understanding or reaction. *(s)* expressionless, deadpan. *(ant)* expressive.

17 **inch** *(v)* move along carefully and slowly. *(s)* budge, edge, shuffle. *(ant)* rush, leap.

'Indeed, you do **desire**[1] to be a knighted Instinctive: that you prove with **continuous**[2] **toil**[3]. Now, let us see you prove your **mettle**[4] as a scholar.'

He pushed the parchment between them on the desk, his narrow eyes **exuding**[5] challenge.

For a moment, she fixed her iron glare on him thinking, *someone must blink first.*

Then picturing her father, Cad settled and pointed to the symbols, explaining to Evans what she thought they meant, but she didn't mention fire-breathing dragons. Again, that detail would be for her father's ears first. Sir Robert listened without uttering a word.

'So you see, sire, we believe it to be some sort of weapon design. One of **potential**[6] devastating **capability**[7].'

Cad's glittering eyes searched his for a reaction. For what felt like ages, he said nothing. Her face twitched. She was sure he'd noticed. She could see it in those crow-black eyes.

Then, he picked up the cipher from the desk and studied it.

'Are you certain of what you see?' he finally asked, his voice **sombre**[8].

'As certain as we … as I can be,' she corrected herself.

Why she didn't **divulge**[9] Rhys's brilliance to Evans, she was unsure. Was it the **serpent**[10] of **pride**[11] uncurling within her, or was it to keep unnecessary detail back from Sir Robert? She hoped the **latter**[12] over the **former**[13] and said nothing.

'I have pondered this puzzle for weeks—' Cad was about to say more but catching herself, she stopped, deciding it prudent to conceal the truth of her stolen ring.

He may not even know I had it in the first place, she thought.

---

1 **desire** *(v)* want something strongly. *(s)* yearn, long.

2 **continuous** *(adj)* without interruption. *(s)* unending, constant, endless. *(ant)* sporadic, intermittent.

3 **toil** *(n)* extremely hard work, especially physically so. *(s)* effort, exertion, labour.

4 **mettle** *(n)* someone's ability to deal with difficulties. *(s)* strength, tenacity, fortitude.

5 **exude** *(v)* display an emotion or quality strongly and openly. *(s)* radiate, convey, emit. *(ant)* absorb.

6 **potential** *(adj)* having the capacity to develop into something in the future. *(s)* possible, probable, likely. *(ant)* unlikely.

7 **capability** *(n)* someone's or something's abilities. *(s)* competence, proficiency. *(ant)* inability.

8 **sombre** *(adj)* deeply serious or sad. *(s)* solemn, grave, sober. *(ant)* cheerful.

9 **divulge** *(v)* make known. *(s)* disclose, reveal, tell, confess. *(ant)* conceal, hide.

10 **serpent** *(n)* a snake. *(s)* viper.

11 **pride** *(n)* the characteristic of excessive self-importance. *(s)* arrogance, conceit, egotism. *(ant)* modesty.

12 **latter** *(n)* the second mentioned of two people or things. *(s)* last. *(ant)* former.

13 **former** *(n)* the first mentioned of two people or things. *(s)* previous, preceding. *(ant)* latter.

'Sir Robert,' she paused to line up her words, 'I cannot fathom the cipher's **creator**[1] from what I see. But, sire, if I might be so **bold**[2] as to ask how you came to possess it?'

There: she'd asked the crucial question. Cad couldn't **discern**[3] the look that flickered in his eyes, for it was fleeting, but she'd seen something **snag**[4] when she'd **posed**[5] that question.

She waited, her eyes levelled straight at him.

Evans cleared his throat as she hoped she'd not **overstepped the mark**[6]. 'Would you care for some water?' he asked.

'No thank you, sire,' she **declined**[7], noticing that he filled his cup with wine.

Cad was now sure he was **procrastinating**[8] over his answer, and her thoughts were **confirmed**[9] when he changed the subject.

'Since Dewi's betrayal, I have purposely **befriended**[10] his associate: the one dubbed Peggy.' Evans spat out the name as if **expelling**[11] a **mouldy**[12] grape. But Cad remembered those weeks back when she'd spied them together. He'd **referred**[13] to Peggy, so called because of his **rotten**[14] stumps for teeth, as Hari. Even if he was **nestling**[15] under Evans's wing, first-name terms between such different **ranks**[16] was highly unusual.

---

1 **creator** *(n)* someone or something that brings an object into being. *(s)* maker, inventor. *(ant)* destroyer.

2 **bold** *(adj)* lacking fear. *(s)* confident, courageous, brave, outspoken. *(ant)* timid, scared.

3 **discern** *(v)* understand. *(s)* recognise, identify, read. *(ant)* confuse.

4 **snag** *(v)* catch or hold back.

5 **pose** *(v)* put forward. *(s)* ask, proffer.

6 **overstep the mark** *(phrase)* go beyond what is allowed. *(s)* transgress, exceed, violate.

7 **decline** *(v)* refuse politely. *(s)* abstain, desist, refrain, turn down, pass up. *(ant)* accept.

8 **procrastinate** *(v)* put off doing something. *(s)* stall, hesitate, delay. *(ant)* accelerate.

9 **confirm** *(v)* establish that something is true. *(s)* prove, affirm, verify. *(ant)* confuse.

10 **befriend** *(v)* become friends with someone. *(s)* support, protect, guide. *(ant)* snub.

11 **expel** *(v)* force something out. *(s)* spit out, eject, issue.

12 **mouldy** *(adj)* covered with a fungal growth (mould) that causes decay. *(s)* rotten, festering. *(ant)* fresh, new.

13 **refer** *(v)* name or allude to (suggest). *(s)* mention, cite.

14 **rotten** *(adj)* decayed. *(s)* bad, spoiled. *(ant)* whole, intact.

15 **nestle** *(v)* settle comfortably. *(s)* huddle, nuzzle. *(ant)* disturb.

16 **rank** *(n)* a position in an organisation. *(s)* standing, status, station.

'One must keep enemies close,' he continued, as if reading Cad's thoughts. 'With me as his protector, he feels safe once more, and crucially, I am in a position to see if Dewi or Siân make contact with him.'

'Sire, as we are alone, would you deem more questions **impudent**[1]?'

With her father gone on his quest to find the Gwalch Gem bracelet, there was no other adult in whom she could **confide**[2]. She cared for the kindly Mrs Hughes, but she could not **inform**[3] Cad of castle business, for she knew nothing of it, or indeed who Cad really was.

'That depends on their **nature**[4],' Evans eventually replied.

Cad relaxed a **tad**[5], **seizing**[6] her moment lest he change his mind. 'Prince Dewi and my mother, Siân, are now absent for weeks. What do you think they will do with the bracelet's powers? Could this cipher be part of their **scheming**[7]?'

Evans pushed his hands together and tapped his lips with his fingertips as if about to pray. 'That is a question I wish I could answer. They may be **plotting**[8]. They may be travelling, building, hiding. They may be learning the **characteristics**[9] of that **fickle**[10] gem. I do not know. But of one thing I am certain: it will not end well.'

Cad swallowed hard, those final words ringing in her head.

'My father,' she said in an almost whisper. 'Do you think he will ever rest from this quest? Is this now his life's work, to ride the lands in search of his brother, rarely resting, **seldom**[11] seeing me and Prince John ...?'

'Callwen,' Evans cooed.

---

1 **impudent** *(adj)* not showing respect. *(s)* insolent, audacious, disrespectful. *(ant)* respectful.

2 **confide** *(v)* trust enough to share secrets. *(s)* entrust, talk, disclose. *(ant)* keep from.

3 **inform** *(v)* tell. *(s)* notify, brief, enlighten. *(ant)* withhold.

4 **nature** *(n)* type. *(s)* kind, sort, style.

5 **a tad** *(adv)* by a small amount or extent. *(s)* a touch, somewhat, slightly. *(ant)* profoundly, considerably.

6 **seize** *(v)* take (an opportunity or thing) quickly. *(s)* snatch, grab, grasp. *(ant)* relinquish.

7 **scheming** *(n)* the activity of making devious (underhand, dishonest) plans. *(s)* plotting, conspiring, conniving.

8 **plot** *(v)* devise a harmful or secret plan (often as a group). *(s)* conspire, connive, contrive, scheme.

9 **characteristic** *(n)* the features and qualities of. *(s)* way, trait, quirk, aspect.

10 **fickle** *(adj)* changeable. *(s)* variable, unstable. *(ant)* constant, stable.

11 **seldom** *(adv)* not often. *(s)* hardly ever, rarely, scarcely. *(ant)* often.

Unwittingly[1], Cad flashed him a half-**scowl**[2].

'I mean, Cad,' he replied softly, with a smile. 'Your father is **enduring**[3] the most painful of betrayals: treachery amongst blood and love is the hardest to **bear**[4]. Perhaps with only his fellow knights and Owain Glyn by his side, it is easier to ignore the **chronic**[5] pain of heart which plagues him.'

Cad pondered his answer, **tolerating**[6] her own internal agonies.

'Do you mean to say John and I remind him too much of our mother?' Cad's voice **trembled**[7].

Evans's face softened to as kind as she'd ever seen it. 'Yes, Cad. I think that is what I clumsily **endeavour**[8] to say.'

Cad felt the tears before she realised they'd appeared. He laid a hand on her shoulder and patted it like he might a dog.

'There, there,' he said, an affectionate tone to his voice. 'This **dire**[9] situation **ails**[10] us all, but we must **strive**[11] to survive it and hope your father retrieves the Gwalch Gem bracelet from his brother before it is too late.'

Those words snapped Cad from her **self-pity**[12]. 'Too late, sire? What do you mean by *too late*? Too late for what?' she asked, **anguish**[13] replacing the **grief**[14] which gripped her chest.

But Cad knew by the look **clouding**[15] Sir Robert's face that their **dialogue**[16] had ended. She saw

---

1 **unwittingly** *(adv)* in an unwitting (unintentional) way. *(s)* accidentally, inadvertently. *(ant)* wittingly, deliberately.

2 **scowl** *(n)* an angry expression. *(s)* glare, glower, frown. *(ant)* smile.

3 **endure** *(v)* suffer pain or difficulty patiently. *(s)* bear, tolerate, undergo, withstand. *(ant)* succumb.

4 **bear** *(v)* tolerate. *(s)* stand, suffer, abide. *(ant)* reject, avoid.

5 **chronic** *(adj)* continuing for a long time. *(s)* persistent, long-term.

6 **tolerate** *(v)* put up with. *(s)* endure, stand, abide. *(ant)* stop.

7 **tremble** *(v)* shake involuntarily (automatically) from fear or excitement. *(s)* quake, quiver. *(ant)* still, calm.

8 **endeavour** *(v)* attempt with effort. *(s)* aim, strive, try.

9 **dire** *(adj)* serious or urgent. *(s)* dreadful, atrocious, drastic. *(ant)* mild, good.

10 **ail** *(v)* trouble or afflict. *(s)* pain, distress, bother, worry.

11 **strive** *(v)* make huge efforts to acquire or accomplish something. *(s)* endeavour, try. *(ant)* shirk, quit.

12 **self-pity** *(n)* excessive interest in one's troubles. *(s)* despondency.

13 **anguish** *(n)* severe mental suffering. *(s)* distress, despair, woe. *(ant)* happiness.

14 **grief** *(n)* intense sorrow. *(s)* anguish, desolation, distress. *(ant)* comfort.

15 **cloud** *(v)* (of the face) show a negative emotion. *(s)* darken. *(ant)* lighten.

16 **dialogue** *(n)* a conversation, especially in a book, film or play. *(s)* talk, discourse, communication.

it close like a **clam**[1]. He'd clearly said too much already. If she pressed him to explain those final words, she may lose the new-found ground she'd just gained with this **distant**[2] man who ruled her father's castle, and therefore her.

'Rise,' Evans said, with a **dismissive**[3] flick of his wrist. Their **audience**[4] was over. 'If you are right about this message then I have much work to do.'

Cad stood, desperate to probe him for more details, but remembering that she'd just avoided the tower, she bowed her head and made for the door. She pulled at the large handle, but it didn't **yield**[5]. Of course, Evans hadn't used the main door, he'd somehow simply appeared … Her heart dropped.

Oh, no! I'm done for!

She had locked the door with her emerald hairpin. How in heaven would she explain that to Evans?

About to turn to face him and the music, a clunking of metal from the door stopped her. To her amazement and relief, it creaked open and in shuffled Peggy, dragging his **maimed**[6] leg behind him.

Before Evans had time to say another word or stop her, Cad flew through the door and sprinted down the passageway back to her friends.

---

1 **clam** *(n)* a marine mollusc with shells of equal sizes that open and close tightly.

2 **distant** *(adj)* cool and reserved. *(s)* aloof, unapproachable. *(ant)* friendly.

3 **dismissive** *(adj)* showing that someone or something is not worth consideration. *(s)* offhand. *(ant)* interested.

4 **audience** *(n)* an interview with an important person. *(s)* meeting, contact, encounter.

5 **yield** *(v)* give way to pressure. *(s)* move, bend. *(ant)* resist.

6 **maimed** *(adj)* injured so as to be irreparably damaged. *(s)* hurt, disabled, incapacitated. *(ant)* healed.

CHAPTER TEN

An Early Return

The thundering of horseshoes **pounding**[1] the moat's **drawbridge**[2] snapped Cad from a horrid dream of hooded monks and **lethal**[3] weapons. Baffled by Cad's sudden awakening and the noise outside, Fishy stood, her hackles raised, a low growl **gurgling**[4] in her throat. Dylan didn't **budge**[5], and who knew whether Rhys actually slept or just pretended to? After all, the sneaky boy **frequently**[6] shared his bed with his pet snake!

On realising it was the sound of **destriers'**[7] hooves, Cad flew out of bed and cracked open the wooden shutter that protected her window, allowing May to fly out through it. The cold light that **precedes**[8] sunlight crept into her room. A shiver shuddered through her. Although he was wrapped in the grey cloak of dawn, Cad recognised him immediately.

'Papa,' she whispered, her heart soaring and **plummeting**[9] at almost the same time. Why the

---

1 **pound** *(v)* hit repeatedly and heavily. *(s)* strike, pummel.

2 **drawbridge** *(n)* a bridge that can be raised to prevent access, especially one over the moat of a castle.

3 **lethal** *(adj)* able to cause death, hugely harmful or destructive. *(s)* deadly, fatal. *(ant)* life-giving.

4 **gurgle** *(v)* make a bubbling sound. *(s)* burble, babble.

5 **budge** *(v)* move a small amount. *(s)* shift, stir, flinch.

6 **frequently** *(adv)* often. *(s)* regularly, habitually. *(ant)* infrequently.

7 **destrier** *(n)* a heavy set, large medieval knight's war horse; also known as the Great Horse due to its importance.

8 **precede** *(v)* come before in order, position or time. *(s)* herald, foreshadow. *(ant)* follow, succeed.

9 **plummet** *(v)* fall or drop straight down at high speed. *(s)* dive, tumble. *(ant)* climb, rise.

early return? He shouldn't be here yet. What was wrong? Cad knew that **haring**[1] out into the bailey to greet Llywelyn would raise suspicions, especially those of Bryn Davis. She must **assert**[2] **restraint**[3] and stay in her quarters until an **apt**[4] time to enter the bailey arose. She quickly pulled on some clothes, hiding her hairpin in a hem, and went back to the shuttered window.

The view from here was **obscured**[5], but she squinted through the wooden slats, observing the unfurling scene.

Llywelyn, Owain and another unfamiliar knight **dismounted**[6] their sweating **steeds**[7], handing them over to **grooms**[8] still dressed in their sleep **attire**[9], who looked surprised and **dishevelled**[10].

As he removed his **helm**[11], Cad saw that Llywelyn's face was **sagging**[12] with exhaustion, his usual upright gait now **stooping**[13] with **fatigue**[14]. He had been gone weeks, and Cad saw how thin he had become; his face brown, **angular**[15] and wrinkled, weather-beaten. Even from this distance, she read the sadness in his **demeanour**[16]. Cad feared her father to be lost in his **sorrow**[17] forever. Just a brief glimpse told her his quest remained **unfulfilled**[18].

In the distance, Cad saw several sleepy-looking squires, including Bryn Davis, pulling on

---

1 **hare** *(v)* run with great speed and agility. *(s)* race, bolt, gallop, fly. *(ant)* dawdle.

2 **assert** *(v)* apply with confidence. *(s)* exert, use, employ.

3 **restraint** *(n)* self-control. *(s)* prudence, moderation. *(ant)* abandon.

4 **apt** *(adj)* suitable in the circumstances. *(s)* appropriate, relevant. *(ant)* inappropriate.

5 **obscure** *(v)* prevent from being seen. *(s)* conceal, hide, mask. *(ant)* reveal.

6 **dismount** *(v)* get off something that one rides. *(s)* descend, alight. *(ant)* mount.

7 **steed** *(n)* a horse that one can ride.

8 **groom** *(n)* someone who is employed (paid) to look after horses. *(s)* equerry, stable person.

9 **attire** *(n)* clothes. *(s)* clothing, dress, outfit, garments.

10 **dishevelled** *(adj)* (hair or clothes) made untidy. *(s)* mussed, tousled, ruffled. *(ant)* tidy, groomed.

11 **helm** *(n)* a helmet, often made from metal and worn in medieval battle and jousting.

12 **sag** *(v)* slump, sink, subside or bulge downwards under pressure or lack of strength. *(s)* droop, drop. *(ant)* rise.

13 **stoop** *(v)* bend one's head or body forward and downwards into a hunch. *(s)* crouch, slouch. *(ant)* straighten.

14 **fatigue** *(n)* extreme tiredness. *(s)* exhaustion, weariness, weakness. *(ant)* refreshment.

15 **angular** *(adj)* having sharp corners. *(s)* pointed. *(ant)* rounded.

16 **demeanour** *(n)* outward bearing or behaviour. *(s)* appearance, attitude, disposition, conduct.

17 **sorrow** *(n)* a feeling of grief or sadness. *(s)* anguish, agony, heartbreak, distress. *(ant)* joy, cheer.

18 **unfulfilled** *(adj)* unsuccessful. *(s)* unaccomplished, uncompleted. *(ant)* fulfilled, successful.

tunics and straightening their hair. They **filtered**[1] into the bailey to **salute**[2] the returning prince and his fellow Knights Hawk. Robert Evans, **notable**[3] by his absence, had clearly not expected her father's arrival.

Why? Cad thought. *Why would the knight left in **sole**[4] charge of my father's realm not know of his early return?*

Cad thought it odd, but then perhaps an **appointed**[5] **herald**[6] had met with **unfavourable**[7] **circumstances**[8] on the road and had failed to deliver Llywelyn's message. It may even be something as **trivial**[9] as a lame horse. Still, the thought of Evans not knowing something this important rankled within her.

As more folks bustled into the bailey to welcome Llywelyn and his **party**[10], Cad, seeing her opportunity and **irked**[11] by Dylan's ability to sleep through a storm, **stooped**[12] to jabbing him with her pin. He shot up, but before he could yell, she threw his clothes at him and barked, 'My father is here. Come now.'

Without questioning her, he grabbed his clothes and pulled them on. Cad still hadn't forgiven him for abandoning her in Sir Robert's rooms yesterday, even though he'd had no choice but to follow Bryn Davis's furious orders at the time. Davis had found Dylan gambling with the guard outside Sir Robert's quarters and punished him with cleaning the ladies' **chamber pots**[13].

Dylan pulled on his boots and hopped along, following Cad out into the now-bustling bailey. Both **exchanged**[14] glances at seeing Sir Robert striding from the high keep flattening his bed-

---

1 **filter** *(v)* move slowly in a specific direction. *(s)* flow.

2 **salute** *(v)* make a formal salute (greeting). *(s)* welcome, acknowledge. *(ant)* ignore, disregard.

3 **notable** *(adj)* worthy of attention. *(s)* significant, conspicuous. *(ant)* insignificant.

4 **sole** *(adj)* one and only. *(s)* solitary, exclusive, lone, solo.

5 **appoint** *(v)* give a job or role to. *(s)* select, designate. *(ant)* reject, dismiss.

6 **herald** *(n)* an official employee who acts as a messenger, especially in medieval times. *(s)* crier, courier.

7 **unfavourable** *(adj)* likely to lead to poor outcomes. *(s)* bad, adverse, negative. *(ant)* favourable.

8 **circumstances** *(n)* the conditions of an event or situation. *(s)* outcomes, events, incidents.

9 **trivial** *(adj)* of little importance. *(s)* minor, insignificant, inconsequential. *(ant)* significant.

10 **party** *(n)* a particular group of people. *(s)* company, contingent.

11 **irk** *(v)* irritate. *(s)* annoy, rattle, vex, aggravate. *(ant)* mollify, please.

12 **stoop** *(v)* lower one's standards enough to do something bad. *(s)* sink, resort, descend.

13 **chamber pot** *(n)* a bowl in a bedroom used as a toilet during the night.

14 **exchange** *(v)* swap. *(s)* transfer.

mussed[1] hair and straightening his clothes. Cad saw beyond the look of fake pleasure fixed on his face. She read his eyes; they **betrayed**[2] his seething anger. Why had he not known of Llywelyn's early return?

Before Evans could speak to him, Llywelyn raised his arm to silence the crowd's excitement and stepped up onto a **mounting block**[3] to address the rapidly filling bailey. Concerned by the **circulating**[4] sickness about which her father knew nothing, Cad hung back, holding Dylan's arm and signalling towards a green-looking Jack Jones, who followed Bryn's **entourage**[5].

'My people,' Llywelyn began. Although **hoarse**[6], his **distinctive**[7] voice immediately commanded the respect of his court, which fell silent at once. The great prince addressed the crowd as equals. Clearly exhausted, and no doubt desperate to rest after weeks of **drudgery**[8] peppered with **perilous**[9] chance out on the road, his being filled the entire bailey.

'As you see, for reasons I will divulge later, we have returned to Catrin earlier than expected. Do not fret about your lack of preparation. We can **overcome**[10] this together quickly. Indeed, let us prepare for a great **feast**[11] tomorrow in the hall, for all.'

A cheer rang around the bailey, for they knew how generous and **lavish**[12] Llywelyn's **banquets**[13] could be.

'He clearly doesn't know of the sickness,' Dylan muttered to Cad. 'That may **scupper**[14] his plans once he finds out. Hopefully, today will present fewer cases,' he added, ever **optimistic**[15].

---

1 **muss** *(v)* make untidy (hair or clothes). *(s)* tousle, ruffle, dishevel. *(ant)* groom.

2 **betray** *(v)* expose (show) information. *(s)* reveal, disclose. *(ant)* conceal, hide.

3 **mounting block** *(n)* a raised step upon which someone stands to help them mount a horse.

4 **circulate** *(v)* move freely in a closed area or system. *(s)* flow, travel, spread.

5 **entourage** *(n)* a group that attends an important person. *(s)* company, associates.

6 **hoarse** *(adj)* harsh and rough. *(s)* husky, croaky, gruff, gravelly. *(ant)* soft, mellow.

7 **distinctive** *(adj)* standing out because of a specific characteristic. *(s)* distinguishing. *(ant)* ordinary.

8 **drudgery** *(n)* hard and dull work. *(s)* toil, labour, slog, grind. *(ant)* relaxation.

9 **perilous** *(adj)* full of extreme risk or danger. *(s)* hazardous, treacherous, precarious. *(ant)* safe.

10 **overcome** *(v)* succeed in dealing with something. *(s)* solve, master.

11 **feast** *(n)* a large celebratory meal. *(s)* banquet, feed, binge. *(ant)* snack.

12 **lavish** *(adj)* sumptuously elaborate, rich or luxurious. *(s)* lush, costly, grand. *(ant)* meagre, poor.

13 **banquet** *(n)* an elaborately formal meal for many people. *(s)* feast, reception.

14 **scupper** *(v)* prevent from working or succeeding. *(s)* ruin, wreck, foil, spoil. *(ant)* help, facilitate.

15 **optimistic** *(adj)* positive and hopeful about the future. *(s)* cheery, sanguine, confident. *(ant)* pessimistic, gloomy.

'Perhaps,' Cad replied, unconvinced by his optimism and deep in thought.

'Cad, I'm sorry I abandoned you last night, but I had no choice. I was distracting the guard with cards, and Bryn appeared from nowhere. Why he'd be in the keep at that time, I don't know,' he added.

'It is odd,' Cad agreed with a nod.

'I couldn't refuse him when he caught me **betting**[1] for **coin**[2]. He could have thrown me in the tower but **opted**[3] for the chamber pots instead.'

Cad **cast**[4] a half-grin, knowing he was right. The pages were strictly forbidden to gamble. Llywelyn **scorned**[5] gambling and his knights never stooped to **partake**[6] in it. Many of the castle's servants and guards, though, seemed **addicted**[7] to losing their money, especially to Dylan, who played a **cunning**[8] hand on the quiet and had **acquired**[9] quite a **stash**[10] of coins. Cad would never inform on Dylan but had warned him of capture one day. She had to admit, though, it was a **crafty**[11] way to distract a guard, especially one with a **penchant**[12] for strong beer.

'Maybe someone warned Davis we might be there?' Cad mused, remembering that Peggy had opened the door to Sir Robert's rooms when she had unwittingly locked herself in there with Sir Robert.

'Who knows?' said Dylan, watching the **bustle**[13].

'Peggy was there too,' Cad added, 'circling for **carrion**[14] outside Sir Robert's rooms, no doubt.'

'He's not got the teeth for that!' Dylan said, chortling.

---

1 **bet** *(v)* risk a sum of money on a chance outcome in a race or game. *(s)* gamble, wager.

2 **coin** *(n)* a flat disc with an official stamp used as money.

3 **opt** *(v)* make a choice. *(s)* choose, pick, select.

4 **cast** *(v)* direct one's eyes or expression at someone or something. *(s)* throw, shoot, send.

5 **scorn** *(v)* express or feel disrespect and disapproval. *(s)* deride. *(ant)* respect.

6 **partake** *(v)* join in. *(s)* participate, engage.

7 **addicted** *(adj)* being dependent on something. *(s)* obsessive.

8 **cunning** *(adj)* having skill in achieving one's objectives by being imaginative. *(s)* clever, intelligent. *(ant)* unimaginative.

9 **acquire** *(v)* obtain for oneself. *(s)* earn, win, amass. *(ant)* lose.

10 **stash** *(n)* a secret store of something. *(s)* cache, hoard, stockpile.

11 **crafty** *(adj)* a clever way to achieve an aim, sometimes deviously so. *(s)* cunning, wily, sharp. *(ant)* naive.

12 **penchant** *(n)* a liking for something. *(s)* fondness, preference, weakness. *(ant)* aversion, dislike.

13 **bustle** *(n)* noisy and excited activity. *(s)* busyness, liveliness. *(ant)* inactivity.

14 **carrion** *(n)* the rotting flesh of dead animals. *(s)* remains.

Cad stitched a smile onto her face, still stumped by everything but not wanting to appear **churlish**[1] at Dylan's **comedic**[2] crack.

'I wonder why your father is back today,' said Dylan. 'It's most unlike him to return to an unprepared castle, and especially so early. Grumpy Evans clearly didn't know.'

Dylan laughed again, eyeing Sir Robert, who flitted about like a puffed-up clown looking **discombobulated**[3] yet trying so hard to hide it.

'I wonder, too,' replied Cad. 'Dylan, I must find my ring,' she added, her heart **leaden**[4] at the thought of telling her father she had lost it. Cad hoped and prayed that the thief would not discover its magic, for if they did, they too could **roam**[5] about the castle **undetected**[6].

At that moment, Rhys **sidled**[7] up to Cad, Fishy at his heels.

'Your father is home early,' he whispered, wide-eyed. 'I hope all is well?' He gazed up at Cad, his curls bouncing about his face.

'As do I, Rhys.' Cad observed the unusual look on her friend's face. 'As do I.'

Desperate to speak to her father alone, she knew that **lobbing**[8] a stone at someone would not work this time. She must be patient, and wait until Llywelyn **summoned**[9] her. Then she would tell him about the secret cipher she'd given to Evans and the weapon plans it concealed within its code.

---

1 **churlish** *(adj)* rude and mean-spirited. *(s)* discourteous, ungracious. *(ant)* polite.

2 **comedic** *(adj)* relating to comedy (something funny). *(s)* comical, witty, humorous. *(ant)* unfunny, sour.

3 **discombobulated** *(adj)* confused. *(s)* disconcerted, flustered. *(ant)* settled.

4 **leaden** *(adj)* heavy and dull. *(s)* weighted, burdened, depressed. *(ant)* light, happy.

5 **roam** *(v)* move about. *(s)* prowl, wander, stroll.

6 **undetected** *(adj)* not detected (found) or perceived. *(s)* unseen, unnoticed. *(ant)* detected, seen.

7 **sidle** *(v)* walk in a furtive (secretive) manner. *(s)* sneak, creep, slink, edge. *(ant)* stride.

8 **lob** *(v)* throw. *(s)* fling, hurl, sling, toss.

9 **summon** *(v)* order or ask someone to be present. *(s)* call, invite, request. *(ant)* dismiss.

CHAPTER ELEVEN

Fun and Jousts

As the castle bustled, readying for Llywelyn's feast, out in the tilt yard, Cad observed Jack Jones's grey **pallor**[1] and **sluggish**[2] movements. **Alas**[3], he still proved to be a worthy **adversary**[4] and knocked Cad down time after time with his **sheer**[5] **heft**[6] as they wrestled. Hand-to-hand combat would always prove tricky for Cad, and though strong, she relied on **guile**[7] and speed to conquer her male adversaries. Once she became a squire, she knew they would prove even harder to overcome.

Preparations were well under way for tomorrow evening's banquet, and Llywelyn had announced a jousting **tournament**[8] for three days **hence**[9], along with wrestling and sword fighting **demonstrations**[10] by the younger pages who trained under the older squires. A **tourney**[11] would

---

1 **pallor** *(n)* a pale and unhealthy appearance. *(s)* sallowness, pastiness. *(ant)* rosiness.

2 **sluggish** *(adj)* slow and lacking alertness. *(s)* lethargic, listless, heavy. *(ant)* sprightly.

3 **alas** *(int)* used to express pity, regret, grief, disappointment or concern.

4 **adversary** *(n)* an opponent (rival). *(s)* challenger, contender, competitor. *(ant)* ally.

5 **sheer** *(adj)* absolute. *(s)* pure, utter, total, downright, outright.

6 **heft** *(n)* weight or heaviness. *(s)* bulk, size, mass, immensity. *(ant)* lightness.

7 **guile** *(n)* clever or imaginative intelligence. *(s)* cunning, shrewdness, ingenuity. *(ant)* candour.

8 **tournament** *(n)* a series of contests with multiple contestants. *(s)* competition, event.

9 **hence** *(adv)* from now.

10 **demonstration** *(n)* a show of how something works or is performed. *(s)* display, presentation.

11 **tourney** *(n)* a tournament, especially jousting set in medieval times. *(s)* contest, bout.

be an excellent opportunity for the older boys, such as Bryn Davis, to prove their skills and **prowess**[1] to Prince Llywelyn, Owain and the other Knights Hawk.

Cad knew Bryn wished for nothing more than to **accompany**[2] Llywelyn on this quest, even though hitherto, Llywelyn had only taken knights with him. All squires currently remained at Catrin Castle, but Davis was **determined**[3] to **excel**[4] and be chosen first. Cad had other ideas.

Now exhausted by the wrestling, and desperate to jab Jack Jones's **buttocks**[5] with her pin to quash his **triumphant**[6] **gloating**[7], Cad was relieved to see the ponies being led into the yard by the younger pages. She would show Jones her riding prowess and wipe that smug grin off his face.

Only recently **graduated**[8] to full **equestrian**[9] combat training, Cad, who'd ridden before walking, proved to be a master rider in the **list field**[10]. She **adored**[11] riding, **shining**[12] in the saddle, at one with her **mount**[13], guiding it with her legs and body, thus freeing up her hands for the **lance**[14] and shield.

Cad found combat training **exhilarating**[15], all the while remembering that Knights Hawk used Instinct for **defence**[16] purposes only, never to attack for reasons of greed or power. This **chivalry**[17] shone a light onto Llywelyn's realm. Not once had he seized lands for **avarice**[18] or

---

1 **prowess** *(n)* remarkable ability in a specific activity or area. *(s)* talent, skill, aptitude, expertise. *(ant)* ineptitude.

2 **accompany** *(v)* go with someone. *(s)* chaperone, attend, escort. *(ant)* abandon, desert.

3 **determined** *(adj)* having or displaying resolve. *(s)* resolute, firm, unwavering. *(ant)* irresolute.

4 **excel** *(v)* be extremely good at something. *(s)* shine. *(ant)* fail.

5 **buttocks** *(n)* the bottom. *(s)* backside, behind, rump, rear, haunches.

6 **triumphant** *(adj)* showing great jubilation (joy) after a victory. *(s)* gleeful, elated, delighted. *(ant)* defeated.

7 **gloating** *(n)* the act of dwelling on one's own success with smug pleasure. *(s)* revelling, celebration. *(ant)* sympathy.

8 **graduate** *(v)* successfully complete a course of training. *(s)* qualify, pass. *(ant)* fail.

9 **equestrian** *(adj)* anything relating to horses and riding.

10 **list field** *(n)* a roped-off area where jousting tournaments take place.

11 **adore** *(v)* love. *(s)* treasure, prize. *(ant)* hate.

12 **shine** *(v)* be very good at something and stand out. *(s)* excel.

13 **mount** *(n)* a horse that is suitable for riding.

14 **lance** *(n)* a long wooden weapon with a pointed steel tip, used in middle-aged jousting and battle.

15 **exhilarating** *(adj)* causing thrill or excitement. *(s)* invigorating, uplifting. *(ant)* depressing, boring.

16 **defence** *(n)* the action of defending or resisting an attack. *(s)* protection, resistance, security. *(ant)* offence, attack.

17 **chivalry** *(n)* polite and courteous behaviour. *(s)* gallantry, consideration. *(ant)* rudeness.

18 **avarice** *(n)* great greed for wealth or gain. *(s)* rapacity, materialism. *(ant)* generosity.

control. He lived peacefully in the kingdom **inherited**[1] from his **ancestors**[2], leaving what was not his to its rightful owners.

However, Cad feared that his brother, Dewi, would not replicate this honour once he **harnessed**[3] the Gwalch Gem's power to his advantage. Sir Robert's words, 'Before it is too late,' **haunted**[4] her, and Cad must understand what he meant.

Now rested and **raring**[5] to go, Cad patted her pony's arched neck and sneaked her an apple she'd pilfered from the **orchard**[6]. Flash, the **chestnut**[7] pony, so named for the streak of white flashed down the centre of her face, had **adopted**[8] Cad as her master. Orphaned at birth and raised by hand, when she **grazed**[9] in the **verdant**[10] **paddocks**[11] beyond the castle walls, Flash would **neigh**[12] and **gallop**[13] to greet Cad the moment she saw her. Yet the **spirited**[14] pony misbehaved for other riders, **bucking**[15] and nipping whenever **disgruntled**[16]. Cad had begged Llywelyn to appoint Flash solely to her, and although it had been an **unorthodox**[17] decision, he had done so, much to the chagrin of Bryn Davis, who had waited years for his own mount.

In case of injury in battle, pages and squires were required to master many mounts, and Cad must **follow suit**[18]. Thus she frequently trained with other horses. But Flash was her favourite, and no one else rode her, for Flash would not let them.

---

1 **inherit** *(v)* receive something from a previous holder on their death. *(s)* acquire, obtain. *(ant)* bequeath.

2 **ancestor** *(n)* a person from whom one is descended. *(s)* predecessor, forefather, foremother. *(ant)* descendant.

3 **harness** *(v)* control and use. *(s)* utilise, exploit, employ. *(ant)* underuse.

4 **haunt** *(v)* always be present in the mind. *(s)* torment.

5 **raring** *(adj)* very eager to do something. *(s)* keen, enthusiastic. *(ant)* reluctant.

6 **orchard** *(n)* an enclosed area used for growing fruit on trees or shrubs. *(s)* grove, plantation.

7 **chestnut** *(adj)* deep reddish brown like the colour of a chestnut. *(s)* rusty, coppery.

8 **adopt** *(v)* choose to take up. *(s)* embrace, approve, endorse. *(ant)* spurn.

9 **graze** *(v)* eat grass in a field or pasture. *(s)* feed, forage.

10 **verdant** *(adj)* green with grass and vegetation. *(s)* lush, flourishing. *(ant)* barren, bleak.

11 **paddock** *(n)* an enclosed field where horses are kept and exercised.

12 **neigh** *(v)* make a high whinnying sound like that of a horse. *(s)* bray, nicker, whicker.

13 **gallop** *(v)* run at the fastest pace of an animal with four legs when all feet leave the ground in each stride.

14 **spirited** *(adj)* having an energetic and determined character. *(s)* lively, vigorous. *(ant)* timid.

15 **buck** *(v)* (of a horse) put the head down between the front legs and kick high with the rear.

16 **disgruntled** *(adj)* displeased or angry. *(s)* discontented, dissatisfied. *(ant)* pleased, contented.

17 **unorthodox** *(adj)* contrary (opposite) to what is usual. *(s)* unconventional, unusual. *(ant)* orthodox.

18 **follow suit** (phrase) do as someone or something else does. *(s)* follow the example of.

A **wilful**[1] pony, if left to Bryn and his grooms, Flash would be punished and **tamed**[2].

As Cad patted Flash, she wondered why her father had decided to **celebrate**[3] in such sad times. Llywelyn's chivalrous jousts were **renowned**[4] in times of celebration, wedding, births and **conquests**[5]. However, it was clear he had not recovered the bracelet, and with John sequestered in Cadwaladr Castle, it seemed **unfitting**[6]. Maybe Llywelyn felt his **subjects**[7] needed some joy. Either way, she would try her **utmost**[8] to **impress**[9] her father, whom she hoped would one day place his sword on her shoulders and **dub**[10] her a Knight Hawk.

Making her way across to the list field, where all jousts occurred, Cad mounted Flash and trotted down the long **runway**[11], its tilt fence separating **opposing**[12] riders. The exercise of **spearing**[13] rings was her favourite warm-up task. Pages stood in a line along the tilt, arms outstretched at both shoulder and head height holding a ring to be speared by the approaching rider's lance. A page she barely knew, Peter Griffith, stood first, with Rhys several feet behind him, and beyond him, a boy she did not know.

In a straight line, Cad spurred Flash into a beautifully controlled **canter**[14]. With ease, she lifted her long spear beside her, her shield before her **breast**[15], and smoothly hooked the first ring over its tip, cantering past Peter, Rhys and then the final boy, and not missing once. The boys let out a cheer as she continued. Then she turned and doubled back for another successful pass before dismounting to prepare for a practice joust.

---

1 **wilful** *(adj)* being determined to do as one wants. *(s)* headstrong, obstinate. *(ant)* compliant.

2 **tame** *(v)* make an animal do as one wishes. *(s)* master, subdue.

3 **celebrate** *(v)* observe a significant event with a social gathering. *(s)* party, revel.

4 **renowned** *(adj)* known or talked about widely. *(s)* famous, esteemed. *(ant)* unknown.

5 **conquest** *(n)* the overtaking of people or a place by military force. *(s)* victory. *(ant)* failure, loss, surrender.

6 **unfitting** *(adj)* not suitable. *(s)* inappropriate, improper. *(ant)* fitting.

7 **subject** *(n)* a person who owes allegiance to a monarch or ruler.

8 **utmost** *(n)* the greatest extent. *(s)* best, hardest. *(ant)* least.

9 **impress** *(v)* make someone admire and respect you. *(s)* influence, affect, inspire.

10 **dub** *(v)* make someone a knight by the custom of touching their shoulder with a sword. *(s)* knight. *(ant)* strip.

11 **runway** *(n)* a long, narrow piece of ground used in a joust. *(s)* list.

12 **opposing** *(adj)* in competition or conflict with. *(s)* rival, combatant, opposite. *(ant)* allied.

13 **spear** *(v)* strike with a pointed (sharp) object. *(s)* spike, stab, poke.

14 **canter** *(n)* the pace of a horse or other quadruped between a trot and a gallop.

15 **breast** *(n)* a person's chest.

In the meantime, Jack Jones, causing both **mayhem**[1] and **hilarity**[2], had thundered by on his mount, almost **skewering**[3] the pages, who had scattered like birds, **fleeing**[4] the tilt area before he killed somebody.

Despite the fact that they trained with **mock**[5] weapons, if they were used carelessly, **fatal**[6] damage was a real possibility. Cad knew Jack wasn't accurate with the rings, but that didn't mean he wasn't a deserving **opponent**[7] in the joust. Although **meek**[8] when around Bryn, Jack was a fearless boy: he rarely failed to present himself and his shield directly to his **rival**[9] and thus was never **disqualified**[10] for lack of **courage**[11]. And again, his heft and excellent riding **stance**[12] ensured he was difficult to **unsaddle**[13]. The joust's main aim was to unseat one's **combatant**[14].

Protection was **paramount**[15] during the joust, and though the pages and squires trained in **partial**[16] armour, even in the **post**[17]-dawn conditions, **temperatures**[18] were **sweltering**[19] beneath the padded **aketon**[20], **chain mail**[21] **hauberk**[22] and metal coverings.

Cad's groom for today, Ellis Williams, a boy she both respected and trusted, attached

---

1 **mayhem** *(n)* extreme disorder. *(s)* confusion, chaos, havoc, tumult. *(ant)* order.

2 **hilarity** *(n)* great amusement. *(s)* laughter, mirth, merriment. *(ant)* seriousness, solemnity.

3 **skewer** *(v)* pierce with something sharp. *(s)* lance, stab.

4 **flee** *(v)* run away. *(s)* depart, escape, leave. *(ant)* linger, remain.

5 **mock** *(adj)* not real. *(s)* imitation, simulated. *(ant)* real.

6 **fatal** *(adj)* causing death. *(s)* lethal, deadly. *(ant)* harmless.

7 **opponent** *(n)* a person competing with another. *(s)* adversary. *(ant)* ally.

8 **meek** *(adj)* mild-mannered, or easily imposed on. *(s)* submissive, quiet, gentle, timid, weak. *(ant)* assertive.

9 **rival** *(n)* a person competing with another. *(s)* opponent, competitor. *(ant)* ally.

10 **disqualified** *(adj)* removed from a competition because of an offence or breaking the rules. *(s)* eliminated. *(ant)* eligible.

11 **courage** *(n)* the ability to do something frightening. *(s)* bravery, pluck, valour. *(ant)* cowardice.

12 **stance** *(n)* a person's posture. *(s)* position, attitude, bearing.

13 **unsaddle** *(v)* dislodge a rider from the saddle when riding a horse. *(s)* unseat. *(ant)* saddle.

14 **combatant** *(n)* someone engaged in fighting. *(s)* fighter, warrior. *(ant)* ally, peacemaker.

15 **paramount** *(adj)* the most important thing. *(s)* major, key, topmost. *(ant)* unimportant.

16 **partial** *(adj)* something incomplete. *(s)* limited. *(ant)* complete, full.

17 **post** *(prep)* after.

18 **temperature** *(n)* the degree or intensity of heat measured in someone or something.

19 **swelter** *(v)* to become overly hot. *(s)* burn, boil, heat. *(ant)* cool.

20 **aketon** *(n)* a padded jacket worn beneath armour.

21 **chain mail** *(n)* flexible armour made of small metal rings that link together.

22 **hauberk** *(n)* a full-length coat of chain mail or military tunic, worn for protection.

Flash's leather **chanfron**[1] in place to protect her face from the lance. He then helped Cad into a metal **breastplate**[2] and finally her helm and **gauntlets**[3], causing her hands to sweat immediately. But Cad knew she must learn to tolerate these conditions, for it was part of a knight's duty.

Her first opponent, a page trained by Bryn Davis, was an easy win, and Cad unseated him on the first pass along the tilt. Today's match was best of three tilts, and although many castles had few jousting rules, here in Llywelyn's kingdom, chivalry was respected. If a page lowered their lance in a **mercy pass**[4], this **gesture**[5] of yielding must always be **adhered**[6] to.

The jousters' helms **camouflaged**[7] the riders, and Cad didn't know this **contender**[8] well. But once he was easily unseated for a second time, he lay still on the ground, and Cad dismounted to make sure the boy was unhurt. He was **winded**[9], and only his pride seeming injured, so Cad patted Flash and led her away for a rest and some water before her next match. Jack Jones would not be quite so easy to unseat.

Sweat trickled down her forehead as Cad removed her helm and partial armour and gave Flash some rest time, leading the pony to a large water tank filled each morning for the horses in the yard. Flash sucked deeply, **guzzling**[10] the water with **gusto**[11].

'Easy, Flash,' Cad said, pulling the pony away. 'You'll be too full to canter. We'll be sloshing about like a **barrel**[12] of beer,' she laughed, leading Flash back to the yard and handing her to Ellis.

'Dylan,' Cad cried, seeing her friend approaching. 'How were the chamber pots this morning?'

---

1 **chanfron** *(n)* a piece of leather or metal armour used to protect a horse's head and face.

2 **breastplate** *(n)* a piece of armour that covers and protects the chest.

3 **gauntlet** *(n)* an armoured glove made from hardened leather or metal.

4 **mercy pass** *(n)* a sign given to indicate that an opponent wishes to end that particular jousting pass.

5 **gesture** *(n)* an action to convey a feeling or intention of something. *(s)* act, indication, sign.

6 **adhere** *(v)* follow closely. *(s)* obey, heed, respect, uphold. *(ant)* flout.

7 **camouflage** *(v)* hide or disguise by means of camouflage. *(s)* conceal, mask. *(ant)* reveal, show.

8 **contender** *(n)* a person competing against others. *(s)* competitor, opponent, rival.

9 **wind** *(v)* cause someone to have difficulty in breathing because of a blow to the stomach.

10 **guzzle** *(v)* eat or drink greedily. *(s)* gulp, swallow, down, swig. *(ant)* sip.

11 **gusto** *(adj)* enthusiasm and enjoyment. *(s)* relish, satisfaction, fervour. *(ant)* distaste.

12 **barrel** *(n)* a cylindrical container usually wider around the middle. *(s)* cask, keg, vat, tub, drum.

she added with a laugh, having just about forgiven him for leaving her **in the lurch**[1] outside Sir Robert's rooms the previous night.

'Delightful,' Dylan replied, his voice **drenched**[2] in **sarcasm**[3]. 'At least I'm done after today.'

'You're in time to catch the next practice match,' Cad said, her face lighting up. 'I'm against Jack Jones, and as he's still **green about the gills**[4], I'm **confident**[5].'

'I'm sure you and Flash will win.' Dylan grinned. 'Don't forget, against Jones, aim high. You hit his shoulders; he's more likely to **topple**[6].' Dylan gave Flash a heavy pat on her neck. 'And little Flashy here is one of the bravest ponies riding into the pass. You won't **falter**[7], will you, gal?' asked Dylan, patting Flash again.

'Come.' Cad grabbed Dylan's arm, 'You can help me into my armour and that **wretched**[8] helm that renders one almost blind.'

Once ready and mounted, Cad warmed up Flash with a couple of canters along the list's runway. When satisfied all was good, Cad pulled Flash to a halt. Then as prepared as she would ever be, Cad signalled to the **marshal**[9] to bring in her opponent and Ellis to ready her lance. She was set, her face adjusted for battle beneath her helm.

Calming Flash, who was jogging with excitement and **anticipation**[10], Cad glanced over towards the holding **stalls**[11] waiting for Jack Jones to emerge on his **cob**[12].

What in heaven? thought Cad, as a stunning grey destrier danced from the stalls. Its rider, partially armoured like her, already with helm, lance and shield, sat **astride**[13] the **magnificent**[14]

1 **in the lurch** (phrase) in a vulnerable state. *(s)* susceptible, exposed.

2 **drench** *(v)* flood with. *(s)* satiate, soak.

3 **sarcasm** *(n)* the use of irony (the opposite) to mock or convey dislike. *(s)* derision, scorn, disdain. *(ant)* flattery.

4 **green about the gills** (phrase) feeling or looking unwell or sick. *(s)* poorly, ailing. *(ant)* hale, healthy.

5 **confident** *(adj)* feeling certainty about something. *(s)* sure, convinced. *(ant)* doubtful, unsure.

6 **topple** *(v)* overbalance and fall. *(s)* tumble, keel, collapse.

7 **falter** *(v)* lose momentum or strength. *(s)* hesitate, stall, delay, waver. *(ant)* rally, continue.

8 **wretched** *(adj)* used to express annoyance. *(s)* loathsome, annoying, despicable. *(ant)* welcome.

9 **marshal** *(n)* a person responsible for supervising an event. *(s)* supervisor, organiser.

10 **anticipation** *(n)* the action of expecting something to happen. *(s)* expectation.

11 **stall** *(n)* a holding compartment for an animal, enclosed on three sides. *(s)* cubicle.

12 **cob** *(n)* a strong horse, but one that is not very tall.

13 **astride** *(prep)* with a leg on each side of something. *(s)* astraddle.

14 **magnificent** *(adj)* spectacular, impressive and awesome. *(s)* superb, superlative. *(ant)* unimpressive.

mount she knew so well – a **dappled**[1]-grey warhorse called Lightning. Bryn Davis's **treasured**[2] stallion.

What on earth is Jack doing riding Lightning? she thought, squinting through the narrow gap in her metal helm. *Jack Jones must have begged Bryn to let him ride his horse*, thought Cad, feeling Flash twitch beneath her, **perturbed**[3] by the much bigger stallion. But as the **gigantic**[4] horse neared, breaking into a gentle canter, Cad could see the rider was somewhat **leaner**[5] and taller than Jack Jones.

'God's blood!' Cad cursed into her sweltering helm, recognising the **crest**[6] the rider wore upon his. It was Bryn Davis, and he was clearly challenging her to a **duel**[7].

From where they watched the match, Dylan and Rhys hared over to Cad, followed by Ellis, who grabbed Flash's **reins**[8], saying, 'Don't do this, Cad. Refuse him. Don't take Davis on. He's daring you to an unfair duel. Flash can't **compete**[9] against Lightning.'

But Cad's mind had set the moment she'd **perceived**[10] the opposing rider and his **intentions**[11] of challenging her to a match. Yanking the reins from Ellis's hand, she turned Flash and made for her side of the runway.

Rhys's agonising **plea**[12] of 'Cad, don't do this!' was the last thing she heard before she cantered over to the list and halted Flash to see Bryn Davis atop Lightning, facing her from the other end of the **strip**[13].

---

1 **dappled** *(adj)* marked with rounded patches or spots, especially appealing on a horse.

2 **treasure** *(v)* value something greatly. *(s)* prize, cherish, adore. *(ant)* dislike.

3 **perturb** *(v)* make uneasy or anxious. *(s)* worry, concern, upset. *(ant)* reassure, calm.

4 **gigantic** *(adj)* great in extent or size. *(s)* enormous, huge. *(ant)* tiny.

5 **leaner** *(adj)* being slimmer or thinner than someone or something else. *(s)* skinnier. *(ant)* fatter.

6 **crest** *(n)* a device which shows a family heritage often worn on a shield or helmet in bygone times. *(s)* emblem.

7 **duel** *(n)* a contest of honour fought between two people with deadly weapons. *(s)* head-to-head.

8 **rein** *(n)* a strap attached to a horse's bit or head-collar, often used in pairs to guide a horse by its rider or leader.

9 **compete** *(v)* be able to rival another or others. *(s)* match, compare with, keep up with.

10 **perceive** *(v)* interpret or view in a particular way. *(s)* recognise, see, discern. *(ant)* misinterpret.

11 **intention** *(n)* a purpose or plan. *(s)* aim, objective, goal, idea, desire, ambition.

12 **plea** *(n)* an urgent and emotional request. *(s)* call, appeal.

13 **strip** *(n)* a long, narrow piece of land or ground.

CHAPTER TWELVE

Blackout

Steeling[1] herself to canter down the runway, just its low fence separating her from Bryn and Lightning, Cad saw her dreams flash before her eyes. Her father would recover the Gwalch Gem bracelet. She would become a Knight Hawk and ride beside him, protecting his realm. And her mother would see sense and return to her family. The three things she wanted more than anything in the world drove her forward towards that goal.

Prepared fully for the joust, but hating herself for scaring her friends, Cad glanced at them huddled together, terror written across their faces. Oddly, she felt little fear. She would rise to Bryn's challenge of a duel. After all, she was not trapped inside an oubliette, **destined**[2] to rot, or blindly crawling through a suffocatingly cramped tunnel. She was where she was born to be: in control of her **destiny**[3], mounted, with lance and shield in hand – a knight.

The world Cad saw through the narrow slit of her helm blocked out the chicken's clucks drifting from inside the castle's walls, **filtered out**[4] the sheep's **bleating**[5] and the cattle's **lowing**[6]. She focused on her task, ignoring the sweet smell of pastries and bread wafting from the kitchen.

---

1 **steel** *(v)* mentally prepare for something difficult. *(s)* strengthen, fortify, brace. *(ant)* weaken.

2 **destined** *(adj)* of a person's future which seems set to a pre-existing plan. *(s)* doomed, fated.

3 **destiny** *(n)* unknown future state or events. *(s)* fate, fortune. *(ant)* past.

4 **filter out** *(v)* remove or reduce. *(s)* refine.

5 **bleating** *(n)* the wavering cry of a sheep. *(s)* baaing.

6 **lowing** *(n)* the deep sound made by a cow. *(s)* mooing, bellowing.

It locked out the delights of roasting meats turned on giant spits by children **fending off**[1] dogs who begged for scraps. Right now, two people **existed**[2] in her world: Cad herself and Bryn Davis, and she was about to unseat him from his magnificent horse.

As she boiled inside her armour, and with one eye on the herald, Cad saw sweat accumulating on Flash's neck. The pony sensed Cad's tension through the saddle: horses always knew their riders' states. Cad needed to relax lest she spook her mount. She saw Lightning **chomping**[3] his bit, white froth **drooling**[4] from his mouth as he danced on the spot, held back by his rider, Bryn Davis.

As **palpable**[5] tension crackled in the air, teetering on the brink of the herald's cry to charge, Cad welcomed the pounding of her heart, her **heightened**[6] **senses**[7], the blood coursing through her veins. Despite the slippery sweat in her gauntlets, Cad gripped her lance, her shield held firmly in the other hand, and waited. Mere moments passed in what felt like aeons, then as the word *Charge!* rang out from the herald, and she spurred Flash on to a canter, her existence **shrank**[8] to nothing but the joust.

At one with the rhythm of Flash's stride, Cad fixed her narrow field of view firmly on the steed charging straight for her. Taller than Flash, Lightning gained ground, but Cad had **accounted for**[9] this and, leaving the tilt of her lance until the very last minute before disqualification kicked in, she lifted its tip and caught Bryn low beneath the **ribcage**[10], before his lance had a chance to hit her. The sheer force of the **blow**[11] striking the armour thwarted any possible contact from Davis, and with a clang of metal and the **splintering**[12] of wood, he **jerked**[13] backwards over Lightning's

---

1 **fend off** *(v)* defend oneself from something. *(s)* stop, repel, parry, discourage. *(ant)* encourage.

2 **exist** *(v)* be. *(s)* be present.

3 **chomp** *(v)* bite and chew noisily. *(s)* champ, gnaw.

4 **drool** *(v)* drop saliva (spit) from the mouth in a uncontrollable way. *(s)* dribble, slobber.

5 **palpable** *(adj)* so intense as to seem almost tangible (real). *(s)* profound, substantial. *(ant)* intangible.

6 **heighten** *(v)* increase. *(s)* intensify, strengthen, amplify, enhance. *(ant)* lessen, reduce.

7 **sense** *(n)* a faculty of the body that perceives the external environment. *(s)* awareness, perception.

8 **shrink** *(v)* make or become smaller (past tense: shrank). *(s)* contract, narrow. *(ant)* expand.

9 **account for** (phrase) consider or regard. *(s)* think, reckon, gauge. *(ant)* disregard.

10 **ribcage** *(n)* the bones that form a frame around the chest to protect the organs inside.

11 **blow** *(n)* a strike with a weapon, hand or hard object. *(s)* punch, thump, thwack.

12 **splinter** *(v)* break into smaller sharp pieces. *(s)* smash, shatter, fracture, crack.

13 **jerk** *(v)* move with a sudden, sharp movement. *(s)* jolt, lurch. *(ant)* glide, ease.

rear, his lance and helm soaring through the air and landing on Cad's side of the tilt with a thud.

Cad, following the **chivalric code**[1], pulled Flash to a halt and signalled the grooms over, but she wasn't too concerned. Bryn, legs **flailing**[2], had just about recovered his seat, but it wasn't pretty. He refused the groom's help with a rude gesture and, grumbling, he regained control of Lightning, his face **livid**[3] with volcanic **wrath**[4] as he signalled his groom to bring his helm. Cad had won the first match with ease. This joust would be the best of three. If she unseated him on the next pass, Cad would take the joust and she certainly planned to do just that.

'Easy, girl,' Cad cooed, patting Flash's sweating neck.

Although the morning temperature was not overly high, Cad was baking inside her armour and Flash **perspired**[5] **profusely**[6]. A tad concerned at her pony's anxiety, Cad gathered the reins and brought Flash around for the second pass. Cad's hands swam in her gauntlets, and gripping the lance proved trickier with each pass. But she knew Bryn would be suffering the same conditions, and he would hurt somewhere, for sure. One could not take such a blow unscathed, especially to one's **confidence**[7].

Quite a lively crowd now **assembled**[8] in the yard. Gossip of a page on a pony almost unseating Davis from his prized destrier spread like wildfire around the castle, and more **curious**[9] folks poured into the yard to **spectate**[10]. Cad rose to the **occasion**[11], cantering Flash to her side of the runway and readying herself while Bryn **regrouped**[12] and trotted Lightning to his. Cad **relished**[13] the crowd, feeling like a great knight in a real joust battling to win the **favour**[14] of their masters.

---

1 **chivalric code** *(n)* a knightly code or system of behaviour developed and followed during the medieval times.
2 **flail** *(v)* swing or wave wildly. *(s)* thrash about, beat about, flap, lash.
3 **livid** *(adj)* extremely angry. *(s)* furious, fuming, seething. *(ant)* calm, content.
4 **wrath** *(n)* anger. *(s)* fury, rage, outrage, vexation. *(ant)* contentment.
5 **perspire** *(v)* sweat through the pores on the skin.
6 **profusely** *(adv)* to a large degree. *(s)* extensively, copiously. *(ant)* barely, hardly.
7 **confidence** *(n)* a feeling of self-assurance and belief in oneself. *(s)* certainty, faith. *(ant)* uncertainty.
8 **assemble** *(v)* gather with others for a common purpose. *(s)* collect, convene. *(ant)* disperse.
9 **curious** *(adj)* keen to know or learn something. *(s)* inquisitive, interested. *(ant)* indifferent.
10 **spectate** *(v)* watch rather than take part in. *(s)* view, observe, look, witness. *(ant)* participate.
11 **occasion** *(n)* an event. *(s)* moment, happening, circumstance.
12 **regroup** *(v)* gather oneself or a group back together after a problem or a defeat. *(s)* rally. *(ant)* disassemble, disperse.
13 **relish** *(v)* enjoy greatly and savour. *(s)* revel, appreciate, delight in. *(ant)* detest, dislike, loathe.
14 **favour** *(n)* approval and support. *(s)* liking, esteem. *(ant)* disapproval.

With aplomb, she took her lance from Ellis and waited, adjusting her face for battle beneath her helm. Bryn snatched his from a scared-looking groom; he looked **rattled**[1]. Cad was so close to making history here in the list field. If she unseated Bryn now, she would win against all **odds**[2], and his call for a duel would fall flat on its face, just where she intended him to be.

Cad was ready for victory, realising she was about to **hurl**[3] a **boulder**[4] into a **millpond**[5]. With her helm affording such **limited**[6] vision, she swivelled her head from side to side, hoping her father had heard and come to watch her compete, but she couldn't see him. A little disappointed, she hoped he might observe from his rooms in the grand tower which offered perfect views of the gardens and tilt yard.

Beneath her, Cad sensed Flash's urgency to charge, so wrenched her thoughts back to the task at hand. She stared **steadfastly**[7] at Bryn and awaited the herald's cry to charge, welcoming her quickening **pulse**[8] and **fluttering**[9] chest. No matter her **humble**[10] beginnings, she was born to this: to be Llywelyn's right-hand knight – a Knight Hawk.

'*Charge!*'

And with that command, fearlessly, Flash hurled down the runway, hooves thundering towards the giant horse. This time, changing **tactics**[11], Cad didn't delay her tilt, swiftly lifting her lance and catching Bryn **squarely**[12] in the shoulder. But, at the same time, Bryn's lance struck her upper arm, **catapulting**[13] her lance **precariously**[14] across the tilt. Cad took a **severe**[15] blow

---

1 **rattled** *(adj)* nervous or irritated. *(s)* perturbed, disturbed, flustered, agitated. *(ant)* comforted.

2 **odds** *(n)* the likelihood or chances of something happening. *(s)* probability.

3 **hurl** *(v)* move or throw in a forceful manner. *(s)* launch, heave.

4 **boulder** *(n)* a large rock. *(s)* stone.

5 **millpond** *(n)* an extremely calm or still stretch of water. *(s)* pond.

6 **limited** *(adj)* restricted in some way. *(s)* inadequate, insufficient. *(ant)* unlimited, ample.

7 **steadfastly** *(adv)* in a steadfast (firm) way. *(s)* unwaveringly, staunchly. *(ant)* weakly.

8 **pulse** *(n)* the rhythm of one's blood pulsating through one's arteries, typically at the wrists or neck.

9 **flutter** *(v)* move with a light, irregular or trembling motion. *(s)* beat, quiver.

10 **humble** *(adj)* of low social rank. *(s)* lowly, poor, ignoble. *(ant)* important, noble.

11 **tactic** *(n)* an action to achieve something specific. *(s)* plan, strategy, ploy.

12 **squarely** *(adv)* directly. *(s)* straight, right. *(ant)* indirectly.

13 **catapult** *(v)* hurl, propel or launch. *(s)* shoot, project.

14 **precariously** *(adv)* in a precarious (dangerous) way. *(s)* shakily, unsteadily. *(ant)* securely, steadily.

15 **severe** *(adj)* extreme or great. *(s)* serious, appalling, dreadful, dire. *(ant)* mild.

below the shoulder, which was protected only by thick leather. Yet, gripping Flash with all her might, and immediately correcting her balance, Cad's backside remained firmly in her saddle. The **steward**[1] would judge this pass, appointing a win based on both equestrian and **martial**[2] skills. Neither rider had unseated the other, but Cad had lost her lance and, to her **vexation**[3], guessed Bryn would catch the win as she had in the prior pass.

Cad steered Flash towards Ellis and pulled her to a halt before the excited crowd. Not wanting to worry them, she **bypassed**[4] her friends and, remaining focused, said to Ellis, 'My arm will hold up.'

Cad lifted the mouth plate of her helm so Ellis might hear her better.

'It's bruised but fine. Still, I am concerned why Flash sweats so.'

'Maybe it is the occasion,' Ellis said, rubbing down Flash's neck with a dry cloth. 'You have drawn quite a crowd. Flash is unused to such a **spectacle**[5].'

'Perhaps,' Cad replied, dropping her mouth plate back down, **apprehension**[6] rising as they awaited the steward's decision, her hidden face **furrowed**[7] with anxiety. If Cad won this pass, the match would be hers. Dare she even contemplate such an outcome against such a skilled squire?

Bryn waited on the other side of the tilt, surrounded by grooms and squires, Lightning pawing the ground with impatience.

The steward approached the herald, who was standing on a mounting block to address the crowd. Cad's breath snagged as he announced, 'I award the win to the squire, Bryn Davis.'

A roar rose from Bryn's camp amid boos from Cad's and the crowd, who clearly favoured the **underdog**[8].

'I think you and Flash can do this,' Ellis said, grinning up at Cad and patting Flash's neck.

'I know we can,' Cad replied, gathering the reins and squeezing Flash with both heels to urge her to the runway's start.

---

1 **steward** *(n)* an official person employed to supervise an event. *(s)* manager, administrator.

2 **martial** *(adj)* relating to fighting (or war). *(s)* military, combative. *(ant)* civilian, peaceable.

3 **vexation** *(n)* the state of being irritated or worried. *(s)* annoyance, exasperation. *(ant)* ease.

4 **bypass** *(v)* go past or round. *(s)* avoid, circumvent, neglect.

5 **spectacle** *(n)* a striking display or performance. *(s)* show, exhibition, pageant.

6 **apprehension** *(n)* fear that something bad may happen. *(s)* worry, unease, anxiety. *(ant)* confidence.

7 **furrowed** *(adj)* (of the face or forehead) marked with wrinkles or lines. *(s)* creased. *(ant)* smooth.

8 **underdog** *(n)* the competitor thought to have no or little chance of winning. *(s)* weaker.

Davis made Cad wait, and clearly savoured doing so, but Cad remained calm, determined not to **succumb**[1] to his delaying tactics and become **riled**[2] as he intended. Cad would love to knock the crest off Bryn's **cocky**[3] helm with her lance. She was accurate enough to do so. It would be just like skewering the rings, but she'd be disqualified immediately in this practice joust where rules were respected. She intended to save that move for a real tourney.

As Cad cantered Flash to the runway, filled with numerous **warring**[4] emotions, she noticed that the pony's stride felt a little flatter than before, heavier.

'Come on, girl,' **encouraged**[5] Cad, leaning down and patting Flash's chestnut neck hard to grab her attention. 'We can do this, girl. I know you're tired, but we have him this time.'

Cad patted harder, reassuring the **stoic**[6] pony, who let out a low **whinny**[7].

Bryn, pushing timing to the limits, eventually cantered Lightning to his start line, and with a high **rear**[8], pulled the stallion to a **spectacular**[9] halt.

He sees that Flash is tiring, she thought. *He's trying to* ***intimidate***[10] *me, but he won't,* she told herself firmly.

The herald stood on the mounting block and, raising his arms to silence the crowd, **bellowed**[11] '*Charge!*'

Cad spurred Flash on, squeezing her knees, doubling her efforts to encourage her mount. But immediately, Cad felt something **amiss**[12]. **Unresponsive**[13] to Cad's commands, Flash barely cantered, let alone charged. And as if the world moved in a strange slow motion, Cad

---

1 **succumb** *(v)* give in or give way. *(s)* yield, submit, surrender, capitulate. *(ant)* withstand.

2 **rile** *(v)* annoy or irritate someone. *(s)* vex, bother, irk. *(ant)* please.

3 **cocky** *(adj)* cheeky or overly bold, conceited or overconfident. *(s)* showy, brash. *(ant)* modest.

4 **warring** *(adj)* of two or more things in conflict with one and other. *(s)* opposing. *(ant)* agreeing.

5 **encourage** *(v)* persuade or support. *(s)* urge, push, spur. *(ant)* dissuade, discourage.

6 **stoic** *(adj)* something or someone that tolerates pain without complaint. *(s)* hardy, tough. *(ant)* weak.

7 **whinny** *(n)* a high-pitched neighing sound. *(s)* nicker, whicker, bray.

8 **rear** *(n)* (of an animal) the act of rising up onto the hind (back) legs.

9 **spectacular** *(adj)* impressive. *(s)* amazing, staggering, dramatic. *(ant)* dull.

10 **intimidate** *(v)* force or frighten into submission. *(s)* threaten, bully. *(ant)* assure.

11 **bellow** *(v)* shout loudly and deeply. *(s)* holler, bark, roar, cry, yell. *(ant)* whisper.

12 **amiss** *(adj)* out of place or not right. *(s)* wrong, awry, incorrect, untoward. *(ant)* right, in order.

13 **unresponsive** *(adj)* nor responsive (reactive). *(s)* unreactive, apathetic. *(ant)* responsive.

felt Flash ailing – not tiring, but failing to **function**[1].

Cad made a split-second decision and, keeping her eyes fixed on the slit in Bryn's helm, did not tilt her lance for the joust. Instead, she swung it out low and to the side, **indicating**[2] an obvious mercy pass to Bryn Davis. She would not risk herself or Flash in this way, no matter the **stakes**[3]. She must **retire**[4] from this joust. But in an instant, and with the shattering of wood against steel, Cad's chest exploded with pain, and her world turned black.

---

1 **function** *(v)* work in a specific way. *(s)* operate, perform. *(ant)* malfunction.

2 **indicate** *(v)* suggest an action or thing. *(s)* show, specify, stipulate.

3 **stake** *(n)* an interest or investment in something. *(s)* prize, award.

4 **retire** *(v)* withdraw from an event. *(s)* pull out. *(ant)* enter, participate.

CHAPTER THIRTEEN

Almost Rumbled

Twinkling lights, ringing bells and chattering greeted Cad. Memories returned in **fractured**[1] jerks. She was **disorientated**[2]; was she feasting in the great hall? It was only when the **searing**[3] pain hit her chest, accompanied by an inability to breathe, that she remembered where she was: the **frayed**[4] edges of her mind were now shocked into **consciousness**[5].

Voices, as if drifting from the bottom of a deep well, swam about her ears. Still **encased**[6] in her helm and viewing the world through its narrow slit, Cad heard Dylan's frantic voice. He was **steeped**[7] in a heated **altercation**[8] with Bryn Davis, who seemed to insist on removing Cad's clothing.

Although in agony, Cad neither cried nor complained, and despite feeling as if a **dagger**[9] was stabbing her ribs and slicing her head, her chest felt light. They'd removed her metal breastplate, hauberk and aketon, and she was down to her woollen hose and linen undergarments.

---

1 **fractured** *(adj)* disordered. *(s)* fragmented, disorganised. *(ant)* orderly.

2 **disorientated** *(adj)* confused. *(s)* confounded, thrown, puzzled, baffled. *(ant)* clear, lucid.

3 **searing** *(adj)* intense. *(s)* excruciating, agonising, severe, extreme. *(ant)* mild.

4 **frayed** *(adj)* showing the effects of trauma or tension. *(s)* frazzled, fragmented.

5 **consciousness** *(n)* the state of being conscious, aware and responsive. *(s)* awareness. *(ant)* unconsciousness.

6 **encase** *(v)* cover or enclose with something tightly. *(s)* truss, enshroud. *(ant)* free, release.

7 **steep** *(v)* immerse in a task or experience. *(s)* absorb, engross, engage. *(ant)* disengage.

8 **altercation** *(n)* an audible (can be heard) argument. *(s)* quarrel, disagreement. *(ant)* agreement.

9 **dagger** *(n)* a short sharp knife with a handle used as a weapon.

Her brain felt like tangled-up wool but, as Cad listened, something worse than pain struck her. The tone in Bryn's voice caught her ear; it didn't add square.

No! she thought, realising with horrid **clarity**[1] why Dylan's voice sounded so frantic.

'Bryn, leave Cad be now. He breathes, so we must carry him inside, and a **physic**[2] will examine him further.' Dylan's voice was thick with pleading.

Mustering **supreme**[3] effort, Cad ignored the fire roaring in her ribs and managed to raise her arm, but it disobeyed and flopped back down by her side. Ever **observant**[4], Rhys noticed and **chimed in**[5]. 'See, Master Cad moves. He is well. Carry him inside,' Rhys begged Bryn, who Cad now saw kneeling beside her.

'No! Call a **physician**[6] out to the field. He must remain here as he would in battle,' Bryn ordered, ignoring the friends' pleas, his voice icy.

Cad realised Bryn's intention: it **assailed**[7] her thoughts like an arrow to her heart. She suddenly felt adrift on a wild sea full of dangerous rocks. If Bryn removed her undergarments to inspect her wounds, which was **commonplace**[8] with injuries in the field, he'd reveal that she was female, and in the most **humiliating**[9] manner possible. Dylan and Rhys knew this and were clearly trying to thwart him without raising suspicion. But Bryn was grasping his chance, and this was a practice joust. No horsemaster existed here, so Bryn **outranked**[10] the pages, ordering them away and taking charge.

Cad fought the urge to scream, wanting to kick Bryn away, but she couldn't even lift her **giddy**[11] head. How long she'd **lain**[12] there, she did not know. As Cad's world imploded before

---

1 **clarity** *(n)* the quality of being understood. *(s)* precision. *(ant)* vagueness.

2 **physic** *(n)* medieval term for a doctor or medicine. *(s)* physician.

3 **supreme** *(adj)* extremely great. *(s)* extraordinary, remarkable. *(ant)* inferior, lowly.

4 **observant** *(adj)* quick to notice or see things. *(s)* sharp, alert, attentive. *(ant)* inattentive.

5 **chime in** *(phrase)* join in a conversation. *(s)* interrupt, comment, contribute, add.

6 **physician** *(n)* a medical doctor. *(s)* medical practitioner, physic.

7 **assail** *(v)* (of an unpleasant feeling) come on suddenly and strongly. *(s)* plague, torment. *(ant)* appease.

8 **commonplace** *(adj)* usual. *(s)* normal, ordinary, routine, conventional. *(ant)* abnormal, unconventional.

9 **humiliating** *(adj)* making someone feel foolish or ashamed. *(s)* mortifying, disgraceful. *(ant)* glorious.

10 **outrank** *(v)* have a higher rank than another person. *(s)* eclipse, dominate.

11 **giddy** *(adj)* dizzy. *(s)* light, faint. *(ant)* steady.

12 **lie** *(v)* assume a lying position (past participle: lain). *(s)* sprawl. *(ant)* stand.

her, she thought only of the **disgrace**[1] she would bring to her father. The kind man who had **indulged**[2] his daughter's wishes. For the first time ever, regret crushed Cad like a curtain of iron.

As Davis loomed above her, a boyish grin masking a hint of malice just beneath the surface, his gauntlets now removed, **snippets**[3] of the joust burst into Cad's head – Flash's faltering performance. Cad had clearly, and in good time, swung her lance off target to ask for a mercy pass. Either Bryn had not seen it, or he'd **blatantly**[4] ignored it.

Then as Bryn moved nearer, panic surged through Cad as his fingers moved to open the buttons on her undershirt. Her stomach turned a sickening twist. The only option now was to scream, and sucking in the deepest breath she could, she almost **choked**[5] when her father's voice boomed, '*Stop!*'

Cad, spluttering beneath her helm, saw Llywelyn's fearful eyes before hers. Tears blurred her vision. An overwhelming relief **gushed**[6] forth, easing her physical and emotional pain at once.

Her father did not address her; he could not. Why would a prince address a page thus? But just one look at his face said everything to Cad, and at this moment, she had never loved him more. She longed to say, 'I am sorry.'

'You. Help me to remove this helm,' Llywelyn ordered, gesturing to a goggle-eyed **blacksmith**[7] who gaped from the crowd.

Cad's fall had **crushed**[8] one side of her helm, jamming it onto her head, and four strong hands were needed to pull out the **dent**[9] and release it. As they removed the helmet, Cad blinked furiously, almost blinded as the dazzling sun hit her bared face. Owain Glyn now joined her father, wearing an equally **anxious**[10] look. Cad turned her head to see Bryn, his face sharp with

---

1 **disgrace** *(n)* loss of reputation. *(s)* dishonour, shame, scandal. *(ant)* honour.

2 **indulge** *(v)* give someone what they want. *(s)* satisfy, entertain, allow. *(ant)* deprive.

3 **snippet** *(n)* small pieces. *(s)* bit, fragment, scrap.

4 **blatantly** *(adv)* in an obvious way, with no shame. *(s)* flagrantly. *(ant)* furtively.

5 **choke** *(v)* have difficulty in breathing due to lack of air. *(s)* gasp. *(ant)* breathe.

6 **gush** *(v)* flow quickly. *(s)* surge, burst. *(ant)* trickle.

7 **blacksmith** *(n)* someone who makes and repairs things in metal by hand. *(s)* smith, smithy.

8 **crush** *(v)* squeeze to the point of damaging. *(s)* squash, compress, press.

9 **dent** *(n) a* small hollow in a surface made by a blow or pressure. *(s)* dint, indentation, depression. *(ant)* lump.

10 **anxious** *(adj)* worried. *(s)* concerned, fearful, uneasy. *(ant)* carefree, unconcerned.

what looked like suspicion. He would be asking how a mere page had drawn Llywelyn and his **deputy**[1] from the castle to the list field.

As she regained a small piece of her **wits**[2], Cad's heart both soared and sank. Her father had saved her, but now she was certain Bryn knew her secret. Had he somehow **contrived**[3] this situation? Cad knew Bryn would not abandon his quest to ruin her chances of a knighthood. Why he **despised**[4] her so, eluded her. But if Bryn brought her down, he would embarrass her father, and that she would not allow.

Bryn came from an **influential**[5] family that Llywelyn would neither wish to disappoint nor cross in battle. He was a problem Cad must live with or control, and at that very moment, she decided on the latter. Bryn Davis would hold her to **ransom**[6] no more.

---

1 **deputy** *(n)* someone's second-in-command. *(s)* number two. *(ant)* chief.

2 **wits** *(n)* capacity for quick thought and understanding, good sense.

3 **contrive** *(v)* create by using skill or artifice. *(s)* engineer, devise, orchestrate.

4 **despise** *(v)* look down upon, view with contempt. *(s)* hate, detest, loathe. *(ant)* love, admire.

5 **influential** *(adj)* having great effect or control over someone. *(s)* powerful, important. *(ant)* unimportant.

6 **ransom** *(n)* a demand for something else in return. *(s)* bribe, payoff.

CHAPTER FOURTEEN

Ribs and Potions

'Callwen, my child, your pallor is wan,' Llywelyn said, looking more **fretful**[1] than she'd ever seen him before. She peered into his blue-green eyes, wondering how a great prince such as he could care for one as **lowly**[2] as she, especially now he had a son of his own.

Since Prince John's birth, nothing had changed between Cad and her adoptive father. When he had briefly returned home from his quest, he had shared his love and time as much as her page-pretence would **permit**[3]. And now it wasn't just her ribs stabbing at her chest; guilt played a large part too. Had her obsession with becoming a Knight Hawk caused any of the current problems? That thought **festered**[4] in her mind like an **infected**[5] wound.

'Papa, I am fine,' Cad lied, propped up in the physician's room as he **diagnosed**[6] broken ribs. Physician Jordan had ordered her to drink a disgustingly **bitter**[7] **potion**[8], **assuring**[9] Llywelyn it would ease her pain.

---

1 **fretful** *(adj)* distressed. *(s)* uneasy, upset, stressed. *(ant)* relaxed, happy.

2 **lowly** *(adj)* low in importance or rank. *(s)* humble, ordinary, simple, common. *(ant)* noble.

3 **permit** *(v)* allow to do something. *(s)* let, enable. *(ant)* prohibit.

4 **fester** *(v)* (of a problem or feeling) become more intense over time. *(s)* rankle, smoulder.

5 **infected** *(adj)* affected by an organism that causes disease. *(s)* rotten, ailing, afflicted. *(ant)* healthy.

6 **diagnose** *(v)* identify a medical condition or injury. *(s)* determine, confirm, pronounce.

7 **bitter** *(adj)* tasting sharp or bad, and not sweet. *(s)* sour, sharp, acidic. *(ant)* sweet.

8 **potion** *(n)* a medicinal liquid. *(s)* drink, brew, concoction, mixture.

9 **assure** *(v)* make someone certain of something positive. *(s)* reassure, promise, guarantee. *(ant)* trouble.

'The ribs will heal in four to six weeks,' stated Llywelyn's personal physician, who had treated Cad since babyhood. '**Refrain**[1] from exercise while they heal – and no riding. Be guided by the pain, and sleep upright for a week or two to keep your chest clear from **congestion**[2].'

'Thank you, Sire Jordan,' Cad replied, nodding begrudgingly as he left the room. But the pain would indeed guide her, for it was **excruciating**[3], and even if she wanted to mount a horse, she doubted she could.

'Callwen, what in heaven were you thinking to duel with Bryn Davis? With him mounted on a destrier and you on a pony, that is simply a death **sentence**[4].'

Although abashed and remorseful, Cad's heart **swelled**[5] with pride hearing Llywelyn call her Callwen. Since beginning her knight's training, she'd missed the closeness of the family she had forsaken, and now with her mother absent, her heart felt even emptier. Yet, she knew Llywelyn's hurt was far more **profound**[6] than hers.

'I was expecting Jack Jones, Papa, as arranged. But without warning, Bryn appeared. That was a direct challenge to duel. I am not **craven**[7], and I could not **concede**[8]. I felt confident I could win, and the weapons were not real,' she reassured him.

'Well, I forbid you to duel with him again, or with any squire, especially one riding a horse several **hands**[9] higher than yours. That match is impossible to win.'

'But Papa, I was winning,' she insisted. 'Flash and I are more **agile**[10] than he.'

Speaking Flash's name stirred fuzzy memories of the joust.

'Papa!' she **exclaimed**[11]. 'My pony, Flash – how **fares**[12] she?'

---

1 **refrain** *(v)* do without something. *(s)* abstain, withhold, keep. *(ant)* continue.

2 **congestion** *(n)* the state of being congested (blocked up). *(s)* obstruction, clogging, choking.

3 **excruciating** *(adj)* very painful. *(s)* searing, agonising, harrowing. *(ant)* painless.

4 **sentence** *(n)* the punishment given for a person found guilty of a crime. *(s)* decision, ruling. *(ant)* liberty.

5 **swell** *(v)* become larger in size. *(s)* expand, bulge. *(ant)* shrink, contract.

6 **profound** *(adj)* (of feelings, qualities, or emotions) intense, deep or great. *(s)* extreme. *(ant)* superficial, shallow.

7 **craven** *(adj)* completely lacking in courage. *(s)* cowardly, gutless, spineless. *(ant)* brave, bold.

8 **concede** *(v)* admit defeat. *(s)* capitulate, surrender, yield. *(ant)* deny, fight.

9 **hand** *(n)* a unit of measurement of a horse's height to its withers, equal to four inches.

10 **agile** *(adj)* able to move easily and quickly. *(s)* nimble, spry, swift, lithe. *(ant)* sluggish, stiff.

11 **exclaim** *(v)* cry out suddenly. *(s)* blurt, proclaim, declare. *(ant)* whisper, mutter.

12 **fare** *(v)* perform or be over a period of time. *(s)* progress, manage, cope.

'I don't know. I accompanied you straight here. My concern was to get you out of the field before Davis inspected your ribs.'

But Cad still pondered Flash.

'Papa, Flash faltered **queerly**[1], as if she were sick ...'

As Cad uttered the word 'sick', the mist **shrouding**[2] her mind lifted more.

'Papa, you know of the sickness **blighting**[3] the castle?'

'I do. Evans has informed me of it, although he says it is **abating**[4] somewhat.'

'You must be careful, Papa. Is it wise to arrange celebrations?'

'The people **crave**[5] **merriment**[6], Callwen. And perhaps you forget?'

Cad's **bleary**[7] mind **trawled**[8] for memories, but none came, and she shook her head.

'This week, your brother, Prince John, will turn one. I think that worthy of celebration.'

Cad's heart **contracted**[9]. 'Oh, Papa. I am so sorry. I am so **selfish**[10], caught up in my desires to be a knight, I forgot,' she cried, feeling truly **desolate**[11].

'I understand,' said Llywelyn, a **wistful**[12] look on his face. 'Please do not be so **harsh**[13] on yourself. You have just been injured, and with your brother now at Cadwaladr Castle for safekeeping, it is easy to forget. The celebrations will go ahead without you riding in the tourney.'

Cad's head drooped with disappointment and shame, her ears still ringing from the fall's **impact**[14].

'To quash suspicion, we will move you back to your quarters, and Goodwife Hughes will

---

1 **queerly** *(adv)* in a queer (odd or peculiar) manner. *(s)* strangely, unusually. *(ant)* normally.

2 **shroud** *(v)* obscure something. *(s)* cloud, veil, envelop. *(ant)* reveal.

3 **blight** *(v)* have an extremely bad effect on. *(s)* disrupt, wreck, devastate.

4 **abate** *(v)* become less severe. *(s)* subside, lessen, ease, decrease, diminish. *(ant)* increase, intensify.

5 **crave** *(v)* feel great desire for. *(s)* want, yearn for, long for. *(ant)* dislike, spurn.

6 **merriment** *(n)* fun, gaiety and high spirits. *(s)* cheer, joy, revelry, jollity. *(ant)* misery, depression.

7 **bleary** *(adj)* unfocused and dull. *(s)* hazy, fuzzy, blurry, unclear. *(ant)* lively, clear.

8 **trawl** *(v)* search thoroughly *(s)* dredge, rake, scout, scour.

9 **contract** *(v)* become tighter, shorter or smaller. *(s)* constrict, shrink, wither. *(ant)* expand, grow.

10 **selfish** *(adj)* lacking thought for other people. *(s)* self-centred, thoughtless. *(ant)* selfless.

11 **desolate** *(adj)* very unhappy, melancholy, gloomy or lonely. *(s)* forlorn, dismal. *(ant)* joyful.

12 **wistful** *(adj)* showing a vague look of regret or sadness. *(s)* pensive, doleful. *(ant)* cheerful, optimistic.

13 **harsh** *(adj)* hard regarding a situation. *(s)* severe, unpitying, unkind. *(ant)* gentle, kind.

14 **impact** *(n)* an instance of one object hitting another. *(s)* collision, blow. *(ant)* avoidance.

tend[1] to you there. It is curious enough that my private physician examines a page.'

'I am sorry to put you in this wretched position,' muttered Cad.

Had she, and her father, **sacrificed**[2] too much for her desire to be a knight? Could it have caused her mother's leaving? Cad's heart **shrivelled**[3] at that thought.

'Do not apologise, my child,' replied Llywelyn. And from his expression, Cad knew he meant what he said. 'I sanctioned this. I will support you to success.'

'Thank you, Father,' she replied, trying to move to hug him but wincing with pain instead.

'Callwen, you must rest, especially in the coming days.'

'Can I at least watch the tourney and attend the feast?'

'I think that unwise. But, as advised by the physician: let the pain guide you. Goodwife Hughes will nurse you once I leave.'

Llywelyn bent down and kissed her forehead.

'Oh, Father!' remarked Cad as he turned to leave, realising that her fall had most definitely affected her memory.

'Yes?'

'Before you go, there is something of the utmost urgency I must share.' She pleaded for his precious time, her eyes sharp and serious.

'What concerns you so?' asked her father, clearly reading the foreboding darkening her face.

'Father, weeks back, whilst you were away and I sought baby John, I took something from Sir Robert's rooms.'

Llywelyn's brow creased as he nodded for her to continue.

'It was a cipher, father. A cipher so troublesome even Evans said he could not **unravel**[4] its meaning.'

'What did this cipher say?' Llywelyn had stopped in his tracks, **mannequin**[5]-still, his gaze levelled straight at her.

'My friends and I, and Sir Robert, are not entirely sure of its true meaning, but it resembled a

---

1 **tend** *(v)* look after, care for. *(s)* attend to, minister to. *(ant)* neglect.

2 **sacrifice** *(v)* give up something for the sake of other things. *(s)* surrender, forgo, forfeit. *(ant)* keep, obtain.

3 **shrivelled** *(adj)* contracted. *(s)* shrunk, withered. *(ant)* expanded.

4 **unravel** *(v)* investigate and solve. *(s)* fathom, decipher. *(ant)* complicate.

5 **mannequin** *(n)* a life-sized human model. *(s)* figure, dummy.

plan. A plan for a weapon which appears to have **destructive**[1] abilities. And uncle Dewi's name appeared in the plans more than once.'

Llywelyn's faced darkened as his flinty eyes met Cad's. Evans had obviously mentioned nothing of this to her father yet.

'Where is this cipher? I must see it.'

The ice in Llywelyn's voice chilled Cad. 'I left it with Sir Robert, Father. He said that if what it stated were true, then there was much work to do.'

Llywelyn focused into the distance, a pensive look on his face as if about to ask another question. But instead, in an oddly **official**[2] manner, with a stiff smile, and a silence clenched between his teeth, he thanked his daughter and left the room, leaving Cad with a most unwelcome sense of **dread**[3]. The look she had seen etched on her father's face was not one she had ever seen there before.

---

1 **destructive** *(adj)* causing huge damage. *(s)* calamitous, injurious. *(ant)* constructive, beneficial.

2 **official** *(adj)* formal. *(s)* proper, authoritative, precise. *(ant)* casual, unofficial.

3 **dread** *(n)* fear. *(s)* apprehension, trepidation. *(ant)* confidence.

CHAPTER FIFTEEN

Suspicions and Shenanigans

'Master Cad, you must rest for at least a week,' Goodwife Hughes clucked, **plumping**[1] up Cad's pillows and topping up her cup from the water ewer she had fetched along with crusty bread fresh from the castle's ovens.

'And get that dog off your bed,' she ordered, wafting Fishy away, who leaped across onto Rhys's bed instead.

If only you knew that a snake lived beneath Rhys's bed, Cad thought with a grin.

'Thank you, Mrs Hughes, I am so grateful for your kindness, but Fishy is my friend, and hers is my only **companionship**[2] in this miserable room.'

'We will stay with you as much as possible given today's chores and training,' said Dylan kindly. 'But Rhys and I must eat midday dinner early, as the hall is being prepared for tonight's feasting, and there is much to do before tomorrow's tournament.'

'Oh, of course! You are busy pages.' Cad ground out the words through gritted teeth, despising her jealousy for surfacing and prevailing. It wasn't their fault that she was injured, and after **brooding**[3] on it for twenty-four hours, she was sure it wasn't her fault either.

---

1 **plump** *(v)* shake and prod something to make rounder and fuller, such as a cushion or pillow.

2 **companionship** *(n)* friendship. *(s)* company, comradeship. *(ant)* solitude.

3 **brood** *(v)* think deeply about something that makes one concerned, angry or unhappy. *(s)* ponder, contemplate.

'Check on Flash for me, please, would you, and ask Ellis to pop by again,' she added, a hint of **ungrateful**[1] **spite**[2] still **tainting**[3] her tone.

'Of course,' Dylan said, either not noticing or ignoring her **ingratitude**[4].

The day before, Ellis the groom had reported back to Cad hourly. Flash had indeed taken ill during the mock joust, almost collapsing before reaching the stables. Cad had not shared with anyone her fears that Flash may have been **poisoned**[5] for fear of being wrong and upsetting Llywelyn's festivities. And now Cad was **bed-bound**[6] and unable to **sleuth**[7] for facts, things could get worse quicker than she'd anticipated. She must have proof of **foul play**[8] before speaking to her father, lest she appear **frivolous**[9] and **incompetent**[10]. The only time she could risk checking the well for signs of **villainy**[11] without raising suspicions would be tonight, when the entire castle, **bar**[12] the odd few guards, would be feasting in the great hall without her.

If only I had my darned ring, she thought, frustrated and wincing with a painful cough. *I could go now before the feasting begins.*

'Drink, Master Cad,' fussed Goodwife Hughes, snapping Cad from her **reverie**[13] and handing her a cup. 'It will speed your recovery, especially in this heat. You look **parched**[14].'

Cad smiled and wet her lips before placing the cup down by her bed.

'What are you gaping at, boy?' Mrs Hughes chided poor Rhys, who was perched on his bed and quietly observing. 'Be off with you,' she added, and as though they were dogs begging at the dinner table, she shooed both boys towards the door she had opened.

---

1 **ungrateful** *(adj)* not pleasant. *(s)* unacceptable, churlish, rude. *(ant)* grateful, appreciative.

2 **spite** *(n)* meanness. *(s)* malice, resentment, malevolence. *(ant)* benevolence, kindness.

3 **taint** *(v)* spoil because of an undesirable (unwanted) quality. *(s)* blemish, contaminate, tarnish. *(ant)* enhance.

4 **ingratitude** *(n)* a lack of caring or thanks. *(s)* thoughtlessness, rudeness. *(ant)* gratitude.

5 **poison** *(v)* give something very dangerous or life threatening to someone or something.

6 **bed-bound** *(adj)* being confined to bed. *(s)* bedridden, immobilised.

7 **sleuth** *(v)* track, search or investigate in secret. *(s)* detect, spy, snoop, stalk. *(ant)* overlook.

8 **foul play** *(n)* criminal behaviour. *(s)* villainy, crime, wrongdoing.

9 **frivolous** *(adj)* superficial and not serious. *(s)* silly, foolish, whimsical. *(ant)* serious, sensible.

10 **incompetent** *(adj)* lacking the skills. *(s)* unable, inept, amateurish, bungling. *(ant)* able, competent.

11 **villainy** *(n)* criminal or bad behaviour. *(s)* wrongdoing, lawlessness. *(ant)* goodness.

12 **bar** *(prep)* except for. *(s)* besides, excluding. *(ant)* including.

13 **reverie** *(n)* a state of being lost in thought. *(s)* daydream, musing, contemplation. *(ant)* concentration.

14 **parched** *(adj)* very thirsty. *(s)* dehydrated, dry, gasping. *(ant)* hydrated.

'That boy is several slices short of a loaf,' **insulted**[1] Goodwife Hughes, banging the door closed behind Rhys and Dylan. She had clearly missed the pouch wriggling away at Rhys's belt. He'd concealed Slippy there lest Goodwife Hughes find the snake and **club**[2] it to death with her broom.

Cad remained mute, leaving Mrs Hughes to her incorrect assumption about Rhys, who was not typical of a boy his age but was incredibly **astute**[3], as Cad now knew.

'How is Hugh?' Cad **chirped**[4], lifting her tired, grey voice, and changing the subject, knowing Mrs Hughes would **gush**[5] non-stop about her beloved son.

But Mrs Hughes didn't gush; her words seeming to struggle to leave her mouth before she eventually said, 'He fares well, Master Cad. Not suffered from this blasted sickness blighting the castle yet,' she muttered, picking up her broom and busying herself in the room.

Cad waited for the oncoming **barrage**[6] of news, but none came. Mrs Hughes, head down, continued her chores, cleaning the floors and rearranging its strewn **reeds**[7].

Confused by the woman's **reticence**[8], yet ever curious, Cad asked, 'Does Hugh enjoy his work with Sir Robert?' Cad eyed Mrs Hughes, sure she'd **detected**[9] a **tic**[10] of **discomfort**[11] at the mention of Evans's name. The Goodwife swept harder, a tight smile fixed on her face, but she avoided Cad's attention.

Even more curious now, Cad waited for an answer, as what felt like a yawning silence fell between them.

'Sorry, what did you say?' Mrs Hughes's voice was thin.

'Hugh, does he enjoy his work?' Cad repeated with perfect honesty.

The woman's face worked for a moment. Then after a slight pause, which Cad found odd,

---

1 **insult** *(v)* speak badly of or to someone or something. *(s)* disrespect, deride, scorn. *(ant)* compliment.

2 **club** *(v)* hit hard with a blunt object. *(s)* bash, bludgeon, clobber, cudgel.

3 **astute** *(adj)* able to quickly assess and turn something to one's advantage. *(s)* sharp, shrewd, clever. *(ant)* dim-witted.

4 **chirp** *(v)* speak in a sing-song way. *(s)* sing, trill. *(ant)* groan.

5 **gush** *(v)* speak quickly and enthusiastically. *(s)* enthuse, effuse, babble. *(ant)* drawl, be silent.

6 **barrage** *(n)* a lot of something. *(s)* profusion, bombardment, deluge, surge.

7 **reed** *(n)* a tall, slim piece of grass, dried out and placed on the ground to adsorb waste or act as flooring.

8 **reticence** *(n)* the characteristic of being quiet or shy. *(s)* reserve, restraint, quietness. *(ant)* exuberance.

9 **detect** *(v)* discern the presence of something. *(s)* notice, sense, perceive. *(ant)* miss, overlook.

10 **tic** *(n)* a twitch. *(s)* spasm, jerk, tremble.

11 **discomfort** *(n)* unease. *(s)* irritation, disquiet, upset, displeasure. *(ant)* comfort.

for Goodwife Hughes usually did not pause for air when **effusing**[1] about Hugh, she eventually answered in a **terse**[2] tone.

'He enjoys his work. He finds it **fulfilling**[3].' Her words seemed to choke out. And with that, she abandoned her broom, gathered her things and, rearranging her **puckered**[4] brow, said, 'I will return with your supper before the feast. I will prepare a special plate, as you cannot attend.'

Then, with a smile that looked in need of **scaffolding**[5], Mrs Hughes left, in what Cad thought was a rather **strained**[6] manner.

'What irks her so?' Cad asked Fishy, who had leaped back onto the bed, causing Cad to yelp in pain. 'I have never known Goodwife Hughes to **forgo**[7] the chance to **harp**[8] on about Hugh.'

Fishy, with whom only Cad now **conversed**[9], as Dylan and Rhys were so busy with tournament practice, tilted her head towards Cad as if listening. Then she licked Cad's face before flopping onto her side, with what Cad suspected was more than just a hint of boredom.

Cad wriggled forward, and anticipating the flame of pain to her ribs, braced herself to stand, adjusting the strapping she had **swaddled**[10] around her ribs once Physician Jordan's potion had worn off. He had strictly **rationed**[11] her intake, stating that folks could develop an unhealthy craving for this **draught**[12] if it were **imbibed**[13] too frequently, and that they might see **demons**[14] and horned **devils**[15] whilst still awake. She doubted that, but as she **hobbled**[16] to her feet, and

---

1 **effuse** *(v)* talk a lot. *(s)* gush, babble, spout, enthuse, rave.

2 **terse** *(adj)* using few words. *(s)* snappy, abrupt, curt, brusque. *(ant)* verbose, rambling.

3 **fulfilling** *(adj)* make to feel satisfied and happy. *(s)* satisfying, rewarding, enjoyable. *(ant)* unfulfilling.

4 **pucker** *(v)* contract into creases or wrinkle. *(s)* crumple, furrow, line. *(ant)* smooth.

5 **scaffolding** *(n)* a temporary support that holds something up. *(s)* framework, support.

6 **strained** *(adj)* showing signs of tension. *(s)* tense, forced, uneasy. *(ant)* easy, genuine.

7 **forgo** *(v)* go without something that you actually want. *(s)* sacrifice, waive, decline. *(ant)* keep.

8 **harp** *(v)* talk in a boring manner about a specific topic. *(s)* witter, prattle, blather.

9 **converse** *(v)* have a conversation (talk) with another. *(s)* speak, chat, discourse.

10 **swaddle** *(v)* wrap tightly in cloth, especially a baby. *(s)* sheathe, bundle, bind. *(ant)* unwrap.

11 **ration** *(v)* allow only a fixed amount of something. *(s)* limit, restrict, control. *(ant)* lavish.

12 **draught** *(n)* liquid with medicinal properties. *(s)* medicine, potion, elixir.

13 **imbibe** *(v)* drink. *(s)* consume, swallow, swig, down.

14 **demon** *(n)* a bad spirit. *(s)* fiend, devil. *(ant)* angel.

15 **devil** *(n)* in some religions and beliefs only, a bad entity or spirit.

16 **hobble** *(v)* walk in a difficult manner. *(s)* limp, dodder, totter. *(ant)* stride.

was then almost forced to flop back in agony, Cad wished she could **swig**[1] a cup full of the **concoction**[2] right then.

That would not be the case though. Tonight, when the physician visited for her evening **dosage**[3], she must distract him again as she had done earlier that morning. Cad must *not* drink all the bitter **brew**[4]; the potion that eased the pain and summoned sleep, but take just enough to carry her through the task that lay ahead. She would save the remainder of the dose until her return from the well, when she knew she would be in agony and desperate for sleep. Then she would guzzle it, welcoming the effects with relish.

If she was to risk checking the well, she must be prepared for failure. With her ribs **protesting**[5] as she moved, she shuffled over to her writing desk and scrawled several notes to her father; one for every possible outcome, and then hid them away in her tunic.

Now it was time to rest, without which her task would be **insurmountable**[6]. She **doddered**[7] back to her bed, hid the hairpin on her person, sent Fishy over to Rhys's bed and gulped the remainder of the morning's draught. If she were to endure a visit to the castle's central well this evening, the **tincture**[8] would ensure she slept away the afternoon, along with the mounting **trepidation**[9] which threatened to scupper her plan.

---

1 **swig** *(v)* drink in big gulps. *(s)* guzzle. *(ant)* sip.

2 **concoction** *(n)* a mixture of ingredients. *(s)* potion, brew, mixture.

3 **dosage** *(n)* the frequency or size of a dose of medicine. *(s)* measure, application.

4 **brew** *(n)* a blended drink. *(s)* beverage, mixture.

5 **protest** *(v)* express an objection to something. *(s)* object, disagree, complain. *(ant)* agree.

6 **insurmountable** *(adj)* too great to overcome. *(s)* impossible. *(ant)* easy, surmountable.

7 **dodder** *(v)* move in an unsteady way. *(s)* hobble, shuffle, totter. *(ant)* stride.

8 **tincture** *(n)* a liquid medicine. *(s)* solution, potion, infusion.

9 **trepidation** *(n)* anxiety or fear about what may happen. *(s)* dread, foreboding, apprehension. *(ant)* assurance.

CHAPTER SIXTEEN

Feast or Famine

'Master Cad. Master Cad, wake up, please!'

The voice echoed as if drifting from afar, smudging the comfortable silence. Something irritating clawed at Cad's arm; she batted it away. Probably just another potion fuelled dream, which she swiftly banished from her mind.

'Master *Cad*!'

The voice rang again, closer, more determined this time, **braying**[1] in her ear.

'Ouch!' Cad cried ripped from sleep and **clutching**[2] her agonising side as the pain wielded its cruel power.

'Heavens, Rhys! What are you doing?' she yelled, fire in her eyes.

Rhys gaped at her, his look **haunted**[3], but said nothing.

'Where in heaven did you find that?' Her eyes flashed towards his hand, which now trembled.

But Cad's question was **wholly**[4] **rhetorical**[5], for she remembered exactly where she'd stashed her precious hairpin, and right now, Rhys, after prodding her shoulder with it, held it in his hand.

---

1 **bray** *(v)* speak or laugh loudly, sound like a donkey. *(s)* roar, trumpet, bellow. *(ant)* whisper.

2 **clutch** *(v)* grab or grasp something tightly. *(s)* hold, grip, seize. *(ant)* release, let go.

3 **haunted** *(adj)* continually distressed. *(s)* anguished, troubled, tormented. *(ant)* untroubled.

4 **wholly** *(adv)* completely. *(s)* entirely, totally. *(ant)* partially.

5 **rhetorical** *(adj)* asked for effect or to make a statement rather than to get an answer.

Cad scowled, her expression travelling from rage to relief and back to somewhere in between. Rhys, looking as dumb as a rock and blinking like a mole, stood **tongue-tied**[1] as Cad fumbled her way through the **receding**[2] red mist of anger.

Realising they could drift on this ocean of silence forever, mumbling noises of frustration, Cad rounded on him again.

'Well?' she spat. '**Whence**[3] did you steal my pin?'

Rhys, like a fly trapped in **amber**[4], handed her the hairpin, then gazed at his feet. 'I ... I thought you were ... dead, from the sickness. I returned ages back, but you didn't wake, even when I shook you, and Fishy pawed your head. We couldn't rouse you.'

'Did you not think to check I was breathing?' snapped Cad, still furious at Rhys for taking her pin from her tunic. How had he known where to look? But then she remembered Lord Nosy missed little. He'd probably known all along where she'd stowed her scribbled notes and precious items.

'I saw you wake Dylan with it many times. I thought its magic might wake you,' Rhys muttered, through a sob.

Magic? thought Cad. *What makes you think this pin is magic?*

A **pang**[5] of guilt at Rhys's burgeoning tears **quelled**[6] her anger somewhat, but not the trepidation now rising in her **gut**[7].

'Rhys,' she said gently, arranging a sunny smile on her face. 'Dry your tears. I forgive you.'

Cad meant it. Rhys had copied her behaviour, and to blame him for that would make her a **hypocrite**[8]. He hadn't known that the power of the potion she'd quaffed that morning had rendered her unconscious for hours.

'Rhys, I know you meant well, and thank you, but please respect my **privacy**[9]. What I hide on my person stays on my person unless I state otherwise.'

---

1 **tongue-tied** *(adj)* too embarrassed, scared or shy to speak. *(s)* speechless. *(ant)* loquacious.

2 **recede** *(v)* move back or diminish. *(s)* retreat, ebb, fade. *(ant)* advance, grow.

3 **whence** *(adv)* from where. *(s)* wherefrom, from what place.

4 **amber** *(n)* a honey-yellow coloured fossilised resin, often used in jewellery.

5 **pang** *(n)* a sudden painful feeling or emotion. *(s)* twinge, stab, ache.

6 **quell** *(v)* suppress (put an end to) and silence. *(s)* subdue, quash, control. *(ant)* incite, intensify.

7 **gut** *(n)* the stomach. *(s)* belly, abdomen, tummy.

8 **hypocrite** *(n)* someone who tells others to do what they don't do themselves. *(s)* pretender, charlatan.

9 **privacy** *(n)* the state of keeping one's business to oneself. *(s)* confidentiality. *(ant)* publicness.

Rhys nodded, his anxiety-**ridden**[1] face softening at her words.

Forcing a casual tone, Cad said, 'Rhys, why do you **consider**[2] my hairpin to be magic?'

Without hesitating, Rhys **piped**[3], 'Because it wakes Dylan. That must be magic, for he sleeps like the dead.'

Cad searched his eyes for flickers of lies but detected none. Rhys's face, framed by his coppery curls, shone with honesty and relief.

'I see,' said Cad, with a half-smile, for what Rhys had said seemed truthful. Dylan would sleep through a lightning storm pouring **hail**[4] the size of ducks' eggs, yet a prod with her pin always did the trick, waking him from **slumber**[5] at once.

Maybe its magic does work on Dylan? Cad reflected, relaxing a tad, then **grimacing**[6] as she moved too quickly.

'Does it hurt a lot?' asked Rhys, his face **sympathetic**[7].

'It's agonising,' she hissed through her teeth, manoeuvring herself into a more comfortable position.

Especially when that potion wears off, she thought, realising that her next draught would have little effect. She planned to take only enough to get her to Catrin's central well without screaming in pain or falling asleep as she walked.

Dry-mouthed and feeling shipwrecked, she said, 'Can you pass me the beer jug, please? I have a **raging**[8] thirst.' Even her tongue felt **gritty**[9].

'Beer?' Rhys questioned. But quickly catching himself, his mouth closed like a trap as he grabbed the jug and filled her cup.

'Helps the pain and **slakes**[10] my thirst,' said Cad, emptying the entire cup in gulps, knowing she

---

1 **ridden** *(adj)* full with or containing something one does not want. *(s)* afflicted, gripped. *(ant)* free.

2 **consider** *(v)* believe to be. *(s)* deem, think, reckon.

3 **pipe** *(v)* speak up in a high voice. *(s)* sound, say. *(ant)* silence.

4 **hail** *(n)* frozen rain. *(s)* hailstones.

5 **slumber** *(n)* sleep. *(s)* a rest, a nap. *(ant)* wakefulness.

6 **grimace** *(v)* make an ugly, twisted expression on one's face. *(s)* scowl, frown. *(ant)* smile.

7 **sympathetic** *(adj)* showing or feeling sympathy (pity). *(s)* consoling, compassionate. *(ant)* unsympathetic, indifferent.

8 **raging** *(adj)* great in effect. *(s)* tremendous, huge, overwhelming. *(ant)* slight.

9 **gritty** *(adj)* covered with or containing grit (dirt or earth of some sort). *(s)* sandy, grainy.

10 **slake** *(v)* satisfy a thirst. *(s)* quench, satiate, relieve. *(ant)* exacerbate.

had requested the weakest beer from the castle **brewery**[1]. She'd not touched a drop of water since seeing Flash guzzle from the tank in the list field the day before. Then, most out of character for her, Cad nodded at Rhys for more.

'Another?' Rhys remarked, astonished, but taking her cup and refilling it for her.

'It's excruciating. I feel I have been torn **asunder**[2],' Cad replied. 'And beer helps me to sleep away the **misery**[3],' she lied, not touching this cup, for she didn't plan to sleep this time. She would save this drink until later, when she was genuinely thirsty again. No way was she drinking castle water until she'd checked the well.

'Where's Dylan?' asked Cad, hearing her stomach growl and feeling the hollow shapes of hunger.

'Bryn Davis has him **skivvying**[4] in the kitchens, turning spits. It seems he is still punishing Dylan.'

Poor Dylan, thought Cad. *He'll be a greasy sweat-soaked shambles by the start of the feasting.*

'I must leave soon, as I am to serve the high table,' Rhys announced, suddenly tall.

'Congratulations,' Cad replied with a wide, white smile. 'Don't tip food on my father, though,' she added with a wink.

Rhys beamed, revealing that gap-toothed grin she knew so well. A warmth flooded her chest, easing her broken ribcage for now.

Then, emerging in a clatter of **melodrama**[5], Mrs Hughes bustling through the door unannounced startled both friends into silence. Taken aback, Cad howled in pain, hoping Goodwife Hughes had not heard her utter the words 'my father'.

'Goodwife Hughes, please knock,' cried Cad.

'Oh, Master Cad, I am so sorry. In my **haste**[6] and excitement, I forgot, but I think you'll forgive me when you see the plate I have for you,' she said, chuckling.

---

1 **brewery** *(n)* a place where beer is made. *(s)* brewhouse.

2 **asunder** *(adv)* apart. *(s)* in two, into pieces. *(ant)* together.

3 **misery** *(n)* distress or discomfort. *(s)* unhappiness, suffering, anguish. *(ant)* cheer, happiness, joy.

4 **skivvy** *(v)* work doing tasks that are thought to be unimportant. *(s)* toil, slave, slog.

5 **melodrama** *(n)* excitement and drama. *(s)* commotion, fuss. *(ant)* calm.

6 **haste** *(n)* speed or urgency, hurry. *(s)* swiftness, briskness, rapidity. *(ant)* slowness.

Mrs Hughes, **adorned**[1] in **festival**[2] **finery**[3], showed no signs of **eavesdropping**[4], or the **disquiet**[5] over Hugh which had been **evident**[6] earlier. In fact, Cad observed that she was acting **positively**[7] giddy with joy.

'Oh, Goodwife Hughes, you treasure,' said Cad, doubting the woman had overheard her say 'father' and eyeing the delights on the tray.

'Well look at you, Rhys Price,' cooed Mrs Hughes, placing the tray on Cad's bed and shooing Fishy off it and onto Rhys's. '**Decked out**[8] like a little lord,' she added, admiring his new **doublet**[9], hose and feathered **velvet**[10] cap. 'Mind you don't go dropping food in their laps, though,' she warned with a tut. 'I know what a **butterfingers**[11] you can be.'

Rhys blushed, looking like a human **radish**[12]. Cad rolled her eyes, giving him a nod to escape while he could, and hoped he didn't have Slippy strapped to his waist for company. A snake appearing at a banquet would not **bode**[13] well for the serpent.

'Enjoy yourself, Rhys. Quaff some small beers to calm your nerves,' Cad said with a fake smile as he headed through the door, for that was not the real reason she wanted Rhys to drink beer. Cad feared someone may be poisoning the castle's central well and she wanted her friend to be safe. She'd agonised over telling the boys, but what if she were wrong? She would ruin her brother's first birthday celebrations, her father's plans and Rhys's golden opportunity to serve at the prince's table.

'Goodwife Hughes, make haste. Go! Join the feasting.' Cad gestured towards the door, wearing

---

1 **adorn** *(v)* make more attractive or beautiful. *(s)* decorate, embellish. *(ant)* strip.

2 **festival** *(n)* a day or period of celebration. *(s)* pageant, jamboree.

3 **finery** *(n)* fancy, expensive things. *(s)* splendour, glad rags. *(ant)* rags, scruffs.

4 **eavesdrop** *(v)* secretly listen in on a conversation. *(s)* earwig, snoop.

5 **disquiet** *(n)* a feeling of worry or unease. *(s)* anxiety, distress. *(ant)* contentment.

6 **evident** *(adj)* clearly understood. *(s)* obvious, apparent. *(ant)* unclear.

7 **positively** *(adv)* certainly the case *(s)* absolutely, extremely. *(ant)* doubtfully, dubiously.

8 **decked out** (phrase) (informal) dressed in a fancy way.

9 **doublet** *(n)* a short, close-fitting jacket, commonly worn by men in the Middle Ages.

10 **velvet** *(n)* fabric woven from silk, cotton or nylon with a dense, short pile on one side.

11 **butterfingers** *(n)* a clumsy person who drops things. *(s)* bungler, fumbler.

12 **radish** *(n)* a small red root that is edible.

13 **bode** *(v)* be a portent (sign) of a certain outcome. *(s)* portend, foretell.

a smile that belonged to a storybook prince. 'I will be more than **content**[1] here with Fishy. I have a chamber pot, **quill**[2] and ink. What more does a boy need?'

Cad let out an earthy laugh as Goodwife Hughes grinned at her, and looking as lovely as a full moon, chirped, 'If you are sure, Master Cad, then I will be on my way. And I will try to forget this darned sickness for a few hours,' she added, removing her **apron**[3] and crossing the room like a ship in full sail.

'Of course. Enjoy the evening,' Cad said, with a **polite**[4] nod. 'And thank you for your kindliness.'

Goodwife Hughes smiled, rubbed her hands together and headed for the door. Just about to leave, she stopped and turned.

'Oh, silly me, what a **scatterbrain**[5] I am,' she sang, her hands floating up into the air. 'In my merriment, I almost forgot. Physician Jordan is **splinting**[6] a lord's untimely leg injury, so he gave me your draught for this evening.'

Then Goodwife Hughes, admonishing herself with a series of tuts, placed a **vial**[7] of the pain-killing potion on the table beside Cad's bed, and with a swoosh of skirts and a cheery wave, left Cad to eat her supper with Fishy.

---

1 **content** *(adj)* peaceful and happy. *(s)* fulfilled, pleased, satisfied. *(ant)* dissatisfied.

2 **quill** *(n)* a pen made from the main wing or tail feathers of a large bird.

3 **apron** *(n)* a garment worn around one's midriff to protect one's clothing. *(s)* pinny, overall.

4 **polite** *(adj)* showing respectful and considerate behaviour. *(s)* civil, courteous. *(ant)* rude, churlish.

5 **scatterbrain** *(n)* a disorganised person. *(s)* birdbrain, featherbrain. *(ant)* organiser.

6 **splint** *(v)* secure an injured limb with something rigid (a splint). *(s)* brace.

7 **vial** *(n)* a small cylindrical glass container. *(s)* ampoule, phial.

CHAPTER SEVENTEEN

Spooky Stables

Cad's supper refused to go down, so she fed some to Fishy, wrapped the remainder in the linen cloth Mrs Hughes had served it in, then stowed it away in her tunic pocket. As Cad tucked it away, she remembered that Physician Jordan had instructed her to **dilute**[1] the potion's **potency**[2] by taking it with food.

Unable to eat, but with that in mind, Cad took care to swallow even less of the draught left by Goodwife Hughes. She must strike a delicate balance between quashing the **fiery**[3] pains that jabbed her ribs and maintaining her wits. If she swigged too much of the potion she would be rendered useless, slipping into a **stupor**[4] as she walked.

To mask the bitter taste, she pinched her nose, and downing one third, placed the vial under her pillow and checked her hairpin was concealed in the hem of her attire, along with the **contingency**[5] notes she'd penned earlier. Then she waited for the brew's **efficacy**[6] to **ooze**[7] through her veins, loosen her limbs and **extinguish**[8] the constant pain in her ribs. As if being

---

1 **dilute** *(v)* make weaker. *(s)* diminish, reduce. *(ant)* strengthen.

2 **potency** *(n)* the power of something to impress or influence. *(s)* strength, force. *(ant)* impotence.

3 **fiery** *(adj)* like fire. *(s)* raging, hot, burning, scorching. *(ant)* cold.

4 **stupor** *(n)* a state of near unconsciousness or unawareness. *(s)* daze, torpor, blankness. *(ant)* consciousness.

5 **contingency** *(n)* something that might be needed. *(s)* emergency. *(ant)* improbability.

6 **efficacy** *(n)* the effectiveness of something. *(s)* benefit, power, potency. *(ant)* ineffectiveness.

7 **ooze** *(v)* gently flow or seep. *(s)* bleed, creep, issue. *(ant)* gush, pour.

8 **extinguish** *(v)* put an end to. *(s)* stop, eradicate, destroy. *(ant)* begin, start.

submerged[1] into a warm bath of water, Cad **embraced**[2] the floating **sensation**[3] she'd expected and relaxed as the pain abated.

Her discomfort now relieved, Cad watched the sun set, the sky streaked a stunning shade of pink and purple. With one **shrill**[4] whistle she called May, who swooped in through the window. Cad fed her friend scraps of dried pork, ever grateful for the hawk's **loyalty**[5]. Then she checked the floor reeds for Slippy, whose absence proved that Rhys had strapped the snake to his belt and taken him to the feast.

Cad knew it was now or never and, armed with her hairpin, she hobbled across the room to leave, thoughts of what lay ahead tickling the edges of her mind, and knowing that her plan would only work if nobody knew that there was one.

'Stay, girl,' she ordered Fishy, using her most commanding tone.

With most guards **revelling**[6] in the great hall, Llywelyn would have doubly **secured**[7] the castle's main gates. Fishy could not stray from Catrin's grounds, so Cad **wedged**[8] a rock at the bottom of the door's **jamb**[9], leaving it **ajar**[10]. If Cad failed to return, and the feasting continued into the early hours, she'd ensured that Fishy could leave the room if need be.

Even with the pain-killing draught coursing through her veins, Cad's fingertips **tingled**[11] with nerves as she tiptoed away from her room amid the **aromas**[12] wafting from the kitchens, which unexpectedly turned her stomach. She entered the bailey, which was remarkably quiet save for the few guards dotted about, who would no doubt ignore a **wandering**[13] page on feast night. Like

---

1 **submerged** *(adj)* located below the surface of something. *(s)* immersed, plunged, sunken. *(ant)* surfaced.

2 **embrace** *(v)* accept happily. *(s)* welcome, receive, seize. *(ant)* reject.

3 **sensation** *(n)* a physical feeling or perception. *(s)* sense, impression, awareness.

4 **shrill** *(adj)* high-pitched in sound. *(s)* sharp, piercing. *(ant)* low, soft.

5 **loyalty** *(n)* the quality of giving constant support. *(s)* faithfulness, reliability. *(ant)* disloyalty.

6 **revel** *(v)* celebrate. *(s)* enjoy, make merry. *(ant)* mourn.

7 **secure** *(v)* fix, attach or fasten firmly. *(s)* lock, seal, close. *(ant)* open.

8 **wedge** *(v)* force into a tight space. *(s)* jam, shove, stuff.

9 **jamb** *(n)* a post at the side or surface of a doorway. *(s)* frame, pillar.

10 **ajar** *(adj)* slightly open. *(s)* cracked, unfastened. *(ant)* closed, shut.

11 **tingle** *(v)* experience a prickling sensation. *(s)* prickle.

12 **aroma** *(n)* a distinctive, typically pleasant smell. *(s)* scent. *(ant)* stench, stink, reek.

13 **wander** *(v)* move in an aimless or leisurely way. *(s)* amble, dawdle, potter. *(ant)* march, stride.

a lame dog she hobbled across the courtyard, which the grooms had thankfully cleared of **dung**[1] and **foul**[2] **fowl**[3] **droppings**[4]. She would visit Flash before **embarking**[5] on her mission to check the well for signs of poison. If Flash were still sick, Cad would know it on sight.

After what felt like miles, at the far end of the bailey, as Cad finally entered her favourite place, her nose twitched with delight, **tantalised**[6] by its **gloriously**[7] familiar **fragrance**[8]. Fresh **hay**[9] and straw, leather and saddle soap and the **indescribable**[10] smell of well-kept, beautifully groomed horses lifted her **spirits**[11]. **Dusk**[12] in the castle's vast stables was her favourite time, and she usually visited Flash every evening without fail. At this hour, as the day gasped its last breath, the horses were content: tired, groomed, fed and watered.

An eerie quiet hushed the stables. Most of the grooms feasted in the great hall, but those on watch tonight would **rotate**[13] duties and not **resent**[14] caring for the castle's treasured steeds, whom most adored. For without happy, healthy horses, a castle and its knights were **ineffectual**[15].

Cad clutched at her strapped-up side as she wandered to the far end of the stables where Flash slept next to Midnight, Dewi's destrier. For some strange reason, the pony had taken to the **massive**[16] warhorse, and they were stubborn stablemates, Flash whinnying up a storm and kicking her stall if a groom moved Midnight away from her. Yet Flash somehow knew if Midnight was saddled and out working, and as gentle as a lamb, would patiently wait for his

---

1 **dung** *(n)* animal poo. *(s)* muck, droppings, faeces, excrement.

2 **foul** *(adj)* offensive to one's senses. *(s)* disgusting, revolting. *(ant)* pleasant.

3 **fowl** *(n)* birds such as chickens, turkeys and ducks. *(s)* poultry.

4 **droppings** *(n)* the poo of certain animals. *(s)* faeces, excrement.

5 **embark** *(v)* begin or start. *(s)* commence, venture. *(ant)* cease, end.

6 **tantalise** *(v)* excite or tease the senses. *(s)* entice, tempt, draw. *(ant)* repel.

7 **gloriously** *(adv)* in a glorious (wonderful) way. *(s)* splendidly. *(ant)* plainly, dully.

8 **fragrance** *(n)* a pleasant smell. *(s)* perfume, bouquet, aroma. *(ant)* stench.

9 **hay** *(n)* dried grass used to feed animals such as horses and cows.

10 **indescribable** *(adj)* too extreme or unusual to describe. *(s)* intense, powerful. *(ant)* definable.

11 **spirits** *(n)* feelings and mood. *(s)* energy, enthusiasm, morale.

12 **dusk** *(n)* the time just before it goes dark at night. *(s)* twilight, sundown. *(ant)* dawn.

13 **rotate** *(v)* take turns. *(s)* alternate, switch, swap.

14 **resent** *(v)* feel bad about something or someone. *(s)* begrudge, dislike. *(ant)* like.

15 **ineffectual** *(adj)* not producing the desired outcome. *(s)* inefficient, ineffective. *(ant)* effective.

16 **massive** *(adj)* big and solid. *(s)* large, huge, enormous, great. *(ant)* small, tiny.

return. But if Midnight were stabled and not **adjacent**[1] to Flash, the grooms would get little rest until the two were **bedfellows**[2] again.

'Ellis, how is she?' Cad asked, startling the groom who was scrubbing away at leather **bridles**[3] with suds of saddle soap.

'Cad! My heart **nigh on**[4] stopped!' remarked Ellis Williams, who had almost **upended**[5] his water bucket in fright.

'I'm sorry to startle you,' Cad said. 'I didn't want to disturb the horses. They seem so content tonight.'

'We gave them extra feed to quieten them whilst the **majority**[6] of grooms feast. Most of them are already asleep on over-stuffed stomachs. Come, Flash is much improved.'

Cad followed Ellis to the far end of the stables. 'I'm surprised you're here. I was worried sick when you fell off Flash in the tilt yard. We all were.'

'Don't tell Physician Jordan I visited, please,' Cad asked with a beseeching look.

'I won't, but I don't want you ailing further.' Ellis regarded Cad, concern etched on his face.

'I'm not planning on jousting, just patting a horse's neck,' she replied, her voice light to hide the pain that pinched at her side.

When she reached the horse's stall, Flash sat there with her legs tucked beneath her.

'Flashy!' Cad cried. 'Stay, girl,' she urged, dropping to her knees in the straw by her pony's head and flinching silently at a stab of pain.

Flash whinnied, turning her face towards Cad and snorting hot breaths of delight at seeing her. The pony's neck shone, soft and sleek. Her nostrils **flared**[7] as she whinnied again, encouraging Cad to continue stroking. Cad studied the pony's **dusky**[8] eyes, round and gentle, **dressed**[9] with

---

1 **adjacent** *(adj)* next to or adjoining. *(s)* beside, neighbouring, alongside. *(ant)* distant from.

2 **bedfellow** *(n)* one that shares a bed or is closely connected. *(s)* friend, mate. *(ant)* foe.

3 **bridle** *(n)* the headgear used to direct a horse to which reins are attached to a bit.

4 **nigh on** *(adv)* almost. *(s)* nearly, about, just about, more or less.

5 **upend** *(v)* turn upside down. *(s)* overturn, flip. *(ant)* straighten.

6 **majority** *(adj)* the greater number of. *(s)* most. *(ant)* minority.

7 **flare** *(v)* spread or widen. *(s)* open, broaden, splay. *(ant)* contract.

8 **dusky** *(adj)* deep and darkish in colour. *(s)* shadowy, hazy. *(ant)* bright, clear, light.

9 **dress** *(v)* decorate. *(s)* adorn, beautify, enhance, *(ant)* strip.

long **sweeping**[1] lashes and **flecked**[2] with **tones**[3] of warm amber. Tears of joy pricked Cad's eyes: her pony was well.

Comforted, Cad turned to Ellis, who smiled gently at the **reunited**[4] friends.

'She's fine,' Ellis reassured her. 'She'll be back on her feet proper **afore**[5] you know it,' he chuckled, his eyes diamond-bright with love for his horses.

'She will.' Cad agreed with a broad grin, and welcoming a palpable sense of relief at his words.

'Where's Midnight?' asked Cad, glancing about, perplexed as she realised the destrier's stall stood empty.

'A fast messenger took him,' replied Ellis **nonchalantly**[6], 'or else Flash would kick up a stink if she thought he was stabled elsewhere.'

Cad **suppressed**[7] her surprise, simply saying, 'Gone? With whom?'

'I don't know his first name,' said Ellis, 'but he's that long-shanked son of **busybody**[8] Hughes.'

Cad's insides turned slushy, but she just lifted her chin, mirroring Ellis's nonchalance, yet feeling none of it. He'd clearly missed the shadow of alarm that had flitted across her face.

Why in heaven would Hugh take Midnight out on a feast **eve**[9]*, and with whose permission?*

In **turmoil**[10], Cad's mind whirled like an ocean storm, but she must focus on tonight's task before the potion wore off and the pain overwhelmed her once more. The mystery of Midnight must wait.

'Ellis, what do you think afflicted Flash so?' Cad asked, her voice flat.

'I'm not certain,' Ellis said, a **mystified**[11] look on his face. 'But with all this unseasonable

---

1 **sweeping** *(adj)* extending in a continuous curve (curved and long). *(s)* wide, full. *(ant)* narrow.

2 **flecked** *(adj)* marked with flecks of colour. *(s)* spotted, streaked. *(ant)* unmarked.

3 **tone** *(n)* the specific quality or brightness of a colour. *(s)* hue, depth.

4 **reunite** *(v)* come or get back together. *(s)* reconcile. *(ant)* separate.

5 **afore** *(prep)* before.

6 **nonchalantly** *(adv)* done in a nonchalant (relaxed) way. *(s)* casually. *(ant)* emotionally.

7 **suppress** *(v)* force something to stop or end. *(s)* repress, quell, quash. *(ant)* encourage.

8 **busybody** *(n)* a person who meddles in the affairs of others. *(s)* gossip, nosy parker.

9 **eve** *(n)* the day or period of time before an event occurs.

10 **turmoil** *(n)* a state of confusion, disturbance or uncertainty. *(s)* chaos, disorder. *(ant)* order.

11 **mystified** *(adj)* completely perplexed or bewildered. *(s)* bamboozled, stumped. *(ant)* enlightened.

weather, I think it could have been too much sun. She has a **fair**[1] **muzzle**[2] and feels the heat.'

Cad contemplated his answer, which was viable, but she'd trained with Flash in hotter weather. Not convinced, Cad asked in her **breezy**[3] voice, 'Is the water tank in the tilt yard filled from the well or the outside **spring**[4]?' Because Cad had never performed well duties, she was not entirely sure.

'It's brought in **pails**[5] from the central well,' said Ellis. ''Tis too far to pump from beyond the walls, and water cannot flow uphill,' he laughed. 'Though it is hardly noticeable, there is too much of an **incline**[6] from here to the list fields and that would mean pumping it across the bailey too. The grooms constantly complain about hauling buckets all the way from the well, but Sir Robert hasn't solved the "uphill problem" yet.'

'No doubt he will,' said Cad, nodding with **resignation**[7], because with rising trepidation, she now knew she must continue tonight's quest for answers. For any other person faced with Cad's **dilemma**[8], visiting a well would be **trifling**[9], but for a child previously rescued from the depths of one, it would be terrifying.

'I'd best return before Physician Jordan's magic potion wears off.' Cad pointed to her ribs with a grimace, still perturbed by Midnight's empty stall.

'I'll take care of Flashy,' reassured Ellis. 'Feasting and drinking don't interest me,' he said **earnestly**[10].

Cad trusted his **sincerity**[11], hearing the smile in his voice. Ellis cherished horses more than humans, for they didn't fail him as his parents had. He too was orphaned, abandoned like her, but he knew not why, nor did he know of Cad's secret, at least not yet.

---

1 **fair** *(adj)* light in colour. *(s)* pale. *(ant)* dark.

2 **muzzle** *(n)* the nose and mouth of an animal. *(s)* snout.

3 **breezy** *(adj)* appearing relaxed and cheery. *(s)* carefree, casual. *(ant)* serious.

4 **spring** *(n)* a place where water wells up from beneath the ground.

5 **pail** *(n)* a bucket.

6 **incline** *(n)* a slope. *(s)* gradient, ascent, rise. *(ant)* decline.

7 **resignation** *(n)* acceptance of something undesirable yet inevitable. *(s)* fortitude. *(ant)* defiance.

8 **dilemma** *(n)* a difficult situation where a decision must be made. *(s)* predicament, plight. *(ant)* breeze, cinch.

9 **trifling** *(adj)* unimportant. *(s)* trivial, easy, minor. *(ant)* important, difficult.

10 **earnestly** *(adv)* in an earnest (serious) manner. *(s)* sincerely, honestly. *(ant)* insincerely.

11 **sincerity** *(n)* honesty. *(s)* truthfulness, candour, integrity. *(ant)* insincerity.

As Cad made to leave for the well, several horses suddenly **shifted**[1], their hooves stamping their stalls. Cad stilled as they reared, kicking and whinnying in shrill tones of terror. Flash clattered to her feet, forcing Cad to step back awkwardly as, **reeling**[2] with surprise, poor Ellis bumped his face on the **manger**[3] he was filling with hay.

As her ribs howled with pain, but suppressing her cries, Cad calmed Flash, whose head had jerked upwards, the whites of her eyes rolling with terror. Ellis had already gone to check and **pacify**[4] the other horses, their hooves clattering in **unison**[5] as they pawed the stone and earth beneath their straw beds.

'Easy, girl,' cooed Cad, gently stroking the pony's white flash until her snorting and stamping stopped, and her breaths eased. Yet, all the while, Cad battled to control her own breathing, as her heart pumped fear through her veins.

'I don't know what spooked 'em,' said Ellis, returning and rubbing his already swelling nose. 'Maybe a fox **slunk**[6] in and back out, spooked one, and then they all **chorused**[7] in panic.'

'Maybe,' said Cad, her voice **quivering**[8] as she soothed a twitching Flash. 'Your nose, Ellis,' said Cad with concern, 'it's swelling like a plum.' **Sympathy**[9] softened her face.

'Had much worse,' said Ellis, waving a dismissive hand and giving a brave smile.

'Whatever it was woke most of 'em, but least they're settling now.' Ellis looked mightily relieved.

'Yes,' said Cad, calmly stroking Flash.

Cad's mind was elsewhere, and nothing about her felt calm, for she had seen exactly what had spooked the **sensitive**[10] steeds. While she was kneeling in the straw next to Flash, a shadowy

---

1 **shift** *(v)* move a short distance. *(s)* reposition. *(ant)* remain.

2 **reel** *(v)* feel bewildered and shocked. *(s)* spin, whirl. *(ant)* steady, stabilise.

3 **manger** *(n)* a trough from which animals feed. *(s)* feeder, crib, fodder rack.

4 **pacify** *(v)* calm the agitation, anger or excitement of. *(s)* soothe, appease. *(ant)* provoke.

5 **unison** *(adj)* all at the same time. *(s)* together, simultaneously. *(ant)* discord.

6 **slink** *(v)* move smoothly and quietly in a stealthy way (past tense: slunk). *(s)* slip, steal. *(ant)* stomp.

7 **chorus** *(v)* say or sing the same thing at the same time.

8 **quiver** *(v)* tremble or shake. *(s)* shiver, quaver, tremor. *(ant)* steady, still.

9 **sympathy** *(n)* feelings of sorrow and pity for the misfortunes of another. *(s)* empathy. *(ant)* callousness.

10 **sensitive** *(adj)* being quick to react to slight changes. *(s)* responsive. *(ant)* unresponsive.

figure had **glided**[1] past her, as if leaving Midnight's **vacant**[2] stall, and headed towards the exit at the back of the long stable block. From the horses' reactions, the figure was clearly **alien**[3] to them, its stance and smell unfamiliar. But what had turned Cad's blood cold was not the figure itself but its attire. The stranger **skulking**[4] about the stables just now had been cloaked in the same monk's **habit**[5] and **cowl**[6] as the person who, weeks back, had trapped Cad and her brother in the oubliette to be forgotten.

---

1 **glide** *(v)* move smoothly and continuously. *(s)* sail, float, drift. *(ant)* hurtle, careen.

2 **vacant** *(adj)* (of a place) not occupied. *(s)* deserted, empty, unoccupied. *(ant)* occupied.

3 **alien** *(adj)* unfamiliar. *(s)* unusual, strange. *(ant)* familiar, usual.

4 **skulk** *(v)* move furtively and stealthily, not wanting to be seen. *(s)* lurk, prowl, loiter. *(ant)* appear.

5 **habit** *(n)* a long, loose overgarment (clothing) worn by someone religious such as a monk or nun.

6 **cowl** *(n)* a large and loose hood, especially as part of a monk's habit.

CHAPTER EIGHTEEN

What's Your Poison?

Cad bade **farewell**[1] to Flash and Ellis. She beamed a wide smile, most of which was a lie, as she was still reeling at the sight of the ghoul-like person. Now more anxious than ever, she left the stables via the same back door as the silhouetted figure. It irked her to know that whoever skulked in that monk's habit would probably be long gone.

By chance, she'd seen the person's hands as they'd held the cowl around their face. They were not the same **slender**[2] fingers that had **slotted**[3] the **grate**[4] over her head all those weeks back. Was the potion fogging her mind, or was it the fear? Fear of the man she'd left for dead in the oubliette. Could it be him, Bryn's assailant, back again? Her mind whirled. The figure gliding from the stables had seemed different though, **fleet of foot**[5]. Cad shook her head, her confidence crashing along with her nerves.

Feeling light-headed, a shadow of pain crossing her face, Cad **shambled**[6] across the bailey towards the **robust**[7] wooden **shack**[8] which housed the castle's central well. The well, the jewel in

---

1 **farewell** *(n)* a parting wish for well-being. *(s)* goodbye. *(ant)* hello.

2 **slender** *(adj)* slim and graceful. *(s)* delicate. *(ant)* chubby, plump, fat.

3 **slot** *(v)* place an object into or over something. *(s)* slide, slip. *(ant)* remove.

4 **grate** *(n)* a screen or grating of metal bars or wires placed in front of something to allow ventilation or observation.

5 **fleet of foot** (phrase) be able to move fast. *(s)* quick, speedy, swift. *(ant)* slow.

6 **shamble** *(v)* move slowly with an awkward gait. *(s)* shuffle, dodder, lumber. *(ant)* bound.

7 **robust** *(adj)* strong. *(s)* tough, sturdy. *(ant)* weak, feeble.

8 **shack** *(n)* a roughly built hut or cabin. *(s)* shed.

Catrin's crown, was why Llywelyn's ancestors had built on this site in the Welsh mountains. It provided a natural **receptacle**[1] for the endless supply of fresh water which gushed down the hills. The mountains ensured an abundance of rain.

Tight with unease, her heart **clenched**[2] as she shuffled along, gently shooing chickens from her path, and feeling floaty despite imbibing just a little of the potion.

Halfway across the yard, Cad nodded at a stockily built man who stood guard at the entrance to the empty keep. The entire court should now be assembled in the hall for tonight's celebrations. The **sentry**[3] lifted his chin and raised a wobbly cup, his beard frothy, his eyes **merry**[4] with beer.

*Not much use you'd be in a **scuffle**[5]*, thought Cad, her eyes darting **hither and thither**[6] for lurking hooded figures. Now she'd seen those differing hands, she was sure several **would-be**[7] monks existed at Catrin Castle, none of which were servants of God.

As she continued towards the well, shaking her head to clear it, two pages exited the keep and **doffed**[8] their caps at the guard. Cad recognised them and quickly turned. To avoid them, she dropped onto one knee, hiding her face and fiddling with her boot lest they see her. Goodwife Hughes would be at Cad's door and clucking like a panicked goose if she thought Cad was out of bed, Physician Jordan being **towed**[9] in her **wake**[10].

Come on! she thought, wishing they would hurry past her. Before she stood, she **scrabbled**[11] in the dirt, fussing with her boot and pocketing a couple of **decent**[12]-sized stones just in case she needed more weapons. Then, with the help of a creamy full moon, she watched as the pages headed towards the great hall to join the other revellers. Struck by pangs of sorrow, she pictured

---

1 **receptacle** *(n)* a hollow object for containing something. *(s)* holder, container, vessel.

2 **clench** *(v)* contract or tighten. *(s)* constrict, tense. *(ant)* relax.

3 **sentry** *(n)* a soldier placed to guard. *(s)* lookout, sentinel, patrol, watchman.

4 **merry** *(adj)* slightly drunk. *(s)* tipsy, squiffy. *(ant)* sober.

5 **scuffle** *(n)* a short fight. *(s)* tussle, rumpus, disturbance, scrap.

6 **hither and thither** *(adv)* in various directions. *(s)* all around, round about.

7 **would-be** *(adj)* desiring to be a specific person. *(s)* potential, aspiring.

8 **doff** *(v)* raise. *(s)* remove, lift. *(ant)* don.

9 **tow** *(v)* pull along. *(s)* drag, haul, lug.

10 **in the wake of** (phrase) following someone or something as a consequence of.

11 **scrabble** *(v)* scratch around trying to hold something. *(s)* grope, scramble.

12 **decent** *(adj)* of a good standard. *(s)* satisfactory, reasonable. *(ant)* unsatisfactory.

her father celebrating John's first birthday without her and her mother, Siân. Cad **longed**[1] to join the festivities with her friends, but she had only this one opportunity to investigate the well without causing her father humiliation. If her hunch proved to be wrong, he would never need to know her thoughts. **Fortuitously**[2], most folks would be supping sweet **meads**[3], beers and wines, because if Cad's suspicions proved true, the water drinkers, by dawn, would be **stricken**[4] by the sickness sweeping through Catrin Castle.

As she made to continue, Cad **surveyed**[5] her locale. Even with the help of the glorious moon, the final breaths of dusk shrouded the bailey, its shadowy **recesses**[6] illuminated by the flickering flames of burning torches. She suspected that ghoulish figure spied from a camouflaged corner. Dare she check the well now? What if that fiend pushed her down its gaping shaft? Cad shuddered at the thought, **tentacles**[7] of **nausea**[8] writhing in her guts.

She had no visual memories of her babyhood rescue, yet some part of that hideous experience had **branded**[9] itself into her mind, leaving black scars of terror. Her fear of confined spaces, especially after her ordeal in the oubliette, threatened her knighthood with failure. To be **initiated**[10] a Knight Hawk and bestowed with Instinctive powers by Llywelyn and the Gwalch Gem, one must be **noble**[11], and afraid of nothing or no one. The former, Cad could master – the latter, she was unsure, for being trapped in the oubliette had **dredged**[12] up feelings she'd since found impossible to manage – feelings she'd shared with no one, not even Dylan.

Now almost there, but stumbling a little, Cad blinked hard against the fading light and packed

---

1 **long** *(v)* to have great want. *(s)* yearn, ache, desire. *(ant)* hate, despise.

2 **fortuitously** *(adv)* in a fortuitous (by chance) way. *(s)* luckily, serendipitously. *(ant)* intentionally.

3 **mead** *(n)* an alcoholic drink made from fermented honey and water.

4 **stricken** *(adj)* gravely affected by a disagreeable feeling or unwanted condition. *(s)* afflicted, troubled. *(ant)* unaffected.

5 **survey** *(v)* look closely at or examine. *(s)* study, inspect, assess, evaluate. *(ant)* overlook.

6 **recess** *(n)* a small corner or hollow place, usually in a wall. *(s)* alcove, bay, niche. *(ant)* protrusion.

7 **tentacle** *(n)* a long, thin part of an animal used for grasping and feeling. *(s)* appendage, feeler.

8 **nausea** *(n)* a feeling of sickness. *(s)* queasiness, biliousness. *(ant)* wellness.

9 **brand** *(v)* mark indelibly (in a permanent way). *(s)* stamp, imprint, burn, scar.

10 **initiate** *(v)* admit someone into a group by means of a ritual. *(s)* inaugurate.

11 **noble** *(adj)* having high morals and good personal qualities. *(s)* honourable, virtuous. *(ant)* ignoble.

12 **dredge** *(v)* bring up something (often unwelcome). *(s)* raise, surface. *(ant)* bury, sink.

her nightmares away. Even though she expelled the **loathsome**[1] visions, her head swam and her skin prickled with sweat.

'Lord save us all!' she suddenly cried, spinning in a circle and almost upending over a stray goose, her heart sprinting at its **belligerent**[2] honks and hisses. Just about gathering her jangling nerves, and nearing the well, she blinked again, the darkening surroundings **playing havoc**[3] and blurring her vision. She paused, her eyes scouring the bailey's darkest corners for **incongruous**[4] silhouettes of monks. Yet, she saw only guards playing chess, dogs missing out on the feast's various titbits, and the castle's wandering fowl, who were now, once more, fouling the bailey.

Cad knew she was not only pausing to check her surroundings but to procrastinate over the **inevitable**[5]: she must enter the wooden shack for the very first time and inspect the castle's central well. Her parched mouth **ironically**[6] **yearned**[7] for the cooling water on the other side of that door. She was so thirsty now, her swallowing had become lumpy; her mouth was gritty and her stomach turned like a **butter churn**[8].

Every part of Cad longed to **retreat**[9] and flee. In a breath, she could be back in her room with Fishy and both could be curled up in her bed. Torn, she pictured her father and friends who might be sick by morning. She thought of Rhys's vile vomit **phobia**[10]. When **bilious**[11] in the past, he'd **spiralled**[12] into **crippling**[13] **bouts**[14] of **melancholy**[15].

If she were right about the well being poisoned, she could stop all this from happening now.

---

1 **loathsome** *(adj)* causing disgust or hatred. *(s)* detestable, abhorrent, repulsive. *(ant)* lovable, delightful.

2 **belligerent** *(adj)* aggressive and hostile. *(s)* threatening, confrontational. *(ant)* peaceful, friendly.

3 **playing havoc** (phrase) causing a large problem or destruction.

4 **incongruous** *(adj)* unusual or out of keeping in some way. *(s)* strange, odd. *(ant)* appropriate.

5 **inevitable** *(adj)* certain to happen. *(s)* inescapable, unpreventable. *(ant)* avoidable, uncertain.

6 **ironically** *(adv)* in a ironic (paradoxical, unexpected or coincidental) way. *(s)* paradoxically.

7 **yearn** *(v)* really want something. *(s)* long, crave. *(ant)* reject.

8 **butter churn** *(n)* a device used to make cream into butter by churning (turning).

9 **retreat** *(v)* withdraw. *(s)* retire, flee, escape. *(ant)* advance.

10 **phobia** *(n)* an extreme or illogical fear of something. *(s)* loathing, dread, aversion. *(ant)* liking, comfort.

11 **bilious** *(adj)* affected with vomiting. *(s)* nauseous, sick. *(ant)* healthy.

12 **spiral** *(v)* fall continuously. *(s)* plummet, plunge, descend. *(ant)* rise, ascend.

13 **cripple** *(v)* cause to become unable to move properly. *(s)* immobilise, paralyse.

14 **bout** *(n)* an attack of illness. *(s)* period, spell.

15 **melancholy** *(n)* sadness. *(s)* sorrow, woe, desolation, gloom. *(ant)* happiness.

But with fear fogging her mind and wobbling legs threatening to buckle, Cad now wished with all her heart that she'd shared her plan and had brought Dylan along with her. Almost **rigid**[1] with a fear she'd not felt before, she battled to clear the muddled daze in her head.

Perhaps this confusion is the price I must pay for a lack of pain? she thought, realising she was without agony for the first time since falling from Flash. But her words struck her like a bad note played in a sweet tune.

Strange to be without ***affliction***[2] *when I swigged less potion than usual. Perhaps I'm healing swiftly?* she thought, trying to reassure herself but feeling blearier with each heavy step she took.

As Cad reached the wooden **cabin**[3], she pinched her nose with **repulsion**[4]. She'd usually find the roasting and baking smells now filling the entire bailey **heavenly**[5], but tonight they turned her stomach. Then without warning and an unexpected retch, Cad vomited where she stood at the well's entrance. Taken aback, she grasped her stomach, coughing up differing variations of foul.

What in heaven! she thought, with her throat on fire and her mouth **sour**[6] as she anticipated a second wave, but none came. *Do I have the sickness?*

As she battled to her senses, she turned to push open the shack's door, when a hand the size of a **shovel**[7] grasped her shoulder in a vice-like grip. Cad froze, her breathing **ceased**[8], and her heart pounded. **Stock-still**[9], she stared at the wooden cabin like a trapped rabbit, her head and stomach whirling in unison as she waited for whatever came next.

'What ails you, young page?' slurred a **gravelly**[10] voice as the heavy hand left her shoulder.

Cad dared not move lest she throw up over whoever spoke.

---

1 **rigid** *(adj)* stiff and unmoving. *(s)* fixed, set. *(ant)* floppy, flexible.

2 **affliction** *(n)* a cause of harm or pain. *(s)* complaint, trouble. *(ant)* wellness, contentment.

3 **cabin** *(n)* a small (usually wooden) hut. *(s)* shed, shack.

4 **repulsion** *(n)* disgust. *(s)* revulsion, loathing. *(ant)* delight.

5 **heavenly** *(adj)* very pleasing. *(s)* glorious, wonderful. *(ant)* dreadful.

6 **sour** *(adj)* possessing a taste like vinegar or lemon. *(s)* acid, bitter, tart. *(ant)* sweet.

7 **shovel** *(n)* a spade for shovelling or digging.

8 **cease** *(v)* stop, end or finish. *(s)* halt, quit, discontinue. *(ant)* start, continue.

9 **stock-still** *(adj)* without motion. *(s)* immobile, unmoving. *(ant)* mobile, moving.

10 **gravelly** *(adj)* deep and rough in sound. *(s)* husky, gruff, raspy. *(ant)* soft, velvety.

'Too much **ale**[1] at the feast?' it continued.

As she fought down nausea, Cad turned to face the man. She lifted her head, forcing a half-smile. Her eyes reached his, and to her great surprise, an overwhelming relief hit her when she realised it was the guard from the keep. Thank goodness he was friendly and thought her **drunk**[2].

'That would be so, sir,' she slurred back, as her voice genuinely **wavered**[3] with relief.

The guard took little notice of her. He carelessly kicked dirt and grit over the spew, saying, 'Get on to bed with you and your **skinful**[4]. Go sleep it off.'

'I will, but first I need water,' Cad lied, as nausea gripped her again.

Just before the vomit reached her mouth, she dived **headlong**[5] into the well shack, kicking the door closed behind her.

As she lay **sprawled**[6] on the floor, coughing and panting, she **willed**[7] the guard to return to his chess, and that she might get to her feet without spewing again.

---

1 **ale** *(n)* a type of beer.

2 **drunk** *(adj)* the state when a person has consumed too much alcohol. *(s)* intoxicated. *(ant)* sober.

3 **waver** *(v)* become weaker. *(s)* falter, wobble. *(ant)* strengthen.

4 **skinful** *(n)* (informal) sufficient alcohol to make one drunk. *(s)* bellyful.

5 **headlong** *(adv)* head first. *(s)* head foremost. *(ant)* feet first.

6 **sprawl** *(v)* fall, sit or lie with one's arms and legs spread awkwardly. *(s)* stretch, flop, loll.

7 **will** *(v)* mentally hope for something to happen or for someone to do something.

CHAPTER NINETEEN

Into the Void

Inside the well's cabin, Cad rolled onto her side, avoiding the pool of sick, stunned that her **lunge**[1] through the door had been painless. Without Physician Jordan's potion, she would be **bedridden**[2], but landing on broken ribs and feeling little pain, seemed **peculiar**[3] when she'd swallowed less than the **prescribed**[4] dose.

To help clear her **befuddled**[5] mind, which whirled like a leaf in a gale, she thought for a moment, picturing exactly how much of the medicine she had quaffed. Confident of her **consumed**[6] dosage, dread and realisation hit her like a club to the head. Physician Jordan had not **administered**[7] tonight's draught; Goodwife Hughes had, and Cad had felt most odd ever since. Water had not sickened Cad, but perhaps the potion had?

Now **buttressed**[8] against the shack's sides for support, Cad hauled herself up, her head rushing, her stomach **waltzing**[9]. Her vomiting may well have saved her mission here, because

---

1 **lunge** *(n)* a forward thrust of the body. *(s)* dive, dash, leap, charge, bound.
2 **bedridden** *(adj)* in bed due to sickness or injury. *(s)* incapacitated, immobile. *(ant)* mobile.
3 **peculiar** *(adj)* different from normal or usual. *(s)* bizarre, uncanny, queer, abnormal. *(ant)* normal.
4 **prescribe** *(v)* (of medicine) advise and authorise the use and dose of.
5 **befuddled** *(adj)* unable to think clearly. *(s)* confused, perplexed, baffled. *(ant)* clear.
6 **consume** *(v)* eat or drink. *(s)* ingest, swallow, imbibe.
7 **administer** *(v)* dispense (give out) or apply. *(s)* deliver, distribute. *(ant)* withhold, deny.
8 **buttressed** *(adj)* placed for support. *(s)* braced, bolstered, propped.
9 **waltz** *(v)* dance a waltz. *(s)* swirl, whirl.

had she not thrown up the brew, she suspected she'd be flat out by now. As that thought settled like a boulder, a **bolt**[1] of terror surged. If she'd not vomited, thus allowing the potion's dose to run its course, would she still be here? Had someone tried to kill her? Surely not Goodwife Hughes?

Not wanting to believe that **preposterous**[2] **notion**[3], yet **grappling**[4] with the thought of it, Cad **tottered**[5] to her feet, her eyes scouring the cramped space, dampness **pervading**[6] its air.

Grateful for some light, she saw a that a single **lantern**[7] lit the well's windowless **interior**[8].

Folks would normally be queueing for evening supplies, but tonight all were still feasting in the hall. Cad suspected that if someone had **sabotaged**[9] the well's water, then it was somehow being deliberately directed, or individual jugs were being targeted, for if not, why was the entire castle not stricken? If she were right, who would the **saboteur**[10] target next? Cad prayed that her father was drinking wine over water tonight, for she suspected that whoever had polluted the well, intended tonight's mass revellers the utmost harm.

Her head now throbbed along to the beat of her heart, and horrified that someone may have poisoned her, Cad paused for thought, her mind still reeling from the effect of the draught's **overdose**[11]. Certain she didn't have the castle's sickness, she suspected the potion she'd swallowed tonight was of a much stronger potency than her previous doses.

Feeling like one foot was nailed to the floor, she braced herself for the task ahead, her vision blurring as the well **shimmered**[12] before her. She shook her head, trying to clear the **haze**[13], but still the well shifted before her eyes. As she stepped towards the circular wall of built-up stones

---

1 **bolt** *(n)* a shock. *(s)* surge, flash, dart.

2 **preposterous** *(adj)* utterly nonsensical. *(s)* stupid, absurd, ludicrous. *(ant)* sensible, reasonable.

3 **notion** *(n)* an idea or something imagined. *(s)* thought, concept.

4 **grapple** *(v)* engage in a struggle. *(s)* wrestle, fight, battle. *(ant)* surrender.

5 **totter** *(v)* move in a feeble or unsteady way. *(s)* wobble, stagger, teeter. *(ant)* balance, stabilise.

6 **pervade** *(v)* spread throughout, be present and apparent. *(s)* penetrate, encompass. *(ant)* evacuate.

7 **lantern** *(n)* a portable (moveable) lamp with a handle. *(s)* light.

8 **interior** *(n)* the inner part of something. *(s)* inside. *(ant)* exterior, outside.

9 **sabotage** *(v)* deliberately damage something. *(s)* wreck, spoil, ruin. *(ant)* aid.

10 **saboteur** *(n)* someone engaged in sabotage (the spoiling of things). *(s)* attacker, foe. *(ant)* innocent.

11 **overdose** *(n)* too much of a dangerous substance or drug.

12 **shimmer** *(v)* shine with a wavering light. *(s)* glisten, glint, dance. *(ant)* dull.

13 **haze** *(n)* mental confusion. *(s)* daze, blur. *(ant)* clarity.

that housed the deep shaft, Cad contemplated her state. The potion had **ultimately**[1] killed her pain yet could have potentially killed her. Praise be she'd expelled most of it when she'd vomited. Still, she worried how much remained in her **system**[2] and what its **consequences**[3] might be.

Maybe I should find Dylan or Rhys, she thought, knowing it was madness to investigate the well alone, and in her condition. However, her brother's birthday celebrations stopped her.

What if I'm wrong about the well and I spoil the feasting? I cannot risk that and ruin my father's attempts to find some joy for himself and Catrin's folks.

So instead, resetting her shoulders, she shuffled to the well, and putting one hand on top of the stones, and then one foot on the base, drew a reluctant breath, and climbed onto its surrounding wall. It was not overly high, and she easily pulled herself up on to it and sat on the edge, facing outwards.

She would inspect the bucket first. To face the **plunging**[4] well head on would be tricky for her, and steeling herself to turn around to face it, Cad sucked in long, steady breaths, trying desperately to calm her sprinting heart. The gentle slosh of the well's water swished in rhythm to the waves sickening her stomach, which threatened to hurl again at any moment.

Now Cad! she told herself, grasping the rectangular wooden frame which held the well's pail in place. She **shimmied**[5] around on her bottom, lifting her legs over so they now dangled inside the well's circular wall. Thankful to be without pain, she fought to shake her fuzzy head and swirling guts. But once she was in the perfect position to begin, she didn't budge; she couldn't move, frozen to the spot.

I can't do this.

Torn, Cad gazed ahead, too afraid to lower her eyes for fear of her reaction. Her legs lost their strength. Unable to move, she sat, rooted like this before finally glancing down the **abyss**[6] in front of her. She must act now, or return to her room. She thought of her father, the castle folks and baby John; innocent Rhys, terrified of getting sick.

---

1 **ultimately** *(adv)* in the end. *(s)* eventually, when all is said and done.

2 **system** *(n)* our body as a whole. *(s)* make up.

3 **consequence** *(n)* a result or effect. *(s)* outcome, upshot, repercussion. *(ant)* cause.

4 **plunging** *(adj)* something falling steeply. *(s)* steep, plummeting, descending. *(ant)* rising.

5 **shimmy** *(v)* shake or sway. *(s)* slide, glide.

6 **abyss** *(n)* a deep hole or chasm. *(s)* depth, void.

With every part of her longing to leave, she inched forward and inspected the underside of the pail, which dangled from the heavy rope. It looked normal: **innocuous**[1], nothing **untoward**[2], just wood and metal strips holding it together, its outer edges glistening and slippery from months of hauling water for the castle's inhabitants. She checked the rope: again, nothing strange, just a slimy, wet cable.

Cad knew she must **persist**[3], though every part of her yearned to flee, so leaning forward, she **peeked**[4] into the void. As a waft of **dank**[5] air hit her nostrils, her queasy stomach lurched again. Now her mind **tortured**[6] her with images of Llywelyn rescuing her, **heaving**[7] her from that well, Owain at his side. But she knew her memories to be false, for no one remembered babyhood, yet the **vivid**[8] images plaguing her now seemed so present she felt she could reach out and touch them.

Blood-curdling[9] screams filled her head. Visions of people fleeing burning huts, their hair and clothes **ablaze**[10], horrified her. The stench was so **pungent**[11], so **grim**[12], she rubbed her nose on her sleeve, closing her eyes, but still the images persisted. Hideous memories of war, her village **razed**[13] to the ground. But she had no memories. These were visions, images, her imagination running wild, inventing its own stories. Then Physician Jordan's words popped into her flailing mind. 'Drink too much, and you'll see demons and horned devils.'

It's the potion. It's the potion, Cad told herself, desperately trying to banish the images blighting

---

1 **innocuous** *(adj)* not offensive or harmful. *(s)* harmless, innocent, safe. *(ant)* harmful.

2 **untoward** *(adj)* unanticipated, inappropriate or inconvenient. *(s)* troublesome, problematic. *(ant)* welcome.

3 **persist** *(v)* continue stubbornly or repeat insistently. *(s)* carry on, push, persevere. *(ant)* stop, yield.

4 peek *(v)* take a quick or secretive look. *(s)* peep, glance, glimpse. *(ant)* stare, gaze.

5 **dank** *(adj)* cold and damp. *(s)* musty, unaired, fusty. *(ant)* warm, dry.

6 **torture** *(v)* to inflict pain or suffering. *(s)* punish, torment. *(ant)* relieve.

7 **heave** *(v)* lift with great effort. *(s)* haul, pull, raise. *(ant)* push.

8 **vivid** *(adj)* powerful or strong. *(s)* graphic, lifelike. *(ant)* vague, weak.

9 **blood-curdling** *(adj)* expressing or causing terror. *(s)* frightening, terrifying. *(ant)* comforting.

10 **ablaze** *(adj)* on fire. *(s)* aflame, burning, blazing. *(ant)* extinguished.

11 **pungent** *(adj)* strong and sharp in smell. *(s)* powerful, pervasive, overpowering. *(ant)* bland, plain.

12 **grim** *(adj)* horrid. *(s)* depressing, wretched. *(ant)* pleasant, amiable.

13 **raze** *(v)* destroy completely. *(s)* demolish, ruin, wreck. *(ant)* build, create.

her mind, for these were her demons and devils: her **origins**[1], her rescue, her **adoption**[2], now dredged up by the concoction coursing through her veins and **warping**[3] her **sanity**[4]. Deeply buried scars re-surfaced – the wounds of two lost mothers tangled amongst the thoughts of losing her father, were unbearable.

'Cad! Control yourself!' she cried, clutching her head and shaking it.

Almost losing her balance, the shock of doing so wrenched her back to reality as she wobbled on the wall's narrow rim. With her body now sweat-soaked, and her limbs light with a floating sensation, Cad ran her hands beneath the well's stone **rim**[5], but felt nothing unusual. Images **bombarded**[6] her mind. There were no obvious signs of poison or anything **dispensing**[7] it. No signs of foul play. She found nothing but a **rickety**[8] wooden ladder attached to the inside of the well.

Cad's mind whirled like a battered **quintain**[9], **addled**[10] by the **chemicals**[11] rushing through her brain.

She eyed the ladder; she could do it.

I cannot return now. I must do this alone.

Yet she feared her judgement to be poor.

Can I think straight with my mind so ***sullied***[12] *by the potion?*

Yet she told herself, as **ridiculous**[13] as it seemed, that she must dig deep and **grasp the nettle**[14]

---

1 **origin** *(n)* someone's background or beginnings. *(s)* heritage, birth, ancestry. *(ant)* ending.

2 **adoption** *(n)* the act of taking another's child to bring up as one's own.

3 **warp** *(v)* change. *(s)* distort, corrupt, colour. *(ant)* improve.

4 **sanity** *(n)* the ability to behave and think rationally. *(s)* mental health. *(ant)* insanity.

5 **rim** *(n)* the upper or outer edge of something. *(s)* lip, edge.

6 **bombard** *(v)* subject to something continuously. *(s)* inundate, swamp, flood, deluge.

7 **dispense** *(v)* distribute or provide. *(s)* supply. *(ant)* collect.

8 **rickety** *(adj)* likely to collapse, poorly manufactured. *(s)* wobbly, unstable. *(ant)* reliable.

9 **quintain** *(n)* a target on a post used for lance game training, typically one that swings and hits an unsuccessful tilter.

10 **addle** *(v)* make someone unable to think properly. *(s)* confuse, muddle, stupefy, daze.

11 **chemical** *(n)* a compound or substance, often artificially prepared.

12 **sully** *(v)* spoil or pollute. *(s)* contaminate, taint, mar. *(ant)* purify.

13 **ridiculous** *(adj)* something deemed to be silly. *(s)* absurd, laughable. *(ant)* sensible.

14 **grasp the nettle** (phrase) bravely do something difficult.

as **befits**[1] a Knight Hawk and **descend**[2] that ladder to inspect for any signs of villainy. Her head swam like the water in the well beneath her, the visions she saw **rampaging**[3] and crushing her **resolve**[4]. But grasp her **grit**[5] and **fortitude**[6] she did. For suddenly feeling superhuman, Cad cast aside her fears and banished her **woes**[7]; she was a Knight Hawk, capable of anything. Cad would save Catrin Castle from its saboteur. She was **invincible**[8].

Without wanting to lose this **empowering**[9] strength she embraced the **mushrooming**[10] confidence and pressed her hands against the stone. Then she wriggled onto her belly, and clutching the top of the wall with her fingers, placed one foot on the ladder's first **rung**[11] and began her **descent**[12] into darkness.

Whether it was the potion, the **elation**[13], or the fear that caused Cad's **demise**[14], she would never know. But as she took a step down the ladder, followed by another and another, her breathing became **ragged**[15], and her heart beat so hard, she coughed. A ringing sound roared in her ears, her grip weakened and her fingers released their hold on the wooden ladder. Then, her vision blacked.

Oblivious, Cad fell backwards, plummeting painlessly through the dank dark air, into the watery depths of Catrin Castle's well.

---

1 **befit** *(v)* to be appropriate for. *(s)* in keeping with. *(ant)* out of keeping with.

2 **descend** *(v)* move or fall downwards. *(s)* go down. *(ant)* ascend, climb.

3 **rampage** *(v)* rush wildly. *(s)* storm, charge, tear, riot. *(ant)* saunter.

4 **resolve** *(n)* firm determination. *(s)* steadfastness, willpower. *(ant)* indecision.

5 **grit** *(n)* strength of character. *(s)* courage, resolve, mettle. *(ant)* weakness.

6 **fortitude** *(n)* courage (bravery) when faced with difficulty. *(s)* mettle, nerve, pluck, valour. *(ant)* weakness.

7 **woe** *(n)* great distress, misery or sorrow. *(s)* anguish, despair, gloom. *(ant)* happiness, joy.

8 **invincible** *(adj)* too powerful to be overcome by anything. *(s)* unbeatable, indestructible. *(ant)* vulnerable.

9 **empower** *(v)* make stronger and more confident. *(s)* enable. authorise. *(ant)* deny.

10 **mushroom** *(v)* increase rapidly. *(s)* burgeon, spread, grow. *(ant)* diminish, shrink.

11 **rung** *(n)* a horizontal support on a ladder for someone's foot.

12 **descent** *(n)* an act of moving downwards. *(s)* climb down, drop. *(ant)* ascent, climb.

13 **elation** *(n)* great joy. *(s)* happiness, exhilaration, euphoria. *(ant)* misery.

14 **demise** *(n)* downfall or fate (sometimes death). *(s)* collapse, failure. *(ant)* success.

15 **ragged** *(adj)* (of sound) uncontrolled. *(s)* uneven, irregular. *(ant)* regular, controlled.

CHAPTER TWENTY

Treading Water

Perhaps it was Cad's unconscious state when **colliding**[1] with the water that saved her. Perhaps it was hitting its depths feet first. She would never know, but when she crashed into its surface, **subsequently**[2] sinking beneath it, the impact and **iciness**[3] of the water roused her at such speed, she had no idea where she was. But in a cruel instant, the memories returned as she frantically kicked her legs and grasped the well's side in the hope of finding **purchase**[4].

She'd either fainted from fear, or the potion's effects, and to her horror, she realised she was at the bottom of the well. Cad wasn't an **elegant**[5] swimmer, but splashing in the moat and surrounding rivers seeing the dogs swim as if born to it, she'd learned to paddle, and now managed to stay afloat.

As her eyes adjusted to the darkness, something brushed her face. With a squeal and a flailing hand, she knocked it away, **thrashing**[6] her legs as she peered up towards the pinprick of light which indicated the well's distant opening. How far she'd plunged, and how she'd not cracked her skull when falling was unfathomable, but she was alive, and beyond her ribs, nothing more

---

1 **collide** *(v)* come into contact with (usually forcefully). *(s)* bump, crash, smash. *(ant)* avoid, bypass.

2 **subsequently** *(adv)* after something has happened. *(s)* then, thereafter. *(ant)* previously.

3 **iciness** *(n)* being extremely cold. *(s)* coldness, chilliness. *(ant)* heat, warmth.

4 **purchase** *(n)* a firm contact or grip. *(s)* hold, toehold. *(ant)* release.

5 **elegant** *(adj)* stylish in manner *(s)* graceful, refined. *(ant)* inelegant.

6 **thrash** *(v)* move in a violent manner. *(s)* thresh, jerk, kick. *(ant)* still.

seemed broken. Her legs and arms worked painlessly, but she was sure that would change once the potion's effects wore off.

With a heaving cough and retching up water, Cad swirled her legs like those of the frogs she'd seen in pools, and fumbled her way around the circular well. Yet darkness shrouded all, even the slimy stone walls, as she grappled to locate the wooden ladder and climb out to safety.

'Arghh!' Cad shrieked, batting away something which poked at her face again, and with another spluttering squeal, splashed it away further. Thankfully, like before, it felt like a piece of wood floating atop the surface. She continued circling the well, **treading water**[1] and scrabbling for the ladder. But on her second **circuit**[2], a chilling terror struck her; it clutched her chest, spreading like poison to her limbs. With a hideous sense of dread, she **accelerated**[3] her kicks and checked the well once more, **swatting**[4] away **debris**[5] from its surface. Horrid realisation shot through her. Like a bear in a trap, she howled, **inhaling**[6] water, **rasping**[7] and choking as she desperately kicked to keep afloat, her arms flailing as she heaved to clear her lungs.

'No! No! No!' she yelled, realising that the objects she batted away from her face, the wood floating atop the water, were **fragments**[8] of the ladder that had broken away from the wall as she'd fallen. There was no way out. She was trapped at the bottom of a freezing well with scant chance of anyone coming until morning, by when she feared it would be too late.

Cad now knew she had never before felt true fear: a consuming terror, which would have **paralysed**[9] her had she not been forced to move her arms and legs to avoid sinking. The torture **constricting**[10] her chest was not physical pain but one of **raw**[11] emotion. Her heart shrank at the thought of not seeing her father again and him never knowing why she was found in the castle's

---

1 **tread water** *(v)* maintain an upright position in water by swirling the hands and feet.

2 **circuit** *(n)* a roughly circular line going from start to finish of something. *(s)* lap, loop.

3 **accelerate** *(v)* increase speed. *(s)* quicken, hasten. *(ant)* decelerate, slow.

4 **swat** *(v)* hit with a blow from a flat object. *(s)* swipe, slap. knock.

5 **debris** *(n)* the remains of anything broken down or destroyed. *(s)* scrap, wreckage.

6 **inhale** *(v)* breathe in. *(s)* suck in, gasp. *(ant)* exhale, breathe out.

7 **rasp** *(v)* make a harsh sound. *(s)* croak, grate. *(ant)* soothe.

8 **fragment** *(n)* a part broken or detached from a whole. *(s)* piece, scrap, portion, bit. *(ant)* whole.

9 **paralyse** *(v)* cause to become unable to act or function properly. *(s)* disable, incapacitate. *(ant)* mobilise.

10 **constrict** *(v)* make narrower. *(s)* tighten, compress, contract, choke. *(ant)* dilate, expand.

11 **raw** *(adj)* (of a feeling or quality) strong, undiluted. *(s)* intense, powerful, vehement, acute. *(ant)* adulterated.

well on her brother's first birthday. Her poor father, alone and tormented by her mysterious drowning, not knowing if foul play was to blame. She had failed him. No, far worse, she had afflicted him with a misery that he'd never shake. The agony now stabbing her chest far surpassed that of broken ribs, for this torment, the grief of a heart torn in two, could not be **cured**[1] by lotions and potions.

Hot tears spilled down Cad's cheeks, to simply **mingle**[2] away with the well water. Her right leg threatened to **cramp**[3], and suddenly fatigue **smothered**[4] Cad like a warm blanket. As she sank beneath the surface, her heavy clothes dragging her down, with all hope gone and **depleted**[5] of energy, she pictured her father one more time.

At once, her lungs burned, desperate to suck in a breath. At least the potion's **remnants**[6] dulled her pain, and as she sank, Dylan, Rhys, Flash and Fishy rushed through her mind. Last of all, she said goodbye to May as she slipped into the water's **murky**[7] depths, the stones she'd forgotten in her pockets helping her on her way.

But as she sank, picturing May, a shock of realisation **jolted**[8] through her like a lance to the chest. With a huge thrust, digging as deep as she had ever **delved**[9], she mustered her last remaining strength, kicked her legs, pulled with her arms, and **propelled**[10] herself back up to the surface, gasping for air as she broke through it.

'May,' she spluttered, 'May.'

In a blind panic, shredding the water with her legs, she put two fingers into her mouth, and taking a deep breath, whistled as loudly as she could. Then, clawing at slippery stones that **protruded**[11] slightly from the well's sides, she hung on for dear life willing May to hear her calls.

---

1 **cure** *(v)* make better or relieve from illness. *(s)* heal, restore. *(ant)* sicken.

2 **mingle** *(v)* mix together. *(s)* blend, unite, meld. *(ant)* separate.

3 **cramp** *(v)* suffer from sudden muscle pain. *(s)* contract, convulse. *(ant)* relax, ease.

4 **smother** *(v)* cover or surround entirely. *(s)* overwhelm, envelop, control. *(ant)* release.

5 **deplete** *(v)* use up. *(s)* exhaust, consume, expend, drain, sap. *(ant)* replenish.

6 **remnant** *(n)* a part of something that is left over. *(s)* remainder, leftover.

7 **murky** *(adj)* gloomy and dark. *(s)* dim, shadowy, obscured. *(ant)* bright, light, clear.

8 **jolt** *(v)* push or move roughly. *(s)* jerk, lurch, bounce, rattle.

9 **delve** *(v)* reach inside and search. *(s)* dig, probe. *(ant)* withdraw.

10 **propel** *(v)* drive or push into a specific direction. *(s)* move, thrust, shoot, force, launch. *(ant)* pull.

11 **protrude** *(v)* extend above or beyond a surface (stick out). *(s)* poke out, jut, project. *(ant)* withdraw.

Desperate, and with the well's wall nigh on impossible to grip, she whistled once more, kicking her legs and **blaring**[1] as shrilly as her lungs would allow.

'Come, May,' she cried. 'Hear my call.'

Cad willed her hawk to come, and although Cad's hidden notes would be **saturated**[2], her hairpin survived, for she had felt it in the secret pocket she'd **crafted**[3] so well. She would send May to find Dylan, carrying the hairpin around her leg, and he would know she was in dire need of help and come looking for her. Cad knew she was grasping at straws, but with nothing else on which to hold, she hoped and prayed, beseeching May to hurry. If May heard, she would **respond**[4] rapidly.

But as time slipped cruelly by, May didn't come, and with sinking **dismay**[5], Cad remembered there was no way into the well's shack for the hawk. No window, just a closed door. Even if May had heard, how would she enter the well?

With a heart as black as coal, Cad accepted her demise, and stared fate in the face. But for her father's sake and her self-pride, as any Knight Hawk would, just like the frogs she'd seen in pools, she continuously kicked her legs and gripped the well's wall with her hands, and this she would do until her fingers finally lost all feeling and failed her.

---

1 **blare** *(v)* make a loud sound. *(s)* boom, roar, bellow. *(ant)* murmur, whisper.

2 **saturate** *(v)* make thoroughly wet. *(s)* soak, drench, waterlog. *(ant)* dry.

3 **craft** *(v)* make by hand. *(s)* work, create, fashion.

4 **respond** *(v)* react. *(s)* answer, reply, acknowledge. *(ant)* ask.

5 **dismay** *(n)* concern or distress. *(s)* alarm, dread, trepidation. *(ant)* contentment, satisfaction.

CHAPTER TWENTY-ONE

Buckets From Above

To Cad, it seemed most odd that singing would steady her shivering, but it did. In the deafening silence, her clattering teeth gave rise to a peculiar sound that echoed eerily off the well's wall. Her muscles **seized**[1] with fatigue. Her lungs lacked air, and her frozen fingers threatened **imminent**[2] release of their grip. As she clung to the last gasps of life, she dared not allow her mind to wander beyond the present, for if she did, she knew she would be **doomed**[3].

I must keep going, she thought, as she battled to stay afloat, and finally emptied her pockets of the stones she'd picked up earlier. Her **sodden**[4] clothes weighed down her body, dragging and **sapping**[5] her strength, but she found not the energy to remove them, and she'd probably freeze to death first if she did so.

Clueless as to how long she'd clung to the wall, Cad's leaden legs **laboured**[6], her arms screamed for respite, and her brain floundered as **debilitating**[7] weakness took hold. Although feeling no hunger, she'd eaten little during the day, and her **meagre**[8] energy stores were rapidly depleting.

---

1 **seize** *(v)* (of a moving part) become jammed. *(s)* stop, cease, cramp, clench. *(ant)* loose, release.

2 **imminent** *(adj)* about to happen. *(s)* forthcoming, immediate. *(ant)* remote.

3 **doomed** *(adj)* likely to have a bad outcome. *(s)* hopeless, condemned, done. *(ant)* blessed.

4 **sodden** *(adj)* soaked through with liquid. *(s)* saturated, sopping, drenched. *(ant)* dry.

5 **sap** *(v)* gradually weaken, erode, destroy or deplete power. *(s)* drain, debilitate. *(ant)* bolster.

6 **labour** *(v)* work with huge effort and difficulty. *(s)* strain, struggle. *(ant)* rest.

7 **debilitating** *(adj)* make weaker. *(s)* draining, exhausting, crippling. *(ant)* fortifying.

8 **meagre** *(adj)* inadequate or scant in amount. *(s)* measly, paltry, insufficient. *(ant)* plentiful.

Rejecting misery, she forced happy thoughts, picturing Bryn Davis topple at the tip of her lance, beating him to the ground in a wrestle, and winning a tourney. She saw Fishy snuggled up beside her in bed, with May perched on its end for the night, and even though blind, watching over them all, **sentinel**[1]-like. Rhys, tucked up in his corner, pretending to snore but missing nothing, and Dylan sleeping soundly through thunderstorms.

She realised a weak grin, but as her father's image crept into view, the smile slipped from her face, replaced by such overwhelming sorrow, she weakened. One hand slipped from the wall, slapping the surface hard. The other struggled for purchase, sliding down the well's slimy **contours**[2], hitting the water. A wave of despair swallowed her.

No matter how hard she tried, her body now refused to listen, failing to function. It seemed **fate**[3] had **foiled**[4] her destiny, her future flipped by the hands of a fiendish poisoner. Yet, anger eluded her, perhaps banished by fatigue and desolation, and as her resolve **dissolved**[5] into the water, Cad hurled back her head and arms as if retiring for bed, **capitulating**[6] to exhaustion. Almost comfortable, she spread into a star shape, relaxed, too tired to panic, too tired to sob.

Then with a **traumatic**[7] sigh, she submitted to the inevitable, her chin pointing up towards the distant **aperture**[8] above her. But Cad didn't see the pinprick of light which had been there before. She didn't see the well's opening, which was now obscured. For a circular shape was descending, growing bigger with each passing moment.

Cad blinked, then blinked again. Were her bleary eyes **deceiving**[9] her? Were the demons **predicted**[10] by Physician Jordan finally arriving. Devils now diving into the darkness for a final dance in her watery grave.

My head tricks me, thought Cad, as the distant barking of dogs drifted into her ears.

---

1 **sentinel** *(n)* a guard or soldier who keeps watch. *(s)* sentry, lookout, protector.

2 **contour** *(n)* an outline representing a shape. *(s)* form, silhouette.

3 **fate** *(n)* the developments of future outcomes that are out of one's control. *(s)* destiny, chance, luck.

4 **foil** *(v)* prevent something from succeeding. *(s)* frustrate, thwart, oppose. *(ant)* assist, aid.

5 **dissolve** *(v)* disperse. *(s)* vanish, evaporate, disappear, mix into. *(ant)* appear.

6 **capitulate** *(v)* stop resisting an opponent or demand. *(s)* surrender, yield, relent. *(ant)* resist.

7 **traumatic** *(adj)* distressing. *(s)* disturbing, upsetting. *(ant)* soothing.

8 **aperture** *(n)* an opening. *(s)* hole, gap.

9 **deceive** *(v)* give the wrong impression. *(s)* mislead, hoodwink, dupe, trick. *(ant)* be honest.

10 **predict** *(v)* say or guess that something will happen in the future. *(s)* foresee, forecast, expect, anticipate.

The potion poisons my mind. But as she floated, staring up at the well's opening, she saw that the circular shape blocking the light was something descending towards her.

The pail! It's the pail!

The bucket dropped downwards, not in a reckless tumble, but as if being lowered carefully by someone collecting water. The dog's barks loudened and, in an instant, she recognised their **timbre**[1]. It was Fishy. No mistake, she heard Fishy's bark, and one so loud and clear, it must be from inside the shack. Fishy was by the well, and with whomever lowered that pail towards her.

'Help! Help!' she shrieked, finding her voice with sudden gusto.

Then Fishy barked so **vociferously**[2], Cad's heart soared.

'Down here!' she bellowed.

'Grasp the bucket,' shouted a voice from above. 'It should hold your weight.'

Cad didn't recognise the muffled voice, nor at this moment did she care to whom it belonged. Someone was there with her **faithful**[3] dog, and they were willing to pull her from this watery grave.

Now thrashing her legs with all her might, Cad propelled her shoulders above the surface and grabbed at the bucket, grasping and clawing, her nails **shredding**[4] and tearing. But her hands slid hopelessly down its sides, too slimy to obtain purchase as the pail, like a **pendulum**[5], swayed back and forth above her head.

'Don't grab it,' shouted the voice from above. 'I'll lower it further.'

In her terror, Cad had forgotten the bucket would lower to her depth with ease. There was no need to snatch at it.

'Hold onto it as tightly as you can, lest you slip as I haul you up.'

Now utterly **devoid**[6] of energy, Cad feared her grip wouldn't hold. But with a **ferocious**[7] kick and stretching until it hurt, she grasped the rope which held the bucket, and then with one

---

1 **timbre** *(n)* the character of a sound or voice independent of pitch and loudness. *(s)* tone.

2 **vociferously** *(adv)* in a vociferous (loud and forceful) manner. *(s)* noisily, stridently. *(ant)* quietly.

3 **faithful** *(adj)* remaining loyal, steadfast, constant and true. *(s)* dedicated, dependable, reliable. *(ant)* disloyal.

4 **shred** *(v)* cut or tear into (shreds) thin pieces. *(s)* rip, slice.

5 **pendulum** *(n)* a swinging, hanging weight that regulates the mechanism of a clock.

6 **devoid** *(adj)* completely lacking or free from. *(s)* empty, without, deficient. *(ant)* full, filled.

7 **ferocious** *(adj)* great. *(s)* strong, powerful. *(ant)* gentle, mild.

timely wrench, grabbed it. At last, Cad rose above the surface and wrapped both legs around the pail, clinging on for dear life.

'Heave!' she yelled. 'Heave slowly, lest I topple.'

And with her arms pleading surrender and legs threatening to unfurl, Cad clung on like a clam, for she knew if she fell back into the well's water, she had not the **reserves**[1] to survive its clutches.

---

1 **reserve** *(n)* a supply of something. *(s)* resource, store. *(ant)* emptiness.

CHAPTER TWENTY-TWO

Green Slime

As Cad clung to the rope like a baby to its mother, her loved ones filled her mind. Familiar faces, **fortifying**[1] her with the resolve to endure the **hoist**[2]; their eyes pleading, beseeching looks **compelling**[3] her to cling to the **slick**[4] rope. Their presence, a force of hope commanding her to ignore her burning hands and weakening legs that clutched at the rope and pail. A task which proved to be the most **arduous**[5] of her young life. Still, the confines of the well paled in comparison to the prospect of plummeting back into its depths.

She dared not speak. As cold as stone, and barely breathing, **riveted**[6], she focused on stillness afraid that if she flinched, her grip might fail. Cad prayed as she progressed at an agonising slow pace, listening to Fishy's worried **whines**[7] of anguish. Fishy knew that her friend faced **peril**[8]: dogs smell fear.

Not once did Cad glance up at the well's opening, and she was still oblivious to who turned the

---

1 **fortify** *(v)* strengthen physically or mentally. *(s)* reinforce, bolster. *(ant)* weaken, debilitate.

2 **hoist** *(n)* an act of lifting or raising something or someone. *(s)* heave. *(ant)* lowering.

3 **compel** *(v)* force or oblige someone to do something. *(s)* impel, drive.

4 **slick** *(adj)* smooth and slippery. *(s)* greasy, oily. *(ant)* rough, grippy.

5 **arduous** *(adj)* difficult and tiring. *(s)* taxing, laborious, toilsome. *(ant)* easy.

6 **rivet** *(v)* completely hold someone's attention so they cannot move. *(s)* absorb, grip. *(ant)* bore.

7 **whine** *(n)* a long high-pitched cry. *(s)* whimper, howl, mewl.

8 **peril** *(n)* immediate danger. *(s)* menace, threat, risk. *(ant)* safety.

crank[1] raising the pail. Instead, she stared straight ahead. Agonising waves of torture gripped her **torso**[2] as the potion's pain-killing properties waned, and her ribs spared no effort in reminding her of their broken state. Yet, like a **limpet**[3] to a ship, she stuck to her saviour, **buoyed**[4] by the nearing sounds of her **devoted**[5] dog.

Bit by bit, she **ascended**[6] as each **harrowing**[7] jerk of the pail, and subsequent halt in the ascent, signalled a complete **revolution**[8] of the crank's handle. They were making slow yet steady progress. But when she remained **static**[9] for a while longer than before, and a voice said, 'Let me help you climb out,' Cad's heart flipped with joy: she'd almost made it.

Fishy, overjoyed, **yapped**[10] so loudly that Cad's ears rang in protest.

But it wasn't over yet, and the situation remained precarious, so when a firm grip took Cad's arm, hauling her and the pail across to the well's wall, she shrieked, almost losing her grip of the bucket. Then without warning, two hands **enveloped**[11] her **midriff**[12], **compressing**[13] her broken ribs. In agony, Cad suppressed her cries of pain for fear the hands would release her. She must bear it. But the determined hands held on, their grip yanking her from the well and onto its wall, where she perched **momentarily**[14] before tilting like a ship in a storm, then toppling to the floor like a sack of **turnips**[15].

Fishy pounced and covered Cad's face with **slobbery**[16] loving licks, pirouetting as her tail

---

1 **crank** *(n)* a lever. *(s)* arm, bar, handle.

2 **torso** *(n)* the trunk (body without head or limbs) of a human. *(s)* upper body.

3 **limpet** *(n)* a marine mollusc that clings to rock, boats and ships.

4 **buoy** *(v)* make optimistic and confident. *(s)* encourage, boost, cheer, hearten. *(ant)* depress.

5 **devoted** *(adj)* loyal or loving. *(s)* faithful, dedicated. *(ant)* disloyal, indifferent.

6 **ascend** *(v)* go up or climb up. *(s)* mount, scale. *(ant)* descend, drop.

7 **harrowing** *(adj)* very upsetting. *(s)* distressing, agonising, traumatic. *(ant)* pleasant.

8 **revolution** *(n)* a turn of something. *(s)* rotation, circle.

9 **static** *(adj)* not moving or changing. *(s)* stationary, steady. *(ant)* mobile.

10 **yap** *(v)* bark with a high-pitched sound. *(s)* yelp, woof.

11 **envelop** *(v)* surround completely. *(s)* encompass, enclose, encircle. *(ant)* release.

12 **midriff** *(n)* the front area between the chest and the waist. *(s)* middle, midsection.

13 **compress** *(v)* squeeze or press. *(s)* squash, crush, constrict. *(ant)* release.

14 **momentarily** *(adv)* for a short time. *(s)* briefly, temporarily. *(ant)* lengthily, languidly.

15 **turnip** *(n)* a round root that is eaten as a vegetable.

16 **slobbery** *(adj)* unpleasantly wet. *(s)* dribbly, sopping, salivating. *(ant)* dry.

whirred in delight, **elated**[1] at seeing her master. Unable to move, Cad stayed on her side, relief rendering her speechless: once more on **terra firma**[2].

As Fishy continued to clean Cad's face, it dawned on Cad that her rescuer had vanished. The shack seemed empty. Gently urging Fishy away, Cad pushed herself onto all fours with a grimace. But utterly robbed of energy, she flopped onto her bottom, where she sat with her back resting heavily into the well's wall, glad it was there, as her feet, numb with cold, refused to **comply**[3].

She sucked in shallow breaths, lest her ribs felt sliced asunder by a sword. Then summoning all her strength, she braced herself to stand for the walk back to her room. Late-night revellers would soon arrive, needing full water ewers to **mollify**[4] their morning **hangovers**[5].

But sapped of energy, she sat silently with Fishy by her side, when a small voice saying, 'Please don't be angry at me,' made her heart almost stop. Because unless Fishy had learned to talk, Cad seemed to be very much alone in this room that housed the well.

Involuntarily[6], Cad jumped, glancing about the cabin, but it was empty. Only she and Fishy were there, sitting by the well. Still **groggy**[7] with potion and unable to gather **rational**[8] thoughts, Cad wondered if those demons had now arrived as voices in her head. Still, when Fishy **promptly**[9] **upped**[10] and sprang across the room, rearing onto her **hind**[11] legs and licking the air, the truth dropped, hitting her like a stone shot from her sling.

'Rhys Price, you took my invisibility ring,' she muttered to herself. 'You did, didn't you? You took it from my tunic somehow.'

Cad's voice then rose several **octaves**[12].

---

1 **elated** *(adj)* extremely happy. *(s)* thrilled, jubilant, ecstatic. *(ant)* devastated.

2 **terra firma** *(n)* firm ground. *(s)* dry land.

3 **comply** *(v)* behave in accordance with a command or wish. *(s)* obey, follow. *(ant)* disobey.

4 **mollify** *(v)* reduce the intensity of something. *(s)* ease, assuage. *(ant)* worsen.

5 **hangover** *(n)* the nasty after-effects of drinking too much alcohol. *(s)* headache, sickness.

6 **involuntarily** *(adv)* done without conscious control. *(s)* unwittingly. *(ant)* voluntarily.

7 **groggy** *(adj)* unsteady. *(s)* dazed, stupefied, befuddled. *(ant)* rational.

8 **rational** *(adj)* logical. *(s)* sensible, reasoned, sound. *(ant)* irrational, illogical.

9 **promptly** *(adv)* with little or no delay. *(s)* immediately.

10 **up** *(v)* get up unexpectedly. *(s)* rise, stand. *(ant)* sit, lie.

11 **hind** *(adj)* back. *(s)* rear. *(ant)* fore, front.

12 **octave** *(n)* eight musical notes or the interval between the top and bottom of these eight notes.

'*You stole my ring!*'

'Please don't be cross. I can explain. Please don't think badly of me,' repeated a quavering voice from where Fishy lapped at nothing, her tail **whisking**[1] the air with delight.

'Rhys Price, you—' Cad muttered, pushing herself up with her hands to straighten her back, and wincing at the spike of pain spearing her side. 'Come here, you noddle head. And you'd better tell a worthy tale, boy,' she added, scowling at the thin air.

Cad knew Rhys was approaching her because Fishy trotted alongside him, stopped, then sat beside her. When Cad sensed Rhys loitering above her, with a bite of impatience, she said, 'Sit down. Tell me what happened, then you can help me back to our room.'

Cad reached out her hand, and there it was, that strange sensation – Rhys's invisible body. Then with perfect timing, Rhys's body began to appear as if **dabbed**[2] by the brush strokes of a master portrait painter.

Cad marvelled. She'd experienced this **transformation**[3] many times, but to view it like this, happening to someone else, and before her very eyes, was utterly jaw-dropping. The drawing of a living human being, from thin air, was magical indeed. But as Rhys's arms, torso, legs and finally, his face, appeared, Cad's stomach filled with a mixture of acid and ice.

It cannot be ...

Her eyes widened, her jaw fell, and what pale colour had lit her face now drained to the hue of raw pastry. Her trusted friend, ally and **confidant**[4], Rhys Price, the boy with whom she shared her deepest secrets and bedchamber, stood before her **draped**[5] in the very same monk's outfit as the people who'd trapped and attacked her in the oubliette. And perhaps even the very same person who had spooked the horses just hours before.

Cad **gawked**[6] at Rhys, **dumbfounded**[7], struggling to find words and unravel her thoughts as her eyes roamed over the **coarse**[8] brown garment, its hood resting back on Rhys's shoulders.

---

1 **whisk** *(v)* turn with rapid movements. *(s)* beat, whip.

2 **dab** *(v)* repeatedly press lightly against something. *(s)* touch, daub, paint, stroke.

3 **transformation** *(n)* a noticeable change in form, nature or appearance. *(s)* alteration, metamorphosis. *(ant)* preservation.

4 **confidant** *(n)* a person another trusts to share in private matters. *(s)* companion. *(ant)* foe.

5 **drape** *(v)* cover with cloth. *(s)* wrap, swathe, shroud, cloak. *(ant)* uncover.

6 **gawk** *(v)* stare stupidly. *(s)* gape, gaze, gawp. *(ant)* glance, ignore.

7 **dumbfound** *(v)* greatly astonish. *(s)* stagger, startle, amaze, flabbergast. *(ant)* underwhelm.

8 **coarse** *(adj)* rough or abrasive in texture. *(s)* wiry, scratchy, prickly. *(ant)* smooth, sleek, silky.

Bewildered, she shook her head, eventually blurting, 'Explain! Everything! Now!' Her stabbing finger **punctuating**[1] each word as she said it.

Rhys's throat visibly tightened, his hands working together in nervous **kneads**[2], as Cad's eyes bored into his. His mouth opened and closed like a landed fish, then it finally fell shut in silence. Purposely mute, Cad blinked, her lips tight, her gaze ablaze with anticipation. But Rhys's stare was now fixed firmly on his feet.

Cad, her eyes flickering with anger, knew she must speak first, and not in a tone that would make Rhys bolt like a rabbit down a hole.

She cleared her throat and rearranged her face into a bright but **brittle**[3] smile, then began, trying her utmost to remain measured. 'Rhys, I cannot tell you how grateful I am that you seem to have saved my life for a second time, but if you don't explain things to me now, I'm not quite sure how I will react.'

Her face flushed with a fury she struggled to conceal, yet she knew it would cause him to **clam up**[4] more. He fiddled with his fingers, not lifting his head.

'Rhys!' Cad finally snapped. 'Explain your clothing now, or I will haul you before my father.'

Rhys's eyes almost doubled in size as he began to stutter, his hands wringing out an imaginary cloth, his stricken face, that of someone caught mid-lie.

'I … I … I took your ring because of Bryn Davis.'

'What?' Cad cried, interrupting him, her expression darkening. 'What's Bryn Davis got to do with you stealing my ring? And how did you fathom how to use it?' she ranted, not taking a breath.

On hearing Cad's tone, Fishy let out a whine, her tail hiding between her legs, her eyes soft with sorrow. Cad, suddenly abashed by her tirade, and realising Rhys was **pallid**[5] and **quaking**[6], finally softened, and paused to let the young boy answer, knowing that a knot is untangled with slow teasing and not sharp pulling.

---

1 **punctuate** *(v)* interrupt, mark. *(s)* break up.

2 **knead** *(v)* work something deeply with the hands, such as dough.

3 **brittle** *(adj)* appearing cheerful but nervous within (or easily broken). *(s)* unsure, anxious, fragile. *(ant)* confident.

4 **clam up** *(v)* stop talking. *(s)* shut up, button up. *(ant)* speak.

5 **pallid** *(adj)* pale-faced. *(s)* pasty, wan, ashen, peaky. *(ant)* flushed, rosy.

6 **quake** *(v)* tremble or shake. *(s)* shudder, wobble, vibrate, rock.

'B–B–Bryn Davis cornered me and said he knew you were hiding something. He said … that … he knew you were a girl. I insisted he was wrong because we shared rooms, and I knew you to be a boy, but he **clouted**[1] me about the ears, gloating and saying he could prove it.' Rhys's words bungled out as thick as **treacle**[2].

Speechless, Cad nodded at Rhys to continue, not wanting to press him too hard, lest he lose his thread along with his nerve.

'The **swine**[3] **bragged**[4], proud he had proof, sniggering and saying he would reveal your secret to the entire court.' Tears trickled from Rhys's eyes, his voice cracked and caught, his face crumpling like creased parchment as he said, 'I'm not lying. I promise you, Master Cad.'

Rhys's eyes met Cad's; she saw they **brimmed**[5] with honesty and **integrity**[6].

Cad's heart melted, and something heavy lifted from her shoulders. Even though he'd not yet explained the monk's outfit he wore, she knew he meant her no harm. Rhys was her faithful friend, and feeling a sharp shard of guilt, she gave him a smile that reflected his braveness.

'Did he reveal this "proof" to you?' Cad's voice faltered as her potion befuddled brain still grappled to grasp Rhys's **revelation**[7].

Rhys shook his head, then said, 'I believed him, though. The look on his face and his **cocksure**[8] tone convinced me. I think, somehow, Bryn knows your secret.'

'Go on,' urged Cad, seeing there was more bubbling beneath the surface.

'For some time, I've suspected Bryn of cheating in jousts. He wins too many when he shouldn't. He stays seated when he shouldn't. I've studied jousts since I can remember, and I suspected his armour to be **bolted**[9] to his saddle in some tournaments. For me to prove his guilt would have been impossible unless I were invisible.'

'I see,' said Cad, her memories of the joust now so sharp they cut like a knife. She lifted her

---

1 **clout** *(v)* strike heavily with the hand or something hard. *(s)* hit, knock, smack, clobber.

2 **treacle** *(n)* a thick, sticky dark syrup made from partly refined sugar. *(s)* molasses, syrup.

3 **swine** *(n)* a pig.

4 **brag** *(v)* talk too highly of one's own achievements. *(s)* boast, gloat, crow.

5 **brim** *(v)* to be full to the top of. *(s)* overflow, spill, flood.

6 **integrity** *(n)* honesty and morality. *(s)* truthfulness, honour. *(ant)* dishonesty, corruption.

7 **revelation** *(n)* a previously unknown fact that has been disclosed (revealed) to others. *(s)* divulgence. *(ant)* concealment.

8 **cocksure** *(adj)* overconfident. *(s)* arrogant, conceited, cocky. *(ant)* humble.

9 **bolt** *(v)* fasten securely. *(s)* lock, fix. *(ant)* unbolt.

chin and fixed Rhys with her iron gaze. 'So you used my invisibility ring and checked his saddle?'

'Yes. And I'm right. Bryn Davis is a craven cheat and a **blackmailer**[1], but now we have our weapon.' Rhys's words tumbled out like a bubbling **brook**[2]. 'Because Bryn cares so much for his **reputation**[3], he won't reveal your secret if we can **counter**[4] his threats with his own dirty little **antics**[5],' he added, his words coming faster and faster, tumbling, and too clumsy to be anything but the truth.

'And your clothing?' asked Cad, marvelling at Rhys's revelations and **valour**[6], but **recoiling**[7] with inner horror as she regarded Rhys attired in the monk's habit.

'I found it in the room where you hid Fishy as a pup,' replied Rhys. 'There were several of them tucked away at the back behind the armour. I feared I might not remain invisible long enough to prove Bryn's guilt. If I appeared before the grooms whilst investigating in the stables, then I hoped the habit might disguise me long enough to flee unrecognised.'

Cad's head shook with **incredulity**[8] and respect for Rhys's hitherto hidden talents. 'So, that was you I saw in the stables tonight when I was visiting Flash,' said Cad, her words **stating**[9] rather than questioning.

But a beat of silence passed between them, and Rhys's bemused face surprised Cad.

'No,' Rhys eventually replied. 'I didn't visit the stables tonight, but I wore the monk's habit when I did so. Tonight I was serving at the feast until May and Fishy entered the great hall. That's how I knew something was **afoot**[10]. They were both so anxious and trying to capture my attention that I left the feast feigning sickness and came to our rooms to find you gone. I **donned**[11] the habit tonight because I lied about being sick and didn't want to be seen. I made

---

1 **blackmailer** *(n)* a person who demands payment for keeping compromising secrets from others.

2 **brook** *(n)* a small, fast flowing stream. *(s)* rill, rivulet, runnel.

3 **reputation** *(n)* the general opinion held about someone or something. *(s)* stature, repute, status.

4 **counter** *(v)* oppose. *(s)* counteract, foil, retaliate. *(ant)* assist.

5 **antics** *(n)* outrageous or foolish behaviour. *(s)* capers, escapades, tricks, stunts.

6 **valour** *(n)* great bravery in the face of danger. *(s)* courage, pluck, nerve. *(ant)* cowardice.

7 **recoil** *(v)* suddenly spring or flinch back in horror or disgust. *(s)* withdraw, retreat. *(ant)* confront, stand firm.

8 **incredulity** *(n)* the state of being unable to believe something. *(s)* disbelief. *(ant)* belief, credulity.

9 **state** *(v)* say something clearly. *(s)* declare, assert, tell. *(ant)* ask.

10 **afoot** *(adj)* in preparation or progress. *(s)* happening, underway.

11 **don** *(v)* put on or get dressed in. *(s)* throw on, slip on, change into. *(ant)* take off, remove.

myself invisible, and Fishy led me straight here. If I made an untimely re-appearance, I could flee as a monk again and not Rhys Price.'

Agog[1], Cad eyed Rhys. How they'd all **underestimated**[2] this taciturn boy. Now so **humbled**[3], that was a mistake Cad **vowed**[4] never to make again.

'I discovered Bryn's secret on the night of your accident, after the joust, before he had the chance to hide evidence of his cheating.' Rhys hesitated, his gaze dropping to the floor.

'Go on, Rhys, I won't get angry, I promise.'

Unable to meet her eyes, he continued. 'It was I who took the ring in the first place. I took it because I always had my suspicions about Bryn, and I wanted a chance to prove it. That chance came quicker than I expected. I used the ring that night because, **sedated**[5] by the potion Physician Jordan administered to you, you slept as deeply as Dylan. I called your name, but you didn't stir, so I knew I'd be safe.'

Feeling no anger towards Rhys, Cad sucked in her cheeks and swallowed over the lump in her throat. If the person she'd seen creeping around the stables earlier wasn't Rhys, then who was it, and where were they now?

Wincing, Cad reached across and hugged Rhys, who immediately stiffened and turned pink.

'Rhys Price, you **astound**[6] me. How in heaven did you work out how to use my ring?'

Turning **puce**[7] and clearly cringing with embarrassment, Rhys muttered, 'I knew how to use it because … because you talk in your sleep, a lot.'

'I do?' asked Cad, astonished at yet another of Rhys's revelations.

'You do,' said Rhys with a half-smile. 'I don't think you should ever sleep elsewhere,' he added. 'Dylan is safe, as he's your friend, and he hears nothing as he sleeps so soundly, but I worry that others will learn your secrets if ever you do.'

Cad considered his comments, amazed at the boy's depth.

---

1 **agog** *(adj)* keen or curious. *(s)* drawn, intrigued. *(ant)* uninterested.

2 **underestimate** *(v)* regard someone as less capable than they really are. *(s)* undervalue, misjudge. *(ant)* overestimate.

3 **humble** *(v)* cause to feel less proud or important. *(s)* abash, shame, mortify. *(ant)* boost, encourage.

4 **vow** *(v)* make a solemn (serious) promise. *(s)* swear, guarantee.

5 **sedate** *(v)* calm or make someone sleep by giving them a sedative drug. *(s)* stupefy, dope. *(ant)* energise.

6 **astound** *(v)* greatly surprise or shock. *(s)* astonish, confound, stun, amaze. *(ant)* underwhelm, bore.

7 **puce** *(adj)* dark red or purple-brown in colour.

'I also watch over you when your … when your nightmares appear,' said Rhys, casting a **coy**[1] glance at Cad.

Cad swallowed hard several times, tears pricking her eyes as they followed Rhys's, whose gaze dropped as they met.

'Oh, Rhys,' she cried, hugging him again. 'To think I could ever doubt your loyalty. Thank you. Thank you,' she gushed as he turned a bright shade of **scarlet**[2].

'You are my best friend, Master Cad,' he whispered, his voice rich with emotion.

Cad's eyes rolled at 'Master'. With a friendly tut, and a ghost of a smile at her lips, she stroked Fishy, and banished the monk's image from her mind.

'And you are my dear friend too, Rhys, not my **inferior**[3]. I am *not* your master.'

'But you're the child of a prince,' said Rhys with complete sincerity and unable to meet Cad's gaze.

'I think you forget,' said Cad, 'I am as you, Rhys, an orphan, fortunate enough to be taken under the wing of a great man. **United**[4], we will **flourish**[5], my friend,' she said with a warm smile.

'Now, *friend*, help me to my feet and support me as I limp back to our rooms for some much-needed sleep.'

Heaving Cad up and desperately trying to avoid squeezing her ribs, Rhys asked in his old, clumsier style, 'Cad, how did you fall into the well?'

Cad was about to answer when she saw Rhys's mouth suddenly gape, followed by a flash of shock striking his face.

'What is it?' asked Cad, perturbed by his sudden changed expression.

'Your arm.' He pointed at Cad. 'It's green, like the spring grass.'

For the first time since being hauled from the well, Cad glanced down and found the answer she'd sought. **Smeared**[6] across her hand was a green **substance**[7], its colour not unlike the slimy

---

1 **coy** *(adj)* reluctant or shy. *(s)* evasive, hesitant. *(ant)* forthright.

2 **scarlet** *(n)* a bright red colour. *(s)* crimson, vermillion.

3 **inferior** *(n)* a person lower in social standing than another. *(s)* lesser, subordinate. *(ant)* superior.

4 **united** *(adj)* joined together to achieve a common purpose. *(s)* unified, undivided. *(ant)* divided.

5 **flourish** *(v)* grow or develop rapidly and successfully. *(s)* succeed, thrive, prosper. *(ant)* deteriorate.

6 **smeared** *(adj)* spread or coated over something. *(s)* wiped, rubbed, streaked, smudged.

7 **substance** *(n)* a particular type of matter which has uniform qualities. *(s)* material, stuff.

weeds found in **stagnant**[1] ponds beyond Catrin's walls; the culprit most likely wielding the sickness upon Catrin Castle continued up Cad's arm – was this the poison?

She caught Rhys's eye and said, 'This is how I came to plummet down the well, in search of the poison polluting our water supply. I couldn't find it. It seemed invisible, but perhaps it is this? Somehow, I think it was administered via that pail that pulled me from the jaws of death. If not the pail, then by a method I've not yet discovered.'

As mute as a well-behaved puppy, Rhys gawped in flabbergasted silence, Fishy sitting by his side.

'Come, Rhys. Before I sleep, we must alert my father without causing **undue**[2] alarm to the revellers, and we must do it quickly before folks come queueing for water. And keep Fishy away from me. You saw what the poison did to Flash, for I fear she drank it too.'

Propped up by Rhys, Cad hobbled from the shack and across the bailey back to their room with Fishy. As they neared their room, May, with a soft swoosh of air, swooped from above, landing on Cad's shoulder.

'Thank you, May,' whispered Cad, to her blind hawk, who'd not failed her after all, and had alerted Rhys at the feast.

As the four friends reached their room, Rhys supporting Cad, none saw the hooded figure slip from the high keep, glide across the bailey, enter the well shack, and quietly close the door behind them.

---

1 **stagnant** *(adj)* having no current. *(s)* still, dirty, foul. *(ant)* fresh, flowing.

2 **undue** *(adj)* not appropriate in the circumstances. *(s)* excessive, extreme. *(ant)* due, appropriate.

CHAPTER TWENTY-THREE

Oblivion

Clad[1] in clean comfortable clothing, her sullied garments now wrapped securely in a sack, and away from the animals in case of **contamination**[2], Cad awaited her father's covert visit.

Desperate to quaff the remaining potion to quell the **inferno**[3] of pain now raging around her torso, Cad pondered Catrin Castle's **predicament**[4]. Why would someone want to poison only certain people, and how would they do it? There seemed to be no **rhyme or reason**[5] to who had become sick. It made little sense to her, but it must **tally**[6] to someone out there.

Even more baffling, who had the means and the **wherewithal**[7] to **invent**[8] and conceal such a **contraption**[9]? One to dispense accurate doses of poison, such that folks fell sick, yet didn't die from it, at least not yet; that thought set fear in her heart, because with the Gwalch Gem bracelet in Dewi's hands, who knew what was possible …?

---

1 **clad** *(adj)* clothed or dressed. *(s)* attired, wearing, cloaked. *(ant)* unclothed, undressed.

2 **contamination** *(n)* the state of being made impure by something. *(s)* pollution, poisoning. *(ant)* decontamination.

3 **inferno** *(n)* something that is extremely hot. *(s)* fire.

4 **predicament** *(n)* a difficult situation. *(s)* dilemma, crisis, plight. *(ant)* solution.

5 **rhyme or reason** (phrase) logical reason. *(s)* logic, explanation, rationality.

6 **tally** *(v)* add up, agree or correspond to. *(s)* match, work.

7 **wherewithal** *(n)* the means or the money to do something specific. *(s)* resources, ability.

8 **invent** *(v)* design or create something never made before. *(s)* devise, develop.

9 **contraption** *(n)* a device. *(s)* gadget, mechanism, apparatus.

Would they target her father next to thwart his ongoing quest, or was there a **broader**[1] plan? She hoped again that Llywelyn had drunk wine with the revellers in the hall, and not the polluted water from the well.

As Cad fingered her invisibility ring, now safely **secreted**[2] in her nightclothes' hem, and with a **solemn**[3] promise from Rhys to ask her permission to use it next time, she willed her father to hurry. She knew it would have been most difficult for Rhys to speak to Llywelyn whilst he feasted with his entire court, but she'd insisted Rhys talk to no one else about her findings, not even Owain Glyn, her father's second in command.

As always, patience eluding her, Cad kneaded Fishy's soft ears and closed her eyes, desperate to swig some potion. But not knowing its specific strength, and along with the effects it had wielded earlier, she decided against it. Instead, she **reclined**[4], striving to ignore the pain shooting through her ribs, and wondered if her father had recovered the cipher from Evans and, if so, whether he had drawn the same **conclusions**[5] as to its meaning. Was it a plan for a weapon, or did it conceal some other nasty little secret? And if so, whose? Evans had **explicitly**[6] told Cad he had not written the cipher. Could he be lying? Her head whirled. Exhausted, she drifted between uncomfortable naps and dark dreams of despair, to be jolted awake by the **piercing**[7] pain stabbing her ribs.

Desperately wishing her father would arrive, Cad contemplated the joyous sounds of revellers leaving the celebrations and heading towards the well for water to quell their morning headaches. They'd be irked and bewildered to find its pail gone, and that they'd need to head down to the stables for spring water from one of the horse's **water butts**[8]. Before leaving the well's shack, Cad had insisted that Rhys **detach**[9] the bucket and hide it from harm's way in case it was the **source**[10]

---

1 **broader** *(adj)* something more extensive. *(s)* wider, expansive. *(ant)* narrower.

2 **secrete** *(v)* hide. *(s)* conceal, stash, stow. *(ant)* display, reveal.

3 **solemn** *(adj)* formal or genuine. *(s)* sincere, earnest, firm. *(ant)* insincere.

4 **recline** *(v)* lean or lie back with one's back supported. *(s)* repose, rest. *(ant)* stand.

5 **conclusion** *(n)* a decision reached by thought and reasoning. *(s)* judgement, opinion, verdict.

6 **explicitly** *(adv)* in an explicit (definite) way. *(s)* openly, clearly. *(ant)* ambiguously

7 **piercing** *(adj)* (of a feeling) intense, typically in an unpleasant way. *(s)* sharp, agonising. *(ant)* dull.

8 **water butt** *(n)* a large container used for catching rainwater.

9 **detach** *(v)* unfasten or release something. *(s)* disconnect, separate. *(ant)* attach.

10 **source** *(n)* from where something originates. *(s)* creator, root, cause.

of the sickness, and to stop castle folks pulling more water. Even while **incapacitated**[1], Cad had ensured no one else would fall victim to the poisoner tonight.

Cad willed her father to hurry, and stared at the medicine vial placed beside her bed. Still nauseous from the draught's earlier dose, and yearning to swallow its contents, she now fully understood how folks relied on pain-killing properties. One swig and she'd float away to a pain-free, happy land, but she must wait. She must remain as sharp as her weary mind and body would permit without the **herbal**[2] remedy.

'Hurry, Father,' Cad called out, hot tears spilling down her face as she **raked**[3] her fingers through Fishy's fur.

'Fishy.' Cad's voice **stalled**[4].

The dog lifted her head, looked at Cad, and licked away the salty tears with huge slurps.

'Sweet girl,' Cad whispered, stroking the top of her dog's broad head and feeling so weak that her hand flopped down beside her.

With longing, Cad peered at the vial that held the cure to her agony. So tempted to **stem**[5] her discomfort, she pushed down with her hand and tried to reach for it with the other.

I'll take the tiniest tad to ease my suffering whilst I wait for Father, she told herself, wincing as the red-hot **pokers**[6] of pain seared her side. Her teeth **ground**[7] together, her muscles **taut**[8], ready to reach for the vial, as a wave of pain swallowed her. But as she stretched towards the **ampule**[9], silver lights swirled before her eyes, beads of sweat soaked her upper lip, and her vision narrowed to a long black tunnel.

Blindsided[10] and sagging into her pillow, Cad fought for her sanity as Physician Jordan's

---

1 **incapacitate** *(v)* prevent from functioning normally. *(s)* debilitate, disable. *(ant)* enable.

2 **herbal** *(adj)* made from or relating to herbs.

3 **rake** *(v)* draw or drag through something with a sweeping movement. *(s)* scrape, pull.

4 **stall** *(v)* stop or cause to stop making progress. *(s)* pause, stutter. *(ant)* continue.

5 **stem** *(v)* restrict or stop something. *(s)* halt, check, staunch, curb. *(ant)* increase.

6 **poker** *(n)* a metal rod used for stirring and prodding an open fire.

7 **grind** *(v)* rub or grate together (past participle: ground). *(s)* gnash, grit.

8 **taut** *(adj)* tight, with no slack. *(s)* stiff, rigid, tense. *(ant)* slack, loose.

9 **ampule** *(n)* a small, sealed glass container. *(s)* vial.

10 **blindside** *(v)* attack unexpectedly. *(s)* ambush, assault, surprise. *(ant)* forewarn.

demons took **refuge**[1] in her head. Now sweating like a hard-run horse, aware something was seriously amiss, and fading fast, Cad knew she would never reach the door to raise the alarm.

The sound of Fishy's concerned barks filtered into Cad's head from far away, and as Cad's eyes found the corner of her fuzzy room, they landed on the sealed sack that contained her contaminated clothes.

Myriad thoughts tugged at the edges of her mind, all **jostling**[2] for a shard of clarity. Then one thought bellowing above the others, suddenly pierced the haze, and like an arrow hitting a **bullseye**[3], Cad realised her dire predicament. Thanks to Rhys and her animal friends, she'd survived the well, but how could she have stupidly forgotten she'd been down there so long, and swallowed so much water, that she probably couldn't survive unscathed … unless someone had specifically targeted her too …

In their haste to return and warn Llywelyn, she and Rhys had not thought to alert Physician Jordan to her **plight**[4]. What now coursed through her veins was a **haphazard**[5] concoction of **herbs**[6] and plants, mixed not by an **apothecary**[7] or physician, but by a callous and murderous poisoner.

With faithful Fishy at her side, Cad fought to focus, as an **ironic**[8] question surfaced in her mind. As she gazed at the sack in the corner of her room, Cad feared her destiny. Tonight, would she, Callwen Cadwaladr, Prince Llywelyn's only daughter, be the first to perish at the hands of Catrin Castle's mystery poisoner?

To be continued.

---

1 **refuge** *(n)* a safe place. *(s)* shelter, sanctuary. *(ant)* hazard.

2 **jostle** *(v)* hustle, push, or bump into something. *(s)* fight, struggle, compete.

3 **bullseye** *(n)* the centre of a target in sports such as archery.

4 **plight** *(n)* a difficult or dangerous situation. *(s)* predicament, bind, dilemma.

5 **haphazard** *(adj)* lacking organisation. *(s)* random, chaotic. *(ant)* methodical.

6 **herb** *(n)* a plant, often used for flavouring food, or in medicine or perfume.

7 **apothecary** *(n)* (archaic) a person who mixed and sold medicines.

8 **ironic** *(adj)* happening in an unexpected way. *(s)* paradoxical, incongruous. *(ant)* logical.

A SNEAK PEEK!

Thank you for reading *The Cadwaladr Chronicles: Book 2 – Cipher*.
I hope you enjoyed reading it as much as I did writing it!

If you did, here's a sneak peek at the first chapter of *Book 3* in *The Cadwaladr Chronicles* series: *Siege*.

S. L. Ager

CHAPTER ONE

A Knighthood

Cad knelt before Prince Llywelyn, one knee on the floor, the other perched on a red **velvet**[1] cushion, her **crested**[2] **helm**[3] placed beside her. The prince **shifted**[4] his attention from the **assembled**[5] **audience**[6] down to his daughter before him. Cad, so proud to be here, **relished**[7] her knight's **attire**[8]. Her body, **clad**[9] **entirely**[10] in **chain mail**[11], **bore**[12] the metal's weight with ease. The heavy **coif**[13], worn beneath the helm to protect the head, now **draped**[14] back between

1 **velvet** *(n)* a fabric woven from silk, cotton or nylon with a dense, short pile on one side.
2 **crested** *(adj)* decorated with a coat of arms, badge or other emblem. *(s)* emblazoned. *(ant)* plain.
3 **helm** *(n)* a helmet, often made from metal and worn in medieval battle and jousting.
4 **shift** *(v)* move a short distance. *(s)* reposition. *(ant)* remain.
5 **assemble** *(v)* gather with others for a common purpose. *(s)* collect, convene. *(ant)* disperse.
6 **audience** *(n)* a group of people who listen or watch something. *(s)* spectators, onlookers.
7 **relish** *(v)* enjoy or like greatly. *(s)* love, delight in. *(ant)* detest, loathe.
8 **attire** *(n)* clothes. *(s)* clothing, dress, outfit, garments.
9 **clad** *(adj)* clothed or dressed. *(s)* attired, wearing, cloaked. *(ant)* unclothed, undressed.
10 **entirely** *(adv)* fully. *(s)* completely, totally, wholly. *(ant)* partially.
11 **chain mail** *(n)* flexible armour made of small metal rings that link together.
12 **bear** *(v)* carry the weight of (past tense: bore). *(s)* support. *(ant)* yield, collapse.
13 **coif** *(n)* a close fitting cap or head covering.
14 **drape** *(v)* arrange (cloth or material) around something. *(s)* cover. *(ant)* uncover.

her shoulders. Over the mail which protected her **torso**[1], she wore a **scarlet**[2]-red **tunic**[3], **intricately**[4] worked in golden thread.

From the **broad**[5] leather belt at her waist hung a **sturdy**[6] **sheath**[7] for her newly **forged**[8] sword.

Siân, Cad's stunning mother, stood alongside her husband, Prince Llywelyn. Her red velvet **gown**[9], which matched Cad's tunic and its gold working, fell in **exquisite**[10] folds. Her long, waved **blonde** hair dazzled, **garlanded**[11] with **miniature**[12] white lilies, and topped with an emerald-studded crown. Both loving parents **gazed**[13] adoringly at Callwen, their **adopted**[14] daughter.

Cad had **yearned**[15] for this day since becoming a **novice**[16] **pageboy**[17] at Catrin Castle. The day for which Cad had **sacrificed**[18] her family and **assumed**[19] a false **gender,**[20] had arrived. She, Callwen Cadwaladr, was to be **sworn in**[21] to the magical order of the Knights Hawk.

Her younger brother, John, now a page himself, stood alongside his parents and beamed with

---

1 **torso** *(n)* the trunk (body without head or limbs) of a human. *(s)* upper body.

2 **scarlet** *(adj)* of a bright red colour. *(s)* crimson, vermillion.

3 **tunic** *(n)* a loose garment, often sleeveless and worn with a belt. *(s)* surcoat, robe.

4 **intricately** *(adv)* done in an intricate (detailed) manner. *(s)* artfully, exquisitely. *(ant)* simply.

5 **broad** *(adj)* physically wide. *(s)* big, large. *(ant)* narrow.

6 **sturdy** *(adj)* strong and solidly built. *(s)* robust, durable, substantial. *(ant)* weak.

7 **sheath** *(n)* a cover for a blade. *(s)* case, sleeve.

8 **forge** *(v)* make a metal object by heating in a fire and hammering it into shape. *(s)* cast, model.

9 **gown** *(n)* a long, formal dress. *(s)* robe, frock.

10 **exquisite** *(adj)* extremely beautiful. *(s)* elegant, graceful. *(ant)* ugly, crude.

11 **garland** *(v)* decorate with a garland (a ring of flowers and leaves). *(s)* festoon, loop.

12 **miniature** *(adj)* small compared to others. *(s)* tiny, diminutive. *(ant)* giant.

13 **gaze** *(v)* look steadily. *(s)* stare, gape, peer. *(ant)* glimpse glance.

14 **adopt** *(v)* legally take another person's child to raise as one's own.

15 **yearn** *(v)* really want something. *(s)* long, ache, crave, desire. *(ant)* reject.

16 **novice** *(adj)* someone new to and inexperienced in a situation or job. *(s)* beginner. *(ant)* expert.

17 **pageboy** *(n)* a boy in training for a knighthood, ranking one below a squire in a knight's personal service.

18 **sacrifice** *(v)* give up something for the sake of others. *(s)* forgo, forfeit. *(ant)* keep.

19 **assume** *(v)* adopt or take on (an identity or manner), sometimes falsely. *(s)* affect, fake, feign.

20 **gender** *(n)* characteristics pertaining to the two sexes; social and cultural identities beyond these established categories.

21 **swear in** *(v)* induct into a position or office by means of an oath (past participle: sworn). *(s)* inaugurate.

pride[1] for his elder sister. Cad's cheeks ached in fellow feeling for him as if they'd smiled for hours.

Cad's dearest friends, Dylan, Rhys and Ellis, sat in **awed**[2] silence, **spectating**[3] from the front row of Llywelyn's princely court. Llywelyn had **summoned**[4] all to Catrin Castle's great hall to **witness**[5] the **dubbing**[6] **ceremony**[7].

May, Cad's blind hawk, perched on Rhys's shoulder, and no doubt Slippy, the toothless snake, slept in a pouch at his waist. Fishy, Cad's **faithful**[8] dog, sat at Dylan's feet, and Cad was sure that if Ellis could have sneaked Flash, her pony, into the back of the hall to view the ceremony, he would have done so.

Everyone Cad cared for was here to see Llywelyn dub her a Knight Hawk. She, Callwen Cadwaladr, the girl **masquerading**[9] as a boy to become a knight, was about to make her father proud. Proud he had saved her from the depths of a well as a baby to raise her as his own.

As she fought back tears of joy, Cad stared into her father's eyes, his enormous sword now raised. Cad dared not peep at her mother, for those eager tears would win the fight if she did. With a **gulp**[10], she swallowed as Llywelyn's sword **descended**[11], her young life's work **culminating**[12] in this moment.

A ripple of delight thrilled Cad as she waited for the touch of Llywelyn's sword on her shoulder. Her green eyes fixed on its silvery tip. But the sword didn't reach Cad's shoulder. In mid-air, it stopped. She **glimpsed**[13] up, regarding her father's face in puzzlement, her eyes

---

1 **pride** *(n)* a feeling of satisfaction. *(s)* pleasure, delight, joy. *(ant)* shame.

2 **awed** *(adj)* filled with wonder. *(s)* amazed, wonderstruck. *(ant)* indifferent.

3 **spectate** *(v)* watch rather than take part in. *(s)* view, observe, witness. *(ant)* participate.

4 **summon** *(v)* order or ask someone to be present. *(s)* call, invite, request. *(ant)* dismiss.

5 **witness** *(v)* see something happen. *(s)* observe. *(ant)* ignore, overlook.

6 **dub** *(v)* make someone a knight by the custom of touching their shoulder with a sword. *(s)* knight. *(ant)* strip.

7 **ceremony** *(n)* a formal occasion to celebrate an event or achievement. *(s)* formality.

8 **faithful** *(adj)* remaining loyal, steadfast, constant and true. *(s)* dedicated, dependable, reliable. *(ant)* disloyal.

9 **masquerade** *(v)* make a false and deceptive show of pretence. *(s)* act, pose, behave. *(ant)* unmask.

10 **gulp** *(n)* a (sometimes audible) swallowing movement of the throat. *(s)* gasp.

11 **descend** *(v)* move or fall downwards. *(s)* dip. *(ant)* ascend, rise.

12 **culminate** *(v)* to reach the highest point or development. *(s)* conclude. *(ant)* begin, commence.

13 **glimpse** *(v)* to see briefly. *(s)* peek, peep. *(ant)* stare.

searching for **clues**[1]. The look in his eyes seemed changed.

Then, as though a spear of ice had passed through it, Cad's heart **lurched**[2] at the sight of Siân **ushering**[3] her brother from the dubbing **dais**[4]. Cad **observed**[5] in horror, seeing that Llywelyn's **expression**[6] had **dramatically**[7] **altered**[8].

The words Cad **longed**[9] to speak refused to form. Beneath Llywelyn's stony stare, her throat turned sandy. For a stunned moment, **bewildered**[10], her thoughts jammed. She looked to her friends for help, but only **blank**[11] faces stared back. Her stomach swirled as she knelt in the centre of a chilly silence, **gooseflesh**[12] running up her arms.

'Father, father,' she mouthed, as Llywelyn placed his **sleek**[13] sword back into its sheath. 'What are you doing?' Her voice was a **mere**[14] whisper.

Yet Llywelyn did not answer. He **uttered**[15] not a word, but turned away and followed her mother and brother from the dais, **accompanying**[16] both from the hall.

Cad watched, confusion **crippling**[17] her, **hopelessness**[18] **paralysing**[19] her **limbs**[20].

---

1 **clue** *(n)* a piece of information about something, especially a crime. *(s)* sign, indication. *(ant)* evidence.

2 **lurch** *(v)* move abruptly without control. *(s)* falter, pitch. *(ant)* steady.

3 **usher** *(v)* show, escort or guide someone somewhere. *(s)* accompany, shepherd, lead. *(ant)* follow.

4 **dais** *(n)* a low platform for a throne or lectern. *(s)* stage, rostrum, stand, podium.

5 **observe** *(v)* watch carefully. *(s)* see, study, regard. *(ant)* miss, ignore.

6 **expression** *(n)* a look that conveys (shows) a certain emotion. *(s)* face, appearance.

7 **dramatically** *(adv)* in a dramatic (powerful) way. *(s)* radically, noticeably. *(ant)* modestly.

8 **alter** *(v)* change in some way. *(s)* adjust. *(ant)* preserve.

9 **long** *(v)* to have great want. *(s)* yearn, desire. *(ant)* dislike, despise.

10 **bewildered** *(adj)* perplexed or confused. *(s)* baffled, mystified, confounded. *(ant)* enlightened.

11 **blank** *(adj)* figuratively showing a lack of understanding or reaction. *(s)* vacant, deadpan. *(ant)* expressive.

12 **gooseflesh** *(n)* small bumps on the skin caused by cold or emotion. *(s)* goosebumps, goose pimples.

13 **sleek** *(adj)* smooth and shining. *(s)* glistening, polished. *(ant)* dull, rough, coarse.

14 **mere** *(adj)* no more than. *(s)* just, only.

15 **utter** *(v)* speak *(s)* say, voice.

16 **accompany** *(v)* go with someone. *(s)* chaperone, escort. *(ant)* abandon, desert.

17 **cripple** *(v)* cause to become unable to move properly. *(s)* immobilise, paralyse. *(ant)* mobilise.

18 **hopelessness** *(n)* a state or feeling of extreme unhappiness or lack of hope. *(s)* distress, anguish. *(ant)* hope.

19 **paralyse** *(v)* cause to become unable to act or function properly. *(s)* disable, incapacitate. *(ant)* mobilise.

20 **limb** *(n)* an arm, leg or wing. *(s)* appendage, offshoot.

A **chorus**[1] of confused noises rose from the audience, **assailing**[2] her thoughts. Unable to move, her heart breaking, her body crumpling and her mind **reeling**[3], Cad **clutched**[4] her head with her hands and sobbed like never before.

---

1 **chorus** *(n)* a group of voices or singers performing at the same time. *(s)* ensemble. *(ant)* soloist.

2 **assail** *(v)* (of something unpleasant) come upon a person suddenly. *(s)* trouble, plague. *(ant)* soothe.

3 **reel** *(v)* feel bewildered and shocked. *(s)* spin, whirl. *(ant)* steady, stabilise.

4 **clutch** *(v)* grab or grasp something tightly. *(s)* hold, grip. *(ant)* release, let go.

LEARN WITH THE CADWALADR SERIES

The Cadwaladr Chronicles: Book 2 – Cipher forms part of *The Cadwaladr* integrated education series.

When you have finished *The Cadwaladr Chronicles* series, it's time to move on to the following trilogy, *The Cadwaladr Quests.*

The Cadwaladr Quests series comprises a trilogy of novels, supporting workbooks and vocabulary revision notebooks.

Find all *The Cadwaladr Quests* books online via your local Amazon store.

The Cadwaladr Quests: Book 1 – Tangled Time

Other supporting books:

The Cadwaladr Quests: Book 1 – Tangled Time – Workbook

The Cadwaladr Quests: Book 1 – Tangled Time – Vocabulary Revision Notebook

11+ Vocabulary, Comprehension and Verbal Skills – Workbook 1

*

The Cadwaladr Quests: Book 2 – Race For The Gold

Other supporting books:

The Cadwaladr Quests: Book 2 – Race For The Gold – Workbook

The Cadwaladr Quests: Book 2 – Race For The Gold – Vocabulary Revision Notebook

*

The Cadwaladr Quests: Book 3 (the finale) – Cat's Eye

PARENTS, GET FIVE FREE COMPREHENSION EXERCISES

Parents, to receive your free comprehensions (with answers) based on *The Cadwaladr Chronicles: Book 2 - Cipher,* please leave a review for *Cipher* on Amazon and email a screenshot to:

freebies@slager.co.uk.

I will add you to my mailing list[1] and send you the comprehensions by email.

1 You can unsubscribe from the mailing list at any time. Further details will be emailed to you as soon as you are added.

REVIEWS, PLEASE!

If you've enjoyed *The Cadwaladr Chronicles: Book 2 - Cipher*,
please leave a review on Amazon.
Thank you!

ERRATA AND INFORMATION

To report any **errata**[1], please email: **errata@slager.co.uk.**
If you would like information about new books in *The Cadwaladr Chronicles* series, please visit:

SLAGER.CO.UK

You can stay up to date with S. L. Ager, author of *The Cadwaladr Chronicles* series, on social media:

facebook.com/SLAgerAuthor
instagram.com/SLAgerAuthor
linkedin.com/in/SLAgerAuthor
pinterest.com/SLAgerAuthor
twitter.com/SLAgerAuthor
tiktok.com/@s.l.agerauthor

---

1 **erratum** *(n)* an error in writing or publishing (plural: *errata*).

Printed in Great Britain
by Amazon

24819859R00106